The Terrible Meek
Religion and Revolution in Cross-Cultural Perspective

The Washington Institute for Values in Public Policy

The Washington Institute sponsors research that helps provide the information and fresh insights necessary for formulating policy in a democratic society. Founded in 1982, the Institute is an independent, nonprofit educational and research organization which examines current and upcoming issues with particular attention to ethical implications.

ADDITIONAL TITLES

Beyond Constructive Engagement: United States Foreign Policy Toward Africa
Edited by Elliott P. Skinner (1986)

Human Rights in East Asia: A Cultural Perspective
Edited by James C. Hsiung (1986)

The Nuclear Connection: A Reassessment of Nuclear Power and Nuclear Proliferation
Edited by Alvin Weinberg, Marcelo Alonso, and
Jack N. Barkenbus (1985)

Central America in Crisis
Edited by Marcelo Alonso (1984)

Global Policy: Challenge of the 80's
Edited by Morton A. Kaplan (1984)

The Terrible Meek
Religion and Revolution in Cross-Cultural Perspective

EDITED BY

LONNIE D. KLIEVER

A WASHINGTON INSTITUTE BOOK

PARAGON HOUSE PUBLISHERS
NEW YORK

Published in the United States by

Paragon House Publishers
2 Hammarskjöld Plaza
New York, New York 10017

A Washington Institute Book.

Library of Congress Cataloging-in-Publication Data

The Terrible Meek.

"A Washington Institute book."
Bibliography: p.
Includes index.
1. Revolutions—Religious aspects.
I. Kliever, Lonnie D.
BL65.R48T47 1987 291.1'77 86-25317
ISBN 0-88702-214-6
ISBN 0-88702-215-4 (pbk.)

Contents

Introduction

LONNIE D. KLIEVER

"Blessed are the meek,
for they shall inherit the earth."
Matthew 5:5

The popular and the pious imaginations have long regarded meekness as an essential if not definitive attribute of the religious life. Divine beatitude rests on those who surrender the powers of earth to the powers of heaven, on those who endure the sorrows of this life for the joys of the life to come. Moreover, this widespread understanding is reinforced by conventional though not entirely accurate views of both Eastern and Western religions.[1] The Orient's metaphysical monism produces religions of mystical renunciation. A fixed cosmic order is mirrored in a static social order. Individuals are compelled to submit themselves uncritically to this one great all–embracing Sacred Reality. By accepting their social place and observing the cosmic law, the religious may eventually achieve a complete spiritual identity with the Sacred Order. The Occident's theological dualism, by contrast, produces religions of moral obedience. A personal God stands over against the universe that he creates and completes. Individuals are required to surrender themselves whole–heartedly to this one all–knowing and all–powerful Sovereign Lord. By learning God's ways and by fulfilling God's will, the religious are promised an everlasting personal relationship with a loving God. Thus, for either broad approach to the religious life, conventional wisdom declares that only the meek inherit the cherished legacy of perfect peace and eternal life.

Of course, Karl Marx (1818–83) turned this conventional wisdom into a philosophical axiom and moral indictment of all religion.[2] Behind his well–known dictum, "Religion is the opium of the people", lies the view that religion glorifies meekness. Marx readily acknowledged that religion originates in the reality of human suffering and as such provides a truthful picture of human privation and alienation. But religion obscures both the social sources and the historical remedies for human suffering. Religion provides a theological justification for the patterns of socio–economic oppression that give rise to most suffering in the first place while simultaneously rechanneling the discontent of the oppressed classes into other–worldly aspirations for some imagined paradise. Given this view of religion, Marx's contention that the criticism of religion is the first premise of the revolutionary imperative is fully understandable. The world can never be changed until the illusions of religion are swept aside and the world of *human* perversity and *human* possibility is confronted directly without false explanations or fantastic consolations.

The social elements of Marx's theory of religion became important building blocks of the modern social scientific approach to religion and society that followed in his wake. Though his negative assessments of religion and his positive commitments to revolution were left behind by most anthropologists and sociologists, Marx's view of religion as the guardian of societal integration and equilibrium was carried over into late nineteenth and early twentieth century scientific studies of cultural systems and social institutions. Indeed, Emile Durkheim (1858–1917) saw societies as religious and religions as social in their very essence.[3] Religious beliefs are collective representations, expressing in symbolic form a given society's shared meanings and ideals. Religious rituals are collective celebrations, evoking through dramatic participation a given individual's social identity and loyalty. Though Durkheim's theory was derived from his study of Australian aboriginal tribes, he insisted that every society is a religious phenomenon. The operative religion and the vital life of a given society are one and the same thing. Every religion exemplifies its own society and every society embodies its own religion.

To be sure, most late nineteenth and early twentieth century social scientists were unwilling to go as far as Durkheim went in identifying religion with the social order or in grounding society in the religious system. Thus, for example, Bronislaw Malinowski (1884–1942) argued that the elemental forms of social life rest on relatively independent systems of religion, magic and science.[4] Every society draws on a body of empirical knowledge and pragmatic skills for meeting the basic needs of human life. Such scientific competence is never fully sufficient or successful in meeting those needs. Magical lore and technique bridge those gaps in everyday understanding and mastery that a given science does not fill. But, beyond the practical concerns of both science and magic, religious beliefs and practices deal with the ultimate questions of human duty and destiny. Or again, Max Weber (1864–1920) devoted considerable attention to religion as a force for social change as well as a source of social cohesion within a given society.[5] Religious ideas are not simply echoes of the dominant social order nor are religious sects simply safety valves for disruptive individuals or deviant classes. Such ideas and groups are forces in the social matrix which interact with other forces in shaping the social order. Sometimes dominant religious ideas or deviant religious groups bring about profound changes in the social order, although such changes are seldom if ever intended by the religious. Nevertheless, despite such scholarly recognition of the relative autonomy and valency of religion within a total social system, the majority of early social scientists regarded religion as an essentially *conservative* factor within society.

Early theories of revolution merely accepted without question either the Marxist critique or the social scientific protrayal of religion as a counter–revolutionary phenomenon. Revolution as the struggle between rival factions or classes within a society for control of scarce resources of property, power and prestige may have occurred in earlier times, but the scholarly study of revolution is a very recent development. Even such classical social scientists as Durkheim and Weber paid no explicit attention to revolution in their writings.[6] Gradually a few philosophers, historians and social scientists outside the Marxist orbit—such as Pitirim Sorokin, Karl Mannheim, George Pettee, Crane Brinton and Hannah Arendt—developed theories of revolution.[7] But, since they concentrated their studies on the great upheavals in Western Europe between the seventeenth and the twentieth centuries, religion appeared primarily in the form of an established state church which supports the ruling power. Thus, religion was for the most part portrayed as either irrelevant or antagonistic to revolutionary movements. Indeed, revolution as an historical phenomena was closely tied to the secularization of modern life and thought. Deicide (the death of religious faith) and regicide (the overthrow of political authority) were portrayed as two sides of the same coin.

But a whole new line of thinking about religion and revolutionary social change began to emerge in the late fifties and early sixties. Leading the way were social scientific studies of millenarian movements, especially among oppressed peoples of the Third World. The writings of such anthropologists as Keneln Burridge, Vittorio Laternari, Anthony Wallace and Peter Worsley, pictured religion playing a vital revolutionary role in the periodic renewal of primitive societies and in the revitalization movements among colonialized peoples.[8] These Third World studies prompted a major re–examination of many European and North American religio–political movements. Political historians such as Michael Adas, Christopher Dawson, Christopher Hill, Quentin Skinner and Michael Walzer and social scientists such as S.N. Eisenstadt, E.J. Hobsbawm, Guenter Lewy, Roland Robertson and Bryan Wilson uncovered surprisingly frequent occurrences of religiously–inspired and legitimated social upheaval and political transformation.[9] Beyond the "accidental" changes in society brought about by conflict within or between religious groups, religion has often been a direct and intentional factor in civil strife and social change.

The essays in this volume belong to this ongoing reappraisal of the positive relationships between religion and revolution. They were originally prepared for a symposium on the topic, "Ideology, Religion and Revolution," which I organized and chaired for The Washington Institute for Values in Public Policy in Washington, D.C. That an educational institute devoted to providing timely analyses of the values underlying policy decisions would fund such research will come as no surprise to readers of the daily newspaper. Religious leaders and religious factions are deeply involved in revolutionary uprisings in every part of the world—in the Middle East, South Africa, the British Isles, Latin America, the Indian subcontinent, Eastern Europe. Even in the United States, a resurgent Religious Right is fueling profound social and economic changes that some commentators have called a revolution. A subject of more timely interest to social theorists, public decision–makers and informed citizens alike can scarcely be imagined.

The topics explored in these essays are as varied as their author's points of view. Anyone familiar with the scholarly controversy surrounding definitions of religion and theories of revolution will recognize the difficulty if not impossibility of reaching consensus on even these foundational issues.[10] Such disagreements are all the more likely when social scientists, historians and philosophers are all brought to the same table to talk about specific revolutionary situations in different cultural contexts! Of course, the present authors broadly agree that revolutions are relatively abrupt and significant changes in prevailing systems of class, wealth or power, that ideologies are sets of ideas which unite and legitimate the organizations or movements built around them, and that religions provide transcendent grounds and sacred warrants for social institutions and human behavior. But each author works with his own concrete definition of religion and reaches his own conclusions about the interaction of religion and social protest within the special historic and geographical context he is investigating. Their differences are particularly acute on the question of whether ideology must be clearly distinguished from religion or whether religion may be understood as an extreme form of ideology. What binds these essays together, however, is their shared concern to illumine the *positive* relationships between movements of religious protest and social dissonance.

The first three essays examine well–known protest movements of the distant and recent past from entirely fresh perspectives. Stanley Johannesen places the American Revolution in the long history of Western piety. This history was marked from the beginning by a tendency for Christianity to be a religion of socially displaced people and of upwardly displaced patronage. Since the Christian God radically transcends time and space, God's people belong to no particular history or territory. Thus, in times of cultural dislocation, and especially the relocation of immigrants to the New World, Christianity fostered religious and political affiliations which were essentially forward and upward rather than backward and downward looking. As a consequence, a sense of individual freedom and manifest destiny became the linchpins of American religion and politics. This emphasis on the single self and the nation as a whole built principles of permanent revolution and prophetic universalism into the very fabric of American life. Herein lies the strength and the weakness of the American system—there are no religious institutions either to compel congruity or to mediate conflict between these two centers of sacrality.

Harvey P. Alper examines three celebrated uprisings which are typically credited with establishing India's nationalistic identity and political independence. He challenges the idea that these uprisings were modeled on either the revolutionary strategies or the Christian pacifism of modern Europe. Neither the eighteenth century Samnyāsī Rebellion nor the nineteenth century Sepoy Mutiny were nationalistic and revolutionary movements. Rather, they fit into a well known pattern of agrarian agitation and regional chaos that regularly occurred when local political leadership changed. Moreover, Gandhi's technique of "non–violent non–cooperation," which did help India gain her independence, was solidly rooted in the ascetic traditions of classical Hinduism. Alper concludes that traditional Hinduism has thus far enabled India to adapt to the changing conditions of modernity without recourse to revolutionary reconstruction of the social order.

Bruce B. Lawrence provides a detailed theoretical analysis of religion, ideology and revolution as a context for interpreting the 1978–79 Iranian Revolution. Carefully distinguishing between the three, he sees religion and ideology as rival expressions of sacral and secular worldviews while revolution is the latterday offspring of their belated conflict. Within this theoretical framework, Lawrence explores the three revolutions that have occurred in modern Iran, the particular events which comprised the 1978–79 Revolution and finally how Iran's Constitutional Revolution of 1905–11, the late Shah's so–called White Revolution of 1963 and the Islamic revolution of 1978–79 compare to other revolutions beyond Iran, including specifically America's nationalistic, constitutional and capitalist revolutions. He concludes that the earlier Iranian revolutions failed and that the 1978–79 Revolution, which unlike other revolutions beyond Iran is a *religious* revolution, is still on its way toward either eventual failure or success.

The next two essays deal with lesser–known contemporary protest movements in Eastern Europe and South America by placing them in deep historical perspective. Martin Rumscheidt connects the on–going but tenuous Christian–Marxist dialogue in Czechoslovakia to the old Hussite tradition stemming from Jan Hus. This fifteenth century religious reformer, who sought reforms in both the ecclesiastical and civil communities of his day, left behind a permanent legacy of revolutionary consciousness. The historical rootage of both Marxist and Christian partners in the Christian–Marxist dialogue in this old Hussite tradition has enabled them to recognize their own weaknesses and to acknowledge the other's strengths in their shared revolutionary goal to make life more fully human for all. Their dialogue thus furnishes a paradigm for pursuing constructive alliances between a revisionary Marxism and a revolutionary Christianity throughout the communist and capitalist worlds.

William W. Stein examines South American revolutionary ferment against the background of two centuries of rural social struggles in highland Peru. The Túpac Amaru Rebellion of 1780–81, the Atusparia Uprising of 1885, the Andahuaylas land invasions of 1974 and the current Sendero Luminoso popular guerilla war demonstrate recurrent patterns of failed revolutionary alliances between urban and rural components. The earlier revolutionary movements demonstrate that different sectors of complex societies were aware of the needs for such social alliances long before the Marxist articulation of proletarian revolutionary doctrine. But these peasant uprisings also demonstrate that the differing religious ideologies of those urban and rural sectors were serious obstacles to achieving their announced goals. Despite the insertion of Marxist theory, the contemporary Sendero "Shining Light" movement has been no more successful than earlier efforts to forge an effective revolutionary alliance between proletarians and peasants. Andean messianism and Maoist utopianism apparently remain too far apart to join city and countryside in common revolutionary cause.

The last three essays deal with specific contemporary situations of revolutionary conflict where both sides appeal to the *same* religion for the moral inspiration and sacred warrants of their respective causes. Richard L. Rubenstein's essay on the American economy reflects the fact that revolutionary conflicts in developed societies typically focus on matters of economic justice and status enhancement rather than upon land reform, universal suffrage or class structure. He analyzes two religiously–inspired but politically–opposed programs for redressing the failures of the American capitalistic economic system. Both strategies seek to mitigate the human costs of unfettered free market competition but they radically disagree on the methods and sanctions required. The U.S. Catholic Bishops' Pastoral Letter advocates a traditional liberal strategy of redistributing the wealth while the New Religious Right champions a traditional conservative commitment to creating additional wealth. Between the two, Rubenstein gives the upper hand in this ideological struggle to the New Religious Right, thanks largely to their powerful if not coherent joining of economic libertarianism, social traditionalism and militant anti–communism.

But he concludes that neither the mainline Catholic–Protestant Left nor the Evangelical–Fundamentalist Right have recognized the threat or learned the lessons of the Japanese "economic miracle," which seems to have solved the chronic problems of a capitalistic system through a highly original union of business and government and business and religion.

William R. Jones deals with the question of the religious legitimation of revolutionary violence in the context of Latin American Liberation Theology. Challenging the portrait of Liberation theology as "Bible and Bazooka Christianity," he offers a detailed analysis of the case for and against this militant theology of social change. Jones contends that the opposing sides in this debate represent rival interpretations of the Christian faith and sharply different understandings of legitimated violence. The critics of Liberation Theology argue that its revolutionary program is at odds with the quietism and pacifism of the biblical faith. But Jones shows that historic Christianity with its "just war" theory and its prophetic moral vision has never supported such social passivity. Moreover, Liberation Theology's opponents condemn its willingness to adopt and approve violent means of social change. Again, Jones demonstrates that Liberation Theology only endorses *counterviolence* as a last resort when other means of social transformation have failed. On either count, Jones sees the case against Liberation Theology as a classic example of ideological mystification. In situations of intransigence, the choice lies between the religiously legitimated violence of the oppressors and the religiously legitimated counterviolence of the oppressed.

Finally, Austin M. Ahanotu provides a South African case study of religion and the problem of power. In this very different religious and cultural context, the lines between the oppressors and the oppressed are also drawn and justified by rival interpretations of the Christian faith. The system of Apartheid rests on a religious and political mythology of a "Chosen People." The Afrikaners believe that they have been given control over the Africans by divine appointment. In sharpest contrast, a swelling tide of South African black Christians insist that Apartheid represents a categorical denial of the Gospel of Jesus Christ. But the African clergy, who are clearly the leaders in this uprising, have reached this conclusion about Apartheid only after years of debate over racism and religion. Indeed, Ahanotu traces out, in patient historical detail, the ever–increasing militancy among African clergymen that parallels the ever–mounting antagonism between the races. Whether South Africa is on the brink of cataclysmic collapse or revolutionary transformation remains to be seen.

What lessons about religion, ideology and revolution can be drawn from these eight essays? They certainly offer a wealth of historical detail and theoretical analysis of specific instances of social upheaval within diverse religious and cultural contexts. As such, they provide impressive evidence of the revolutionary potentialities of religion, regardless of the prevailing form of a religious tradition and social order. Religious "meekness" is always a double–edged sword, whether such acquiescence is conceived of as renunciation of the earthly or as obedience to the heavenly.[11] On either reckoning, the "meek" answer to some nobler reality or higher authority than this world. To be sure, that highter loyalty has more often sustained rather than undermined the status quo. But religion's utopian vision and iconoclastic fervor can promote dissent as readily as compel assent to the kingdoms and rulers of this world. Religion always harbors within its beliefs and practices this profound ambivalence about social cohesion and social conflict. The "temperate meek" are apparently content to exchange this world for the next world—to swap earth for heaven. But the "terrible meek" remain resolutely determined to change this world into another world—to create heaven on earth!

NOTES

1. For a summary statement of this conventional view, see Joseph Campbell, *Myths To Live By* (New York: Viking Press, 1972), pp. 61–104.
2. For primary references to Marx's views on Religion, see *Karl Marx and Friedrich Engels on Religion,* introduced by Reinhold Niebuhr (New York: Schocken Books, 1964).
3. Emile Durkheim, *The Elementary Forms of the Religious Life* (New York: Free Press Paperback Edition, 1965).
4. Bronislaw Malinowski, *Magic, Science and Religion and Other Essays* (Garden City, New York: Doubleday Anchor Books, 1954).
5. Max Weber, *The Protestant Ethic and the Spirit of Capitalism* (New York, Charles Scribner's Sons, 1958).
6. Roland Robertson, "The Development and Modern Implications of the Classical Sociological Perspective on Religion and Revolution," in *Religion,*

Rebellion, Revolution, edited by Bruce Lincoln (London: The Macmillan Press Ltd., 1985), pp. 236–65.

7. Pitirim Sorokin, *The Sociology of Revolution* (Philadelphia: Lippincott, 1965); Karl Mannheim, *Ideology and Utopia* (London: Routledge and Kegan Paul, 1936); George Pettee, *The Process of Revolution* (New York: Harper & Row Publishers, 1938); Crane Brinton, *Anatomy of Revolution* (New York: W.W. Norton, 1938; 3rd Edition 1965); Hannah Arendt, *On Revolution* (New York: Viking Press, 1963).
8. Kenelm Burridge, *New Heaven, New Earth* (New York: Schocken, 1969); Vittorio Laternari, *Religions of the Oppressed* (New York: Alfred Knopf, 1967); Anthony F.C. Wallace, "Revitalization Movements, "*American Anthropologist* 58 (1956), pp. 264–81; Peter Worsley, *The Trumpet Shall Sound* (New York: Schocken, 1968).
9. Michael Adas, *Prophets of Rebellion* (Chapel Hill: University of North Carolina Press, 1979); Christopher Dawson, *The Gods of Revolution* (New York: Minerva, 1975; Christopher Hill, *Puritanism and Revolution* (London: Secker and Warburg, 1958); Quentin Skinner, *The Foundations of Modern Political Thought, Volume Two: The Age of Reformation* (London: Cambridge University Press, 1978; Michael Walzer, *Revolution of the Saints* (Cambridge: Harvard University Press, 1965); S.N. Eisenstadt, *Revolution and the Transformation of Societies* (New York: Free Press, 1978); E.J. Hobsbawm, *Primitive Rebels* (Manchester: Manchester University Press, 1959); Guenter Lewy (New York: Oxford University Press, 1974); Roland Robertson, *Meaning and Change* (New York: New York University Press, 1978); Bryan Wilson, *Magic and the Millenium* (New York: Harper & Row, 1973).
10. For representative definitions of religion, see J. Milton Yinger, *The Scientific Study of Religion* (New York: Macmillan Publishing Company, 1970), pp. 1–23. For full survey of competing theories of revolution, see Mark N. Hagopian, *The Phenomenon of Religion* (New York: Dodd, Mead & Co., 1974).
11. In *The Protestant Ethic and the Spirit of Capitalism,* Max Weber drew a distinction between "other–worldly" and "inner–worldly" views of reality and between "mystical" and "ascetic" paths to salvation. Mystical piety calls for *adjustmemt* to the world, ascetic piety for *mastery* of the world. Weber cross–tabulated the distinction between mysticism and asceticism with the distinction between other–worldly and inner–worldly viewpoints to produce four distinctive types of religion. Of these four types, Weber believed that only *inner–worldly asceticism* provided enough leverage to bring about revolutionary social change since only inner–worldly asceticism provides a basis for both collective and historical action. Recent studies of religion and revolution, including the essays in this volume, call this classical view into question. All types of religion—whether other–worldly or inner–worldly, whether mystical or ascetic—may and have become religions of resistence.

1

American Republicanism and Christian Piety

STANLEY JOHANNESEN

In a democratic community individuals are very powerless; but the State which represents them all, and contains them all in its grasp, is very powerful. Nowhere do citizens appear so insignificant as in a democratic nation; nowhere does the nation itself appear greater, or does the mind more easily take in a wide general survey of it. In democratic communities the imagination is compressed when men consider themselves; it expands indefinitely when they think of the State. Hence it is that the same men who live on a small scale in narrow dwellings frequently aspire to gigantic splendor in the erection of their public monuments.

. . .Thus democracy not only leads men to a vast number of inconsiderable productions; it also leads them to raise some monuments on the largest scale: but between these two extremes there is a blank.

Alexis de Tocqueville.

Behold the great illusion which the goddess at the port of New York symbolizes, shedding her light without favour on all the children of men. Watch her more closely: the goddess in the abstract, so much the more sentimental. She appeals to religious feelings, referring, not without pathos, to emptiness.

Denis de Rougemont.

I

A common difficulty in joining together in the same conceptual framework the social experience of religion and other social experiences is a lack of precision about what religion is. An entrenched disposition of modern ways of thinking is to make the religious apprehension of reality a mere intensifier, a signal that something is emotionally important, or that it has a compulsive quality for an individual or a group not easily accounted for on rational grounds. An instance of such an operation occurs when we say that football is the religion of the sports fan. Another occurs when we say that religion is whatever is of "ultimate concern" or is in some sense "transcendental." The popularity among American historians, of Clifford Geertz' famous definition of religion as persistent "moods and motivations," owes less perhaps to Geertz' own rigorous insistence on the autonomy of religion as a system, and the necessity for "thick description" of the particular system, than to the attraction of a formula that authorizes virtually any use of popular enthusiasms, popular ritual practice, widespread gestural usages, and the like, as a self-evidently explanatory field.[1] We seem further than ever from a characterization of American Christianity, or the relationship of particular social developments to it, and even further from a characterization of American social history in the context of the history of Christendom as a whole.[2] It is this last issue I want to address in this essay.

A point of departure for the reflections that follow is the discussion that has surrounded the concept of "civil religion." The phrase was given currency by Robert N. Bellah in a celebrated essay,[3] but the idea of it was perhaps implicit in the idea of the state as an Enlightenment project from the very beginning of such projects. The founders of both the French and the American republics were conscious of the power of religious forms in legitimizing the secular state, yet were also themselves caught up to some degree in the practice of the piety thus cynically invented.

The practices and forms of civil religion were not unknown before the democratic revolutions; *La religion royale,* to take only one notable example, was the cornerstone of the monarchical state in France. What does appear to be new in the democratic revolutions is the loss of sacramental and penitential concerns in the articulated premises for loyalty to the state. Here we have had available two interpretive strategies: we may point to the loss of power of traditional religious institutions and symbols, and say that the secular state reflects a general secularization of culture; Christianity may survive but not Christian culture. Or, we may emphasize the persistence of certain fields of collective perception and practice involving a strong sense of collective honor, and transcending local and short-term interests, and say that the religious impulse in society has found a new mythic and symbolic context in civil life. This last is the strategy of the "civil religion" writers.

The criticism I want to make of this line of argument is not of its description of the cultic practices it assigns to civil religion. There have certainly been, in American and in other modern national societies, unprecedented phenomena of cultic elaboration of membership in political society, and these phenomena need to be explained. The criticism I want to make of the typical analysis of civil religion is rather of the implied sense that a point in cultural history can be determined at which people's collective perceptions and practices have ceased to be Christian, or have ceased to exhibit vital links with past ages of Christian civilization. Whether it is assumed that this point is revealed in the impotence of theology in the modern world, or in the processes of political and economic modernization, such a narrative of modern history must assume that it knows what the limits of a Christian civilization are, and what the evidences of its death must be. I want to argue here that there is a way to conceive of American collective self-perceptions, particularly those born in revolutionary experience, as lying in a central vein of spiritual and social development in the Christian West. American civil religion is not only, or even primarily, an inauguration of a new religion, but rather a phase of popular religious practices and collective perceptions in the West extending backward to antiquity. What, in brief, is the appropriate narrative context for this reconsideration of the American experience? It is, I shall argue, the long history of remissions, beginning with the Grand Remission of Calvary itself, from penitential service to the dead and because of the dead, and remissions from moral responsibility based solely on natural affiliation and propinquity. The very idea of America, the New World, was a remissive assertion, a religious and metaphysical invention, that broke the hold of the Adamic curse, by extending the sphere of human activity beyond the limits of the fallen world.[4]

If remission—what the Americans called liberty—is the theme of American history in its widest historical context, let us consider, still preparatory to the main argument from the history of Latin Christianity, some comparisons with contemporary societies in which civil religion is significant, but remissive values are not dominant.

The striking instance of the revolutionary invention of civil religion in modern times has been described by Nina Tumarkin in her book on the cult of Lenin and of Lenin's body in the Soviet Union, a cult all the more remarkable in that Soviet social theory is officially materialist and atheistic.[5] The soviet leaders who decided to embalm Lenin's body and create a quasi-religious cult in perpetuity did so with the understanding that features of the cult were congruent with features of early Russian folk religion, and to that extent the new practices were cynically motivated. Yet it is also clear that the cult of Lenin's body remains a vital part of the legitimacy of the regime even in its inner self-understanding and spiritual motivation.

On a superficial view, we might say that this cult of the founder resembles the cult of the founding fathers of the United States, and in particular the veneration that surrounded Washington in the early years of the Republic. We might notice that both Moscow and Washington are notable as capitals in that they are dominated by funerary monuments. Yet details are everything in such comparisons. Lenin's tomb is a mausoleum, a public building with a body in it, a body which symbolizes the claims of the dead on living polity. Washington, on the other hand, is a city of cenotaphs. There are no bodies on view. Furthermore, while one may speak of Leninism as the voice of orthodoxy—the counterpart in dogma of the embalmed corpse in visual imagery—one does not speak similarly of Washingtonism or Jeffersonism. Indeed, if one were to invoke Jeffersonism it would include nothing more prominently than the vociferous repudiation of the claims of the dead on the living.

Another remarkable modern example of civil religion that is both like and unlike the civil religion of America is the case of Israel.[6] Here it was not a question of making up an appropriate cult, but rather of adapting traditional Jewish forms and practices by people whose beliefs were not traditional but radical and socialistic, for the purpose of affirming an ethnicity, and the legitimacy of the state. There is certainly conflict, and deep suspicion and misunderstanding, between the party of traditional religion and the party of enlightenment and of modern radical politics, but there can be no doubt that the state of Israel is legitimized by Judaism.

The case of Israel underscores the importance of long-term continuities of religious tradition even when the evidence might tempt us to see change as the outcome of consciously manipulated, even wholly fabricated, symbols. The case of Israel also suggests that a consideration of the binding power of traditional identities may be useful in reconsidering the religious implications of the American Revolution, not least because Americans have frequently thought of themselves by analogy with the children of Israel.[7] In both cases, a religious tradition prepared the ground for hope of redemption in a settler state, a hope articulated in the act of fulfillment as a hope of individual and collective security, material well-being, and spiritual and political freedom. In both cases there has also been deep partisan division between the agents of self-consciously religious institutions and attitudes, and agents of enlightenment and other secular values. Yet these divisions have, in both cases, masked broad agreement about the appropriateness of a certain generalized religious purpose, and a language of theologically vague invocation on public occasions. The deployment of such language in the Kennedy inaugural address in 1960 occasioned Bellah's essay and the ensuing debate.[8]

The American experience is not, however, the Jewish experience. One cannot say that America is to Western Christianity as Israel is to Judaism, and the reason takes us deep into the heart of what I want to say about American religion and the American Revolution. The Jews were scattered among strangers, and founded Israel, to put it in the starkest human terms, to live and to die among their own ancient dead. Israel was the gathering of a sundered community, called to witness to the moral claim on the living, not only of the dry bones of Ezekiel, but of the six millions of the Jewish holocaust. The United States, on the other hand, was the reverse of this social and cultural process. People left the abode of their dead for good, and created forms of association on new principles. America is the aggregation of the permanently uprooted.

The last comparison I want to make is with South Africa. The United States and the Afrikaner societies were both Puritan in origin, both evolved racial doctrines based in part on covenant and dispensational thinking, and both possessed strong feelings of territorial destiny.[9] Both, furthermore, achieved political identity in armed resistance to the British Empire. Nevertheless, as in the comparisons with civil religion in the Soviet Union, and in Israel, the comparison of South Africa with the United States at once suggests that the difference, among other things, lies in the uniquely remissive character of America, as an idea and a practice. Unlike the westward movement of Americans, the trekking of the Boers intensified the urgings of blood-bonds. Racialism worked against the national idea in America, and was always vulnerable to the remissive premise of the Revolutionary tradition. In South Africa, racialism gained ground in nationalism, because nationalism was in itself a claim of racial memory. The true parallel case in North American history is the history of the Mormons, whose trek toward the interior of the continent was accompanied by a similar emphasis on the claims of blood-kinship. Mormons elaborated a racial myth of origins, a doctrine of white supremacy, and cultic practices emphasizing variously the religious importance of genealogy, and the inclusion of the dead in social membership—almost as if in detailed, conscious rejection of the Revolutionary and republican ethos, an ethos that was indeed an anti-ethos, a gospel, a message of remission. The American was to be a man with no history, only a future.

The civil religion debate tended to see the social and cultural process of American history largely in terms of the institutional transformations of modernization. It assumed that the modern world is cut off from the traditional world by an impassable gulf, that the divide between the traditional and the modern is such that we must stand on one side or the other, in interpretive strategy and in affective commitment. The question therefore was not "What has happened to Western religion under these circumstances?" but rather "What is this new phenomenon?" "Is it a counterfeit religion?" "Is it useful?"[10]

When questions are asked in this way, it becomes inevitable that one will take civil religion to be in competition with the institutional and intellectual remnants of traditional religion, or the "real" religious element in society. It will then be inevitable that these "real" elements will be seen to be in retreat. Without entering into the territory of the institutional history of religion in America, it must be left at least open to possibility, that a history which takes the churches, and the creeds and platforms of the clerical tradition, to be the history of religion in society, has merely confused clerisy with piety. The religious aspect of the Revolution in America should not be prematurely interpreted as having set in motion something to be examined only in its own terms, as though piety is a portable mood, or motivation, seeking only to attach itself to the prevailing social system, or to ascendant aspects of the social system. One should also allow the possibility that the social organism in revolution experiences reorientation of the whole field of piety and affect, in a way that is determined partly by the particular resources of the inherited religion. There will be an element of moral luck, both in the range of adaptable mechanisms in that religion to begin with, and in the state of exhaustion of symbols in that religion throughout its remembered or recorded history. One may have the moral ill-luck to be at the wrong point in the cycle of decay and renewal; the nourishing tradition may be tired, used-up, sucked dry, its atmosphere too thin to support life. This is not a question of psychological or spiritual energy. It rather points to that side of the collective mentality in a society that inherits a content, which is just so much and no more, under conditions of social memory, or lack of social memory, that cannot be made other than what they are merely by thinking about them positively.

If American republicanism is to mean anything other than a certain worshipful demeanor in relation to the public symbols of the American state, one must show both what republicanism entailed as an association of the deracinated and with what effect and with what materials the stream of Western Christianity flowed into this situation. What was blocked off? Into what channels did the surviving stream flow? Can we map this elusive movement?

II

In an interesting and important book by Patricia Caldwell on the conversion narrative in early New England, we learn that the only truly distinguishing feature of American Puritan experience, the practice that separated congregations in the New World from practices in the very places these congregations came from, was that the Americans instituted as an integral part of the process of church membership and full civil participation the requirement that postulants recite a kind of spiritual autobiography.[11] These of course quickly acquired conventional features, and in literary form became the leading prose genre in American colonial letters, culminating in such classics as the autobiographies of Cotton Mather, John Woolman, and Benjamin Franklin. The point of the conversion narrative and the spiritual autobiography would be lost in a society of thick communal memory. Even Christ, it will be remembered, could not tell his story to good effect in Nazareth. But in a society in which the characteristic social relation is one of self-presentation in the company of strangers, or in which the forms of piety must reckon on the likelihood, the ordinariness, of confronting strangers as applicants to membership, the autobiographical narrative is basic. Self-made persons do not, as types, have self-evident stories of origin. They are constrained to tell their stories by the need to be known, but they tell their stories at a certain distance, in conventional terms, in order to protect the illusion of the possibility of community, without exposing the fragility of the personal claim to legitimacy.

The fragility of a personal claim to legitimacy is precisely what binds the experience of various colonial types in America into a single intelligible whole. The society of Virginia planters had not only by the eighteenth century invented a myth of social origins that obscured the individualistic and competitive modes of early Virginia society, but was, as Edmund Morgan has recently demonstrated, profoundly affected by slavery in a manner that suggests how unstable a presumably patriarchal society could be. Far from creating the class confidence and conservatism one would suppose in a master class, the regime of slavery created an obsession with freedom, and a tendency to perceive any check on personal or collective autonomy, any regulation for any purpose, as a vital threat. Slavery represented the ever-present abyss: loss of manhood, loss of dignity, loss of will.[12] The condition of slavery was the exact moral equivalent of the condition of spiritual reprobation. Freedom and sainthood alike required constant vigilance and introspection, lest the foot slide, even as one slumbered in complacency.

The American Revolution was precipitated when these temperaments had also to confront the question of political honor in the attempt by the Parliament of Great Britain to control the colonies after the Seven Years' War. What came to the fore at every stage of testing and response was a growing sense of impotence and fury in the American colonies that legitimacy at every level was determined abroad. Americans had an inferior culture as long as it was provincial; a frustrated political life as long as it was colonial; a trade constrained artificially as long as it was managed on mercantile principles. Republicanism as ideology—that is, the alignment of historical learning, political science and moral sense philosophy in the Revolutionary cause—determined some of the forms of resistance at critical points, but in the end the American colonists rebelled for the reason that men everywhere in the Western world rebelled in exactly the same period. Men who are removed from communities of memory, and form instead communities based on legal rights, and rights according to natural justice, form their honor, their legitimacy, their sense of membership in the company of those who assert these rights. America was distinctive only in that in America the old regime was foreign. The "myth of origin," as Bellah would later put it, could go back no further than July 4th, 1776.[13] America was also distinctive, however, in the degree to which community had become a question of personal rights. One of the characteristics that all observers of America agreed on was that its people were litigious, constantly engaged in lawsuits. It was even a ground for the Americans' own complaint about the Stamp Act: that people who have incessant recourse to lawyers experience a real hardship when legal papers are taxed.[14] Such a characteristic suggests the weakness of communal and consensual opinion.

All this is not to say that there was not an "internal" old regime of sorts, a Protestant insularity, pockets of community self-sufficiency, a domestic economy still firmly oriented to family strategies. But these conservative pockets were fragile, and were outpaced by fecundity and scarcity, which together wrecked the traditional strategies of families and farms, however these modes of calculation persisted.[15]

Consider now the specifically religious context of this revolutionary turn toward a future that embraces displacement as a strength rather than a weakness. The immediate context has been often and well told: The rise of revivalism, which in fact preceded the political revolution, gave new cultural authority to the man without a church, without a parish, who wills to be saved, who becomes literally a "new man," not identifiable to his former companions; the decline of the state-churches to the status of denominations, and the dreary and very nearly blank pages of their subsequent cultural history; the extraordinary cultural status but limited social authority of the considered and genteel forms of religion: deism, immanentalism, transcendentalism; and of course the eventual appearance of those militant utopian and millenarian sects, whose very literal-mindedness in disciplined community suggests how little of settled and self-forgetful community was available in the society at large. It is out of these local contours of American religious history that the issue of civil religion arises in its characteristic form. Is it a religion alongside these other religions? Does it have a constituency for which it is the sole religious experience? Does it occupy a place in a scattered spectrum of religious fragments in modern culture?

Let us forget for a moment the local features of this field of religious activity, however, and ask instead: what features of the religion of Western European societies are likely to be germane to the experience of a dislocated population seeking a form of legitimacy in legal and constitutional terms that will cover a vast territory and a practically limitless influx of strangers? Put this way, the question invites us to consider Christianity itself as a mechanism which has had to adapt itself repeatedly to dislocated populations, and to express the character of political societies under all conditions of expansion, assimilation, exile and so forth.

III

The Western Church, as the custodian of the spiritual and narrative traditions of early Christian people, and increasingly as a force in all aspects of the lives of believers, is unique in the history of the world religions. Beginning even in the canonical writings, particularly in *Acts* and the epistle to the *Ephesians,* we can readily observe the process of "catholicization" in which the hope of imminent *Parousia* of the risen Christ gives way to an organizational and expansionary intention that, taking advantage of the *Pax Romana,* eventually supercedes it.

In a fine work of scholarly synthesis of the available evidence, Jack Goody explains how the social history of the West was fundamentally shaped by the existence of Christian churchly institutions and by the logic of the Church's multiform and sometimes unconscious intentions.[16] He shows in particular how the growing demand by the church that marriage be contracted only outside the prohibited degrees of consanguinity—growing by the early medieval period to a burdensome seven removes of cousinship—altered the ancient customs of all Mediterranean peoples, including the Jews and the Romans, that permitted, and frequently required, marriages that the Church defined as incestuous. The effect, if not the direct intention, of these prohibitions, is not easy to overstate: It provided the characteristic elements of the ethos of the new Western, or Latin, societies. The difficulty in finding suitable mates drove people out of the circle of life-long familiars—all of whom were likely to be kin within the prohibited circle. This physical removal of a large number of people from the vicinity of kin, and the ease with which innocently contracted unions might be declared incestuous upon investigation, funneled extraordinary power over inheritance, testamentary practices and penitential fees and penalties, into the hands of the Church. Goody shows that in the long run, the net transfer of capital wealth, largely as land, to the Church, equalled what might have been predicted by the rate of illegitimacy and disinheritance occasioned by the prohibited degrees (plus, certainly, the similar effects of clerical celibacy and depopulation by war and crusade). He also shows that the accession of wealth by the Church was not unconnected with the assumption of responsibility by the Church, from an early date, for those people rendered helpless or marginal, in a turbulent and peregrinating society. The point we want to stress here is not the one that has to do with the sociological implications of the existence of the church, but rather the one that has to do with the cultural implications of these facts for Christian populations. That is, considered even from the standpoint of the family, the most basic of social institutions, Christianity has functioned as a mechanism, or within mechanisms, characterized by dislocation, expropriation, alienation of wealth and affect, and life among strangers. Where symbols were offered that mitigated to some degree the loss of the comforts of consanguinity—as when the language of family was applied to religious persons, as father, sister, brother, for priests, nuns, monks; or in the creation of the institutions of god-parenthood—those symbols were not permitted to reify into self-perpetuating communities: The clergy and monastic orders were celibate and formed a separate culture; god-parents and god-sibs were placed within the prohibited degrees of relationship for marriage, thereby excluding nearly everyone in one's circle of acquaintanceship, not otherwise related, from the circle of potential mates.

It was not only in its evangelical phases and moods that the Christian religion closely identified itself with dislocation, although it was certainly in such phases that dislocation is most explicit. The call to come out from among one's kin and familiars and live set apart echoes through the earliest accounts of Christian experience. It could scarcely have been otherwise for a people whose literary and spiritual inheritance so closely identified illumination and beatitude with exile, whose founding god-prophet and his disciples reveal their missions through successive renunciations. We know little in detail of Christ's spiritual methods. But we have many acts and sayings that portray the outlook of the wanderer, the man with no permanent home or settled domestic arrangements. His genealogy contains no woman of unsullied sexual reputation, including his own mother. He left no progeny and no tomb. All these things suggest, in the context of practices in all ancient and modern Mediterranean societies, a radicalism more far-reaching than the economic or ethical radicalism of his teachings, aiming as it does at the very basis of human association.

An intriguing implication of recent scholarship on the origins of monasticism is that the earliest manifestations of ascetic withdrawal from worldly interests did not arise in Egypt—which is to say in an area of stable and static social life—but in the Syriac-commercial world of the levant, where such practices were associated with peregrination and with the direct imitation of Christ. It appears in fact that the origins of the Church itself must be sought in clusters of believers surrounding an elite of such ascetic imitators. Throughout late antiquity, Peter Brown has explained, Christianity was embodied in holy men, in particular individuals so marked with personal authority that they *were* Christianity.[17]

Thus Christianized populations were, from the very beginning, separated from social and cultic practices that emphasized communities of memory, or that emphasized the value of intercourse with, or memory of, the dead or the culture of the dead. For the converted Jew the dead were members of a superceded covenant. For the converted pagan the dead were as nothing. Evangelization, where it did not encounter and address a pre-existing displacement and alienation, created them in the very terms of the new association.

This process became even more acute as Latin Christianity crossed the Alps, and particularly under conditions of forcible conversion. Germanic people cut off from their ancestral dead received in their midst a new population of elite dead in the form of relics of foreign saints—themselves now posthumously peregrinating classical holy men and women, or, in the case of romanized peoples, dead clerics from among themselves, but celibate and therefore both biologically and socially neutered.[18]

IV

The consideration of saints leads to a second characteristic of Christian piety: if Christian piety entails a challenge to the implicit comforts of settled, tribal existence, it also holds out the promise of membership through a vast historical accumulation of sodalities under a variety of supernatural patronages, as various as Christian populations have been: according to language, occupation, civic association, mission, vocation, opinion, or any other distinguishable social category.

It is not remarkable that the religion of peoples who experience multiple layers of sovereignty as the ordinary condition of social life would contain beliefs in supernatural beings arranged in hierarchies, from local, personal and household gods, through tribal and clan gods, to high gods and indifferent, remote creator gods, or that such a system would express in narrative a variety of mediating and intercessory functions, both instrumental and penitential.[19] What is remarkable in Western Christianity is the dynamism and flexibility of the system of supernatural beings. It not only expresses lines of cleavage within populations, but provides a system of revolutionary transformations whereby assertions of personal and collective rights, or the need to mobilize against danger, or simply the need to accept violent or irreversible change, find their natural patrons in the constellation of beings in the vast supernatural firmament of the Christian religion.[20]

Take a small detail from a tiny corner of Christendom: the *pays* of the Bigoudens in Armorican Brittany, as described by Pierre-Jakez Hélias in his remarkable books on this now-vanished peasant culture which still flourished in the early decades of this century. The Bigoudens were a complete society unto themselves, regarding neighboring Breton communities (perhaps barely distinguishable from one another to an outsider) as foreign places, with strange customs and costumes.[21] "France" to such people may as well have been China. Hélias explains that the patron saint of the Bigoudens was St. Fiacre. This saint was the chief point of contact with supernatural power and cured the residents of the *pays* of illness, and forestalled domestic strife on proper application at his shrine. Other communities had other patron saints who performed similar wonders in the vicinity of their cults. Now one of the things that happened when people from these communities came into contact with the French Republic was that they also came into contact with wider structures of Catholic culture, with, for example, the reputation and more fabulous powers of Our Lady of Lourdes. It was only then that the Bigoudens came to understand, what the local priest knew, but prudently kept to himself, that St. Fiacre as the patron saint of sufferers from hemorrhoids was a humble specialist, a bush-league saint.[22] Such knowledge paralleled similar revelations about the place of one's own *pays*, now no longer a "country," but a district, or a hometown.

Here in miniature is perhaps the most highly significant point of contact between religion and the social history of Western societies. People thrust into memberships that were formerly alien, and which encompassed people not bound by the self-evidency of deeply-charged, over-determined collective memory, found legitimacy in these new memberships through loyalty to higher symbolic representations. This would be true whether the upward displacement in identity was the result of pilgrimage experience, large-scale rural protest, external pressures to collectivize, or dynastic and national centralization. In every case there is some form of movement from a legitimizing potency connected with a locale—classically, the vicinity of the relics of a saint—to a legitimizing potency which is portable: as heavenly figures who left no remains, the persons of Jesus and Mary; or the direct spiritual experience of the divine in mystical discipline; or treasuries of merit available according to a universal dispensing authority; or festivals and rituals that summarize sacrality, such as All Saints and All Souls.

Perhaps most interesting of all is the clear recognition throughout the history of Western theology and spirituality of a form of extreme danger attaching to the ultimate upward transference of allegiance within the orthodox structure of supernatural beings, that is, an explicit attachment to the Holy Ghost. This repeatedly expressed fear of illuminism, quietism, antinomianism, immanentalism and the savagery with which such spiritual elitism is typically suppressed, suggests an implicit understanding of the revolutionary potential in the entire structure of transferences and correspondences of allegiances to supernatural beings. The Holy Ghost, not being representable (although he may be symbolized in a trinitarian context), tends to elude the public (and therefore controllable) domain altogether. The epiphany of the Holy Ghost on the day of Pentecost indeed threatened to undo what God had done at the Tower of Babel, in that every man could hear every other in his own tongue. The event also gave unprecedented power to each separate individual baptized in the Holy Ghost. That is, a transfer of allegiance specifically to the Holy Ghost meant a peculiarly dangerous dual claim to personal certainty and universal membership. Yet this claim remains alive as marking the outer boundary of sanity and social responsibility in a structure that has always functioned to define simultaneously an individuality of consciously chosen attachment, and collectively guarded honor in relation to supernatural personality.

V

What is sketched to this point is a somewhat abstract but historically plausible mechanism that allows us to see the American revolutionary process in the longest possible setting, the setting of a Western mentality shaped both by dislocation and by revolutionary displacement, generally upward and outward, of symbols of attachment. A clear gain in stating problems from within this perspective is that the issue of civil religion and the religion of the churches may be seen to be facets of a single issue which for want of a better term we will call the history of piety: piety being all those practices and perceptions that legitimize social forms by connecting them with supernature. To construct a history of piety in this sense is to ask first of all what social forms lack legitimacy, or are in process of acquiring legitimacy, and secondly, to ask what in the repertory of sacred lore can be entrained for the purpose of conferring legitimacy without danger of overshooting the mark, of creating the monstrous or the blasphemous. Such a history cannot automatically assume that a symbolic solution is by definition tailored to the need it addresses. It must remain open to the possibility of historical tragedy: that there are dead ends, exhaustions, inherent limitations, both in the ability of given social forms to achieve stability or confer blessing, and in the ability of a given religious mechanism to extend its reach without attenuation.

What would be the outlines of an account of American republicanism, seen from this perspective? The issue of revolution was, in a central way, the upward displacement of symbols of affiliation. A key element, or symbol, in the map of American republicanism, and one easy to criticize as only marginally religious, is the figure of God, that is, the God of the Enlightenment, the God of Newton, of the deists, the figure referred to in the political literature of the period as the Almighty, the Creator, Nature's God and so forth.

This figure bears closer scrutiny than it is usually given, precisely because it lies in the path of a clear upward displacement of symbols of affiliation. The particular names of God employed in these invocations, redolent as they are of the fashions of thought of a scientific and rationalistic age, should not obscure the fact that this symbol was not cut out of whole cloth, but stood always at the apex of an orthodox, if somewhat juridically slanted, pyramid of celestial and supernatural beings. The deist God is still in some sense the first person of the Trinity. The emotional point of the isolation of the Father-God is perhaps best articulated in Unitarian piety, where this isolation rests on the unacceptability of a doctrine of atonement, but it is a point that profoundly permeates the age. Good fatherhood was one of its obsessions, and a key emotional factor in the political and social controversies of the 1760s.[23] The Creator is also a father. And the Creator, as father, is the appropriate supernatural patron of a revolutionary displacement of affect in favor of the most general and inclusive of social forms, the society of nothing but orphaned persons.

Here we may be in danger, however, of tending toward certain psychologistic interpretations of the Revolution, some more-or-less Freudian and some concerned with the structure of ritual behavior.[24] They have value in understanding motivation and pattern in certain types of behavior. But such explanations do not deal with specifically religious constraints, with the *dramatis personae* of supernature, and received ways of deploying its favors. Political and cultural movements in sophisticated societies may draw on the whole array of human types in pursuit of their ends. They may fill the empty vessels of ritual procedures with consciously designed tokens and emblems in rich abandon. But such movements cannot invent religious resources, partly because that level of creativity belongs to a different order of cyclical renewal, to a much longer period of time than the time of Revolution; and partly because religion is prior to culture and remains, as T.S. Eliot explained in a classic essay, largely unconscious.[25] Americans might choose to adopt as political ideology the views of John Locke and the Harringtonian opposition writers, rather than the views of Robert Filmer and the Hanoverian court party. They might, with some obvious limitations, choose the persuasions of the Evangelical temperament over the alternative modes of social and intellectual bearing available.[26] But they could not, while sane, choose to place themselves, say, under the protection of the Virgin Mary. Nor, actually more to the point, could they make themselves center rather than periphery, or early rather than late, in relation to the history of Western piety. Both the stock of social forms and the stock of supernatural patrons had already a very long history, in the old centers, and in other peripheries, that shaped not only what was practicable, but what was thinkable.

The simplifications that Americans introduced to the science of government may fairly be said to have been made possible by the peripheral situation of American society and culture, in several senses. Being physically remote they had the time and isolation for radical experiments. The balance of uniformity and variety in ethnic and class mixture was just such as to make compromise both necessary and possible, and both were marks of provinciality, of marginality to any center of European culture. But simplification in the objects of piety, being relatively unconscious, did not lend itself to an orderly redisposition in the way that simplifications in politics did, and led straight to a catastrophe.

Consider only those passages in the Declaration of Independence which are frequently pointed to by those commentators who see in them the adumbration of civil religion. In two places God is mentioned. In one "Nature's God" presides over the severing of the bonds that join one nation to another, giving to each "the separate and equal station" they are entitled to. In the other, the "Creator" endows individual men with "certain unalienable Rights." God is here invoked to bestow rights—which is to say, he bestows legitimacy—on only two social forms: on the nation, and on the person. The nation has no duty, in this formulation, except to be born. The message of God is revealed and exhausted by this epochal turn of affairs. The nation is massively authenticated in this brief but resonating perception, but there are no practices that follow. Likewise with the single person, the Creator's act of endowment entails quickly the premise that the object of this endowment, the single person, is weightier than the political forms he may create. There is here as well a religious perception without a corresponding religious practice. The nation and the self are sacralized but there is no cult to occupy the space left between the nation and the self, and to regulate the claims of both. What in practice occupies this space, in such a society, is the law. But the law, operating only in situations of conflict, cannot have the integrative effect of collective practices. The Constitution, which never mentions God, does prohibit, in the first amendment, any such cultic establishment. Here then is the great "emptiness" Tocqueville and de Rougemont speak of. All that is sacred lies either in the immediate surroundings of the isolated person, or in the ineffably huge, in the nation conceived without features other than its right to be, and to attract to itself a monopoly of honor.

If religion is prior to culture, in some sense of Eliot's subtle distinction, may we not find here some clue to certain paradoxical patterns in American cultural history? One such pattern is apparent in the fact that a nation with no establishment of religion exhibits such a gaudy variety of separate religious expressions. Sidney

Mead, in several thoughtful and illuminating essays, addressed this question, and came to the conclusion that Americans had created a new form of religious organization, namely the *denomination,* and that the significant thing about the religious life of the nation was the equality of all sects and churches; an equality that flowed from the commitment to personal equality, but which in fact fulfilled the first promise of the Church in Christendom: to be universal.[27] Mead has different purposes from Bellah and other writers on civil religion, but like them he is concerned to delineate religious culture in terms of the field of religious organizations: the nation constituting either a separate site of religious institutionalization (Bellah), or the nation as an instrumentality in the hands of a religious people for ordering religious institutions in a revolutionary way (Mead). Neither takes in enough of the field to notice the tensions between the extremes of religious expression, or the specific character of American popular piety.

On one side lies clear evidence of the decline in the intellectual quality and precision of American religious opinion, even while Americans were and remain the most committed to general Christian beliefs of any population in the West. Two very shrewd books on American culture (one on the nineteenth century, and one on contemporary America), make this point from very different perspectives. Daniel Calhoun traces the decline in the relevance and vigor of preaching as an index of the decline of verbal intelligence in America after the Revolutionary generation, but his remarks are extremely telling about the general state of religious culture in the age of Beecher—as opposed, say, to the age of Edwards. Theodore Caplow and his associates, writing of Middletown in the 1970s say that the religion of both pastors and people may be characterized uniformly as "diffuse, hopeful, absorbed in personal experience and moral self-improvement within the narrow sphere of family and local church"—language that might well have described Beecher and his congregation 100 years earlier.[28]

On the other side lies the phenomenon of lush religious invention and experimentation in forms of community, in the era of Mormonism, Brook Farm, the Millerites, New Harmony, and so on down to the present day. America has been a fertile ground for experimentation. It is, however, an experimentation in that special sense, itself an Americanism, which is a synonym for not-too-serious, a bit wild. Arthur Bestor, in a well-known essay, says that the utopias were "patent-office models," trials in miniature for an age to come.[29] But neither the utopias nor the cults were ever thought of as serious experiments in this sense by the main religious tradition.

Tocqueville's image of the great empty middle, the cavernous nothing between the sacralized busy-ness of the private person and his awe of things vast, may help to explain both ends of this paradox: The ordinary, or typical man, in a society whose authentic religious perception is narrowed to himself and to his doings—his "pursuit of happiness"—is both subject and object of his religious cult. In such a condition, disbelief would be as absurd as a rigorously defined belief. Without religious practices there is no contact with others, at the primary religious level, only at the level of the constructed cultures of work and leisure, which, among other things, certainly excludes the dead, the unborn, and the different, from the moral community, and from the field of collective perceptions. The upward displacement of symbols of affiliation, when this moves beyond the patrons of cognizable and affective community—the patrons of guild, village, ethnic group—to embrace general and universal gods, is in danger of a qualitative transformation in which displacement upward becomes evaporation, and society itself disappears. Paradoxically, without society there is no temptation to atheism, because there are no social forms to be modified or destroyed by such a gesture. Indeed, social life is not representable in religious terms except for the single self and the nation as a whole. The celestial patrons of these domains, in traditional terms, are, respectively, the Holy Ghost and the Almighty—the warrior/clock-maker of the American Enlightenment. It is along these lines, as a matter of fact, that religion is conceived in the United States as a matter of public interest. The party of the Holy Ghost is the party of the fundamentalist and evangelical attitude toward society and social reform, and its attitude is characteristically individualistic and morally self-assured. The party of the Almighty, whether left or right ideologically, conceives of moral community in relation to defense (the warrior), and in relation to the economy (the clock-maker). The man of visionary temper, or the seeker, will on the other hand feel the terror of the great empty middle and seek to fill it with parodied versions of religious materials from near and far.[30]

To summarize the argument of this paper: Behind national ideologies, properly so called, lies a territory of historically determined spiritual identifications that constitute limitations on the forms of affective powers in society. In America that territory is Christian, but Christian beyond any previously conceived pale of remissive dispensations, beyond any previous mechanisms of upward displacement of supernatural symbols of affiliation. The legacy of an individualistic and antinomian piety on the one hand,[31] and the legacy of a Revolutionary tradition that fused the God of Calvinism and the God of the Enlightenment on the other, has produced a religion of perceptions without practices, and of membership without society.

The implications of these reflections for social policy lie outside the scope of this paper, but the nature of the problem suggests the direction in which hope, if not solutions, may be sought. If the problem is a Christian problem, that is a problem of Christendom, lying as it does in the whole history of Christian people, then the answers are to be found there, in all the institutional and spiritual resources of the past, or, to put it more simply and graphically, among the dead. The myth of origin must go back behind July 4th, 1776. The Church must not be confused with the denominations of "the lively experiment." The universities must not conceive of themselves as trustees solely for the interests of the living. For these are the institutions, with other, popular ones, whose care is the piety untouched by republicanism, whose historic service is the conservation of the symbols of affiliation in that vital space between self and nation.

NOTES

1. Henry F. May discusses the necessary difference between intellectual and religious history, with a remark about Geertz, in "Intellectual History and Religious History," in John Higham and Paul Conkin, eds., *New Directions in American Intellectual History* (Baltimore, 1979), pp. 105–115. See also Clifford Geertz, *The Interpretation of Cultures: Selected Essays* (New York, 1973), especially "Religion as a Cultural System," pp. 87–125.
2. See John Bossy, *Christianity in the West, 1400–1700* (London, 1985), for a survey suggesting that the social history of Western Europe and the history of Christianity are essentially the same.
3. "Civil Religion in America," *Daedalus* 96 (1967): 1–21.
4. Edmundo O'Gorman, *The Invention of America: An Inquiry into the Historical Nature of the New World and the Meaning of Its History* (Bloomington, 1961). The theme of Adamic innocence in American literature is treated by R.W.B.

Lewis, *The American Adam: Innocence, Tragedy and Tradition in the Nineteenth Century* (Chicago, 1955).

5. Nina Tumarkin, *Lenin Lives: The Lenin Cult in the Soviet Union* (Cambridge, Mass., 1983).
6. See Charles S. Liebman and Eliezer Don-Yehiya, *Civil Religion in Israel: Traditional Judaism and Political Culture in the Jewish State* (Berkeley, 1983). A convenient chart on pp. 218–220 lists "central values and beliefs of Israeli civil religions" through successive regimes of Zionist-socialism, statism, and "new civil religion." The general impression is of progressive solidification and ritualization of fragmentary beliefs and attitudes sometimes inconsistant with one another.
7. A collection of documents with a brief but representative essay on the significance of civil religion in American history is Conrad Cherry, *God's New Israel: Religious Interpretations of American Destiny* (Englewood Cliffs, 1971), esp. pp. 1–24.
8. Russell E. Richey and Donald G. Jones, eds., *American Civil Religion* (New York, 1974), is a convenient collection with a very good introduction. For an older, thoughtful, and gloomy assessment of civil religion in the United States see Will Herberg, *Protestant, Catholic, Jew: An Essay in American Religious Sociology* (Garden City, 1960).
9. George M. Frederickson, *White Supremacy: A Comparative Study in American and South African History* (New York, 1981).
10. Catherine L. Albanese makes a similar point. In speaking of the writings of Sidney Mead, Will Herberg, William Lloyd Warner, Martin E. Marty, and others, she says, "much of it appears as woven of the same thread as the myth of Revolution. Is civil religion good and to be fostered, or idolatrous and to be decried?" But Albanese is herself more interested in modernity, and in the trajectory of the American national experience in itself, than in the relationship of that experience to continuing themes of Western piety. She emphasizes the radical discontinuities of the Revolution and the "fictive" qualities of religion, "a system of meaning-making which may or may not center on the life of God." *Sons of the Fathers: The Civil Religion of the American Revolution* (Philadelphia, 1976), pp. 5–6, 223–225.
11. Patricia Caldwell, *The Puritan Conversion Narrative: The Beginnings of American Expression* (Cambridge, 1983). See also Daniel B. Shea, *Spiritual Autobiography in Early America* (Princeton, 1968).
12. Edmund Morgan, *American Slavery, American Freedom: The Ordeal of Colonial Virginia* (New York, 1975).
13. Robert N. Bellah, *The Broken Covenant: American Civil Religion in Time of Trial* (New York, 1975), p. 3.
14. See, for example, John Dickinson, *The Late Regulations Respecting the British Colonies . . .* (1765), in *Political Writings,* vol. 1 (Wilmington, 1801): 67–68. An extremely interesting essay by J.A. Sharpe, " 'Such Disagreement betwyx Neighbours': Litigation and Human Relations in Early Modern England," in John Bossy, ed., *Disputes and Settlements: Law and Human Relations in the West* (Cambridge, 1983), pp. 167–187, demonstrates that what appears to be

a similar phenomenon in the context of English social life actually functioned quite differently. In the cases he cites, litigiousness concealed anxiety about conflict, and a wish to restore harmony quickly, through mediation.

15. This is the theme of James A. Henretta, "Families and Farms: *Mentalité* in Pre-Industrial America," *William and Mary Quarterly,* 3d ser., 35 (1978): 3–32.
16. Jack Goody, *The Development of the Family and Marriage in Europe* (Cambridge, 1983).
17. Robert Murray, "The Features of the Earliest Christian Asceticism," in *Christian Spirituality: Essays in Honour of Gordon Rupp* ed. Peter Brooks (London, 1975), pp. 63–77; Peter Brown, "The Holy Man as Exemplar in Late Antiquity," *Representations* 1 (1983): 1–36.
18. Here and at several other points in what I have to say about Christian piety, and the relationship of Christian populations to their dead, I am indebted to Lionel Rothkrug, *Religious Practices and Collective Perceptions: Hidden Homologies in the Renaissance and Reformation* (Waterloo, Ont., 1980).
19. See Guy Swanson, *The Birth of the Gods: The Origin of Primitive Beliefs* (Ann Arbor, 1960), for a full and interesting analysis of the connection between perceptions of social structure and the population of supernatural beings in a culture.
20. See also Lionel Rothkrug, "Icon and Ideology in religion and rebellion 1300–1600: *Bauernfreiheit* and *religion royale*" in Janos M. Bak and Gerhard Benecke, eds., *Religion and Rural Revolt* (Manchester, 1984), pp. 31–61.
21. See particularly *Les autres et les miens* (Paris, 1977), pp. 11–34.
22. Pierre-Jakez Hélias, *The Horse of Pride: Life in a Breton Village,* trans. June Guicharnaud (New Haven, 1978), pp. 77–79.
23. Jay Fliegelman, *Prodigals and Pilgrims: The American Revolution Against Patriarchal Authority, 1750–1800* (Cambridge, 1982).
24. Good examples of the former are Bruce Mazlish, "Leadership in the American Revolution: The Psychological Dimension," in *Leadership in the American Revolution* (Washington, D.C., 1974); James H. Hutson, "The American Revolution: The Triumph of a Delusion?" in *New Wine in Old Skins: A Comparative View of Socio-Political Structures and Values Affecting the American Revolution,* ed., Erich Angermann and others (Stuttgart, 1976). On ritual behavior see Peter Shaw, *American Patriots and the Rituals of Revolution* (Cambridge, Mass., 1981).
25. *Notes towards the Definition of Culture* (London, 1948). On orders of time, see George Kubler, *The Shape of Time: Remarks on the History of Things* (New Haven, 1962).
26. Cf. Philip Greven, *The Protestant Temperament: Patterns of Child-Rearing, Religious Experience, and the Self in Early America* (New York, 1977).
27. Sidney E. Mead, *The Lively Experiment: The Shaping of Christianity in America* (New York, 1963); and *The Nation With the Soul of a Church* (New York, 1975), particularly the title essay, pp. 48–77.
28. Daniel Calhoun, *The Intelligence of a People* (Princeton, 1973), pp. 210–230,

256–291; Theodore Caplow, Howard M. Bahr, Bruce A. Chadwick and others, *All Faithful People: Change and Continuity in Middletown's Religion* (Minneapolis, 1983), p. 108.

29. Arthur E. Bestor, Jr., "Patent-Office Models of the Good Society: Some Relationships Between Social Reform and Westward Expansion," *American Historical Review* 58 (1953): 505–526.

30. I take this to be an implication, although not the thesis, of Catherine L. Albanese, *Corresponding Motion: Transcendental Religion and the New America* (Philadelphia, 1977).

31. Like the work by Patricia Caldwell, cited above, a recent book by Charles E. Hambrick-Stowe, *The Practice of Piety: Puritan Devotional Disciplines in Seventeenth-Century New England* (Chapel Hill, 1982), will profoundly affect our understanding of the depth of the theme of spiritual life in America. It certainly renders almost useless some of the conventional contrasts between Puritans and Quakers.

2

Order, Chaos and Renunciation: The Reign of Dharma In Modern India

HARVEY P. ALPER

I. Dharmarājya, The Classical Order of Hindu Society, Ideal and Actuality

Introduction

In India, in distinction from many "third world" nations, there has been no revolution, no civil war, no military *coup d'état*.[1] The nationalist movement triumphed without "armed struggle"—in large measure because it embraced a style of "moral combat," Mohandās K. Gāndhi's *satyāgraha,* which was at once indigenous and *sui generis*. The obvious explanation for these peculiarities is cultural: India, having an ancient and distinctive civilization has responded to the crises of modernity in ways which reflect its traditional worldview. India is not peculiarly spiritual. Nonetheless, there can be no doubt that a sense of "sacred order"[2] is central to traditional Indian civilization.[3] Therefore, it makes sense to explore some of the so-called revolutionary movements in modern India from the perspective of India's religious history.

In the first section of this paper I shall briefly depict the structure of traditional Indian society in terms of the ideology of *dharma,* the "preordained social order" of the Hindu world. In doing so I shall explore traditional Indian mechanisms for change in light of the caste system, a pervasive fear of chaos, the tradition of institutionalized "renunciation" *(saṃnyāsa),* and certain paradigmatic Hindu myths.[4]

In the remainder of the paper I shall focus upon three apparently revolutionary movements: (1) The so-called Saṃnyāsī Rebellion of 18th century Bengal, (2) the North Indian Rebellion of 1857, that is, the "Sepoy Mutiny," and (3) *satyāgraha,* the Gāndhian component of the Nationalist Movement. I shall attempt to explicate these three movements in terms of traditional Indian attitudes towards continuity and change, and as responses to the trauma of colonial occupation.

My thesis is that in traditional India political, economic and social change routinely took place under the umbrella of a theoretically sophisticated, practically efficacious social "theory." According to this theory, change of a certain sort was to be accepted as natural because its occurrence was necessary and predictable. It could be accounted for in terms of an encompassing reality which was understood to be transcendental and, thus, sacred.

If this thesis is correct, then the question of ideology and revolution in modern India may be formulated as follows: to what extent has the traditional Indian social order been able to assimilate and adapt to the admittedly new military, technological, cultural and moral conditions of modernity, that is, to the conditions created by the imposition of Western, scientific order upon India. My conclusion is that the traditional Indian social order has so far worked remarkably well in allowing the subcontinent to cope with the stresses of enforced modernization. It would be foolish to say that India does not face perilous days ahead. I believe, however, that an examination of Indian revolutionary movements since the late eighteenth century, in the context of the traditional Hindu ethos, gives one ground to avoid despair. The Indian social order may yet collapse in the face of modernization, but the historical record, properly understood, by no means forces one to conclude that it shall.

The Dharmic Model: The Eternal Order of Caste Society

The Indian tradition employs the word *dharma* to refer to that proper ordering of groups which is Indian society.[5] It names that society which *is* a society, that is to say, which is, well-ordered, luminous and *"āryan,"* that society which is a "clearing" offering protection from the dark, threatening jungle beyond.

The basic unit of this society is not the individual, it is the group.[6] To the extent that the concept "individual" is even applicable to the Indian social world, the individual is subordinate and perceives himself to be subordinate to the group. It is the group which provides individual identity and makes possible meaningful individual lives. It is the group which delimits the most significant parameters within which each individual lives: traditional occupation; eating habits; social, ethical and ritual duties.[7]

The communities out of which traditional Indian society is woven are deemed to be as distinctive from each other as different species of animals. They are ranked in a complex symbolic hierarchy largely, but not exclusively, in terms of their relative purity or impurity.[8] A given group is considered pure in comparison to those below it, and impure in comparison to those above it.[9] If Dumont is correct, the structure of Hindu society may in large measure be derived from the overriding concern to set the pure apart from the impure. For the concept of impurity itself demands the hierarchical ordering of society as a *gestalt* of discrete groups of varying status.[10]

Indian society has presented itself as if it were an unchanging, immutable, monolith. Westerners, overawed by the ideology of caste and the multitudinous ritual practices employed to minimize pollution, have almost always accepted this self-presentation. What the Indian self-presentation ignores, and what most Western observers have failed to notice, is that Indian society's self-presentation as an eternal, dharmic order is a structural fiction. The dharmic system itself accommodated traditional patterns of change. While the structure of traditional Indian society has remained astonishingly stable, the society itself has evolved significantly. In other words, in the Indian scheme of things social change of certain sorts was perfectly normal. It was necessitated by the dharmic system, and legitimated by the concept of *dharma* itself. On the other hand, according to the dominant religious ideology it was culturally gauche to comment upon the very changes which were, in fact, taken for granted.

Philip Rieff's Sociology of Sacred Order And Its Application to the Study of Traditional India

As an aid in explicating the pattern of social change in traditional and contemporary India I shall employ certain concepts developed by Philip Rieff. Rieff understands culture as a sacred order whose authority is fundamentally expressed through primal prohibitions. These Rieff dubs "interdicts." He summarizes:

> Culture, our ingeniously developed limitations, is constituted by two motifs which are dialectically related. These two motifs, which have shifting contents, I call "interdicts" and "remissions" from interdicts. Every culture is so constituted that there are actions one cannot perform; more precisely, would dread to perform. . . . These interdictory-remis-

sive complexes are more or less compelling; human action is organized in their terms.[11]

Developing Freud's critique of culture, Rieff sees each society as radically limiting "the primacy of possibility." It is not that he imagines that any group of human beings can live perfectly interdictory lives. On the contrary, the content of a culture is predominantly made up of actions which relate dialectically to the interdictions upon which the cultural order is founded:

A raising act, I shall call *interdictory*. A lowering act, I shall call *transgressive*. Mixed acts, what is not done, yet done, I have already called *remissive*. Much of our lives are spent in a remissive flux. The order of that flux is unchanging—I daresay, sacred.[12]

Expressing this in my own words, the interdictory is the complex of absolute (or ultimate) prohibitions which define that which is meant to be unthinkable for a given culture. The remissive and the transgressive are, in turn, responses to the interdictory. A remissive act is a tolerated violation of an interdict which yet, by its very nature, tends to support and reaffirm the validity of the system of interdicts as a whole. A transgressive act is different in degree: it carries a remission to its "logical conclusion."

Ambivalence in Hindu Cosmogonic Myth as a Precedent for Change:

One finds in Hindu mythology a pervasive dualism and a deep ambivalence. The duality expresses itself in the conviction that there is "over against" the world in which we live "another world." The ambivalence expresses itself in the conviction that, while the ordinary world is in one sense superior to the alternative realm, it is in a higher sense its inferior. This ambivalence in values expresses itself socially in a contrast between the "householders," ordinary people, and the "renouncers" *(saṃnyāsīs),* that influential minority who devote themselves fully to the religious life. As a dharmic society, traditional India presupposes that the ordinary world is good. It stresses behavior which will minimize the threat of an outbreak of disorder, of that primal chaos which is represented mythically as a demonic realm and which is conceived of symbolically as a source of pollution. As a society of renunciation *(saṃnyāsa),* India presupposes that the ordinary world is baneful. It demands behavior which inverts the norms and interdicts of ordinary Hindu society. For this reason it is, by the interdictory standards of *dharma,* transgressive.

This axiological dualism first appears in the *Ṛgveda* (c. 1000 B.C.), the oldest extant Indian text. There it informs a creation myth which accounts for the genesis of a twofold world. Our world is a world of *sat,* order, existence, being; the netherworld is a world of *asat,* disorder, non-existence, non-being. The lived, human world is portrayed as a realm of diversity, fertility and growth. Change is intrinsic to it. The counter-world is, in contrast, a dead, impotent monad; a monad which, by its very nature constantly seeks to subvert the world of *sat*. The *Veda* symbolizes this constant threat of chaos in terms of a multitude of anonymous demons who sneak out of the netherworld and attack the human realm under the cover of the night.[13]

The worldview delineated by this body of myth resurfaces again and again. It provides one key for deciphering the traditional Indian social world. The myth portrays the lived human world not only as a world of diversity, but as a world which, by its nature, becomes increasingly diverse. Proliferation is of its essence. This world is, however, threatened by two sources of impending chaos. On the one hand, there is an explicit threat of being overwhelmed or subverted by the *asat*. On the other hand, there is an implicit threat that the world would become so complex, so diversified, so populous that it would in and of itself revert to chaos. On the one hand, our world is good, and the other world is not. On a closer look it emerges that the netherworld with its population of seductive, enticing demons, was at once an object of dread and of fascination. *Asat* was at once the term for that chaos from which the ordered world emerged, and that ultimate return to which one might come to desire. In this ambivalence the dialectic of classical Hindu society is prefigured.[14]

Mechanisms For Remissive and Transgressive Change in Traditional India

For India the interdictory is that web of social regulations which is *dharma*. The world of *dharma* is the ordered world which is yet constantly threatened by outbreaks of disorder; normal change, "remissive change" is the well-contained inner threat, the threat that the dharmic world would become so complex that it would collapse; what I shall call "transgressive change" is the miraculously contained external threat, the threat of a society of "men" who utterly subvert the interdicts of *dharma*. For the traditional Hindu social world this threat is not represented symbolically by demons but concretely by the counter-society of *saṃnyāsīs,* men who have renounced the interdicts of the ordinary world of *sat*.

In the Indian dharmic context remissive acts are those which, while not based on the ideology of purity and impurity, nonetheless, have the surprising effect of strengthening the caste system which is the major social expression of the interdictory force of the dialectic of the pure and the impure. Indeed, I shall argue that certain key remissions from the ideal scheme of *dharma*—the phenomenon of regionalism, the multiplication of *jātis,* the intervention in caste of Dharmic Kings—made normal change both possible and necessary in traditional India. These remissive acts had such an effect because they provided relief from the ceaseless demand for an absolute absence of impurity while respecting and protecting the structure of dharmic society as such. It was, in other words, the remissions from *dharma* which allowed it to appear as unchanging, that is, sacred.

A transgressive act is, in contrast, a violation of the interdictory that is so extreme that it tends to subvert the whole complex of a society's foundational prohibitions. In the context of the dharmic society of traditional India there is, I shall attempt to show, one major form of *institutionalized* transgression: *saṃnyāsa* ("renunciation").

I shall interpret it as transgressive, as a subversive act which is, nonetheless, not allowed to have a subversive effect. I shall further suggest that it is this agile ability to clear a space for individual acts of transgression—acts which explicitly repudiate the whole notion of purity and impurity—while preventing them from getting out of hand which gives traditional India its uncanny social strength and flexibility. It also suggests the unlikelihood—I do not say the impossibility—of either a fundamental moral revolution or an organized, violent, political and social revolution in contemporary India.

Normal, remissive change has been an integral part of the traditional Indian social order. It was not, however, acknowledged directly in the ideal scheme of the textual, Brahmanic tradition. For this reason Western observers have tended to overlook the actual pattern of change—the internal balance—of caste society.

Four major factors lent traditional Indian society a capacity to change which was consistent with, if obscured by, the dominant ideology.

(1) Caste society is intrinsically fissiparous. The multiplicity of types of impurity and the bias of the social order in favor of small-scale, local, exogamous groups *(jātis)* made it possible for the number of such groups to proliferate. From the few original *varṇas* (Vedic social orders) there evolved a society consisting of thousands of communities each of which functioned as if it was a molecule in a stable social compound. These new groups emerged through several "under the table" historical processes. Older communities were subdivided when one portion of the group migrated to a new region; local elites, not originally subscribing to the *varṇa* system were incorporated into the Brahmanic order in what looks very much like a series of political-cultural deals;[15] one or another sort of "deviant" group (tribal people) gradually sought or were constrained to accept "legitimacy" within the caste system; movements within "Hindu" civilization which in one sense or another attempted to dissent from the caste system typically wound up becoming new castes themselves, e.g., the Vīraśaivas. The traditional ideology of *dharma* provided a ready source of alibis to account for this proliferation of communities. The violation of interdicts, especially those relating directly to the rules governing purity, the mixing of communities through illicit marriages, the progressively deteriorating moral atmosphere of the *kaliyuga* (the dark age) could all be invoked to provide a mythic lineage to account for the "hereditary" and "unvarying" status of any community.[16]

(2) The various communities were not autonomous, but were locked into a complex web of economic, social and ritual interdependence. This tended to give every group some interest in the general order, to personalize the relationship between communities within a limited geographical range, and thus to control the sting of low status. Often this web of hereditary interdependence was largely tacit. It did not necessarily achieve formal recognition.[17] The pattern of interdependence between communities changed over time and varied from region to region. Here again, Indian society tolerated a mechanism for change precisely when it gave the appearance of being immutable.

(3) Governments in traditional India—irrespective of the ostensible religious identification of a dynasty—typically understood that the protection of *dharma* was one of their chief duties.[18] The

Indian king was a sacred king not in the sense of being a deity, but in that he was obligated by *dharma* to defend and protect *dharma*. Kings were not limited to the passive support of *dharma*. They could alter the status of a community by decree.[19]

(4) The single most important factor giving traditional Indian society flexibility within the system of *dharma* was regionalism. Although there was a pan-Indian cultural and social system in the pre-modern period, the effective organization of the society was into regions. These regions tended to be smaller than the political units of the nineteenth and twentieth centuries and do not usually correspond to contemporary borders. It appears to be within each region that the system of inter-dependence worked, that dynasties ruled effectively, that the ranking of communities functioned harmoniously. To the extent that this is true, the conventional view of Indian history must be turned on its head. The British prided themselves on having brought unity to India. Nationalist historians prided themselves on demonstrating that certain indigenous empires had come close to achieving that unity. The periods of imperial unity were routinely taken as the high points of Indian history, the norms against which the remaining centuries, the majority of the Indian past, were denigrated as periods of disorder. Recent work calls this view into question: it is possible that the real genius of the Indian social order was regional rather than imperial; that it was in the regions that the dharmic system functioned at its best, there achieving a balance between tolerance of change and loyalty to a transcendent order.[20]

II. The Case of the Warrior Ascetics: The Saṃnyāsi Rebellions of 18th Century Bengal

In January 1985, as the unofficial returns began to make clear the election victory of Rajiv Gandhi and the Congress-I, crowds could be heard in the cities of north India chanting, "Indira Gandhi amara hai," in effect, "Indira Gandhi has become immortal." It is not accidental that an originally religious chant was here pressed into service in an apparently secular, political context. Nor should it be thought that the use of this chant was just a perfunctory political ritual. On the contrary, the Indian populace chanted the name of the recently martyred Prime Minister rather than that of her son and successor precisely because she had come to be viewed—even by some of her political opponents—as an embodiment of India itself.

One can sense something of the emotional context of this "deification" of Indira as the mother of her country by considering the song which served as the "national anthem" of pre-independent India. Written in the Bengali language, the song is entitled "Bande Mātaram," ["Hail to the Mother"]. It is a hymn of obeisance to the land of India conceived of as a manifestation of an omnipotent, multi-faceted mother goddess:

Mother to thee I bow.
Who hath said thou art weak in thy lands,
When the swords flash out in twice seventy million hands
And seventy million voices roar
Thy dreadful name from shore to shore?
. . .
To thee I call, Mother and Lord!
Thou who savest arise and save!
. . .
Thou art wisdom, thou art law,
Thou our heart, our soul, our breath,
Thou the love divine, the awe
In our hearts that conquers death.
Thine the strength that nerves the arm,
Thine the beauty, thine the charm.
Every image made divine
In our temples is but thine.[21]

The song comes from Baṅkim Candra Chatterjee's *Ānandamaṭh,*[22] one of the first novels written in an Indian language.[23] The novel, an historical romance deeply influenced by the work of Sir Walter Scott, appeared in 1882, three years before the first meeting of the Indian National Congress, the fore-runner of the Congress Party. In *Ānandamaṭh* Baṅkimcandra took as his subject the *saṃnyāsī* rebellion of late eighteenth century Bengal. Indeed, one may credit the novel with creating that insurrection, for it established something like an official mythology of the rebellion and won for it a place in the lore of the independence movement. *Ānandamaṭh* portrays the resurgence of Indian nationalism as a direct concomitant of the renaissance of traditional Hinduism. One might even date the conception—I would say, the misconception—of the Hindu tradition as a potentially revolutionary political force from the portrayal of the *saṃnyāsī* rebellion in this work.

To understand the appeal of Baṅkimcandra's novel one must see it in its historical context. The last quarter of the nineteenth century saw the emergence, for the first time in Indian history, of a pan-Indian national consciousness. The novel *Ānandamaṭh* exemplifies that strand in this new consciousness which was known as Extremist.[24] For the Extremists, "politics" and "religion" were necessarily intertwined. The British would be driven out of India, they argued, only when the English speaking elite mobilized the Hindu masses by speaking the language of religious fervor which they understood. The portrayal of the *saṃnyāsī* rebellion in *Ānandamaṭh,* a work written in the vernacular for a popular audience, was thus intended to appeal to the Indian people's innate love of Mother India. Today one can appreciate it for what it was: a brilliant work of literary propaganda which helped create precisely the feelings which it ostensibly took as a given.

Ānandamaṭh is set in the 1770's. Its heroes are a band of *saṃnyāsīs* who have taken up arms against their rulers—the Muslim inheritors of Mughal authority—in the name of the sacred land of Bengal and the goddess Durgā with whom the land is identified. In the novel land, deity and mother are tied together so totally that disloyalty to one is seen to be disloyalty to the others. "The mother and the land of birth are higher than heaven," the warrior ascetic Bhavananda says. The Muslims and the British are both condemned as illegitimate rulers precisely because they do not—and by birth cannot—fulfil the primary duty of kings, upholding the order of *dharma:*

> "In every country the bond that binds a sovereign to his subjects is the protection that he gives; but our Mussulman king—how does he protect us? Our religion is gone; so is our caste, our honor and the sacredness of our family even! Our lives even are now to be sacrificed. Unless we drive these tipsy longbeards away, a Hindu can no longer hope to save his religion."[25]

In Baṅkimcandra's romantic revisioning, the *saṃnyāsīs* of eighteenth century Bengal became the vanguard of a new, independent India, a purified, Hindu Bhāratavarṣa. Obviously, the portrayal of the *saṃnyāsī* revolt in *Ānandamaṭh* is historically anachronistic.[26] It was, however, enormously influential and it is worth asking whether there was anything like a religiously inspired revolutionary movement in eighteenth century Bengal.

The events which historians have tended to treat indiscriminately together as *the* rebellion of the *saṃnyāsīs* occurred roughly between 1765 and 1790, a period of instability and disruption in Bengal which also saw, in 1770, a traumatic regional famine. The British historian J. N. Farquhar—ironically, he cites the appendix to Bankimcandra's novel as his source—describes the outbreak from the colonialist perspective:

> For several years, before and after 1770, great hordes of armed sannyasis infested Bengal. Appearing suddenly in a district, they would burn, plunder and ravage without mercy or measure. On one occasion they plundered Dacca, which was then a wealthy city. The income of the British Government in Bengal was seriously curtailed in consequence more than once. The memory of this horror still survives in Bengal and is called The Sannyasi Rebellion. Hastings finally put them down.[27]

Farquhar's language is revealing: just as Baṅkimcandra presupposes that the rebellious *saṃnyāsīs* must have been religiously inspired revolutionaries, so Farquhar presupposes that they must have been a horde of religious fanatics. In fact, neither account is credible. Upon examination, the *saṃnyāsī* Rebellion turns out to have been neither religious nor a rebellion.[28]

According to Lorenzen, the disturbances in Bengal seemed to have involved "three quite separate phenomena."[29] The first and most significant of these involved the Madārīs, a group of Muslim mendicants *(fakīrs)* who annually went on pilgrimages to certain sites in northern and central Bengal. They relied for "income" on the traditional "contributions" of the villages and *zamindars* (large landowners) through whose lands they passed. After 1765 when the East India Company won the right to collect taxes in Bengal the local population found itself in a "financial squeeze in which they were unable to pay both the British and the fakīr pilgrims." Eventually, after a period of intermittent "warfare" the Madaris were excluded from Bengal by the combined pressure of the local elite and the regional power, that is, the *zamindars* and the Company. There is some evidence that the Madaris gathered into their ranks peasants who were disaffected or had been displaced from the land. Nonetheless, Lorenzen is surely correct in concluding that "the Madaris never led what could realistically be called a popular rebellion of the lower classes."[30]

The second phenomenon in the so-called *saṃnyāsī* uprising involved armed bands of *bona fide* Hindu renouncers. During the long period of Muslim domination in north India (the 13th to 18th centuries) certain groups of organized renouncers had armed themselves. Some of these eventually became mercenaries and, opportunistically, marauders. In the late eighteenth century some of these groups—technically *Daśanāmī nāga saṃnyāsīs*—became involved in a dynastic struggle in the region of Cooch Behar, a principality today located between Bangladesh and Bhutan. Because the *saṃnyāsīs* were usually allied with claimants for the throne who were opposed by the British it could have appeared as if they were involved in revolutionary activity. Such a reading would be anachronistic, and, in any case, the groups involved departed Bengal around 1775 "to participate in the wars of central India."

Finally, the third phenomenon in the rebellion was an "attempt by Dasnami sannyasis resident in local monasteries to collect debts owed to them by many zamindars." Here, again, the British, desiring to maximize their own revenue and, one may assume, desiring to create a native Indian gentry, allied themselves with the large landowners and used their authority to cancel or reduce the zamindari debts.[31]

The disturbances in Bengal seem to have oscillated between three poles: the defense of local interests by armed mendicants, the involvement in petty dynastic struggles by mercenary ascetics, the descent into brigandage by one and all as opportunities presented themselves.

Neither a nationalist nor a colonialist perspective helps elucidate the situation. The "insurrections" were not even remotely anticolonial, they were not rebellions against a foreign, occupying power. Similarly, the East India Company in restoring order to the Bengali countryside was not defeating an incipient revolution. On the contrary, the British were responding opportunistically to the collapse of imperial Mughal administration in the eastern Gangetic plain. They were adventurers vying with a number of indigenous powers for regional supremacy. Like these native groups, like the "warrior ascetics" themselves, the Company was predominantly motivated by the desire to maximize revenues which were, by and large, derived from taxes on land. They thus were behaving in a classically Indian manner.

What role did traditional religious ideology play in this situation? The evidence suggests that religion most probably played no explicit role at all. It neither encouraged nor retarded Indian nationalism, which in any case was an idea that had not yet been planted on the subcontinent. It would appear not to have been a factor—certainly not a significant factor—in prompting the *saṃnyāsī* rebellion.[32] On the other hand, we can speculate that the Hindu understanding of *dharma*—in the broad sense I have outlined—predisposed the population of Bengal to defend the traditional social order during an interregnum, a period of expected social chaos. In the first instance it would have tended to legitimate the defense of "local" interests, those of the *zamindars* and those of the peasants, as well as those of the "warrior ascetics." In the second instance, however, it would have tended to legitimate the acceptance of British rule once it was clear that the Company had, in fact, managed to establish effective *regional* suzerainty. If, on the other hand, anyone in Bengal had been able to conceptualize anything like an organized, pan-Bengali social and political revolution, the traditional Hindu social order would have functioned to minimize the possibility of its outbreak, no less its consummation.[33]

One may, on the other hand, discern in the *saṃnyāsī* rebellion the seeds of that religious militancy which was cultivated first by the Extremists and then by Gāndhi. Once the idea of a single Indian nation arose among Western educated Indians in the second half of the nineteenth century it was natural to extend the concept of *dharma* so that it encompassed loyalty to national as well as local and regional order. It was natural to conclude that its defense entailed struggling for the independence of India. By this marriage of *dharma* and the idea of a free India the nationalist leaders were able to marshal sufficient mass support to drive the British out of India. At the same time, the nationalist movement took upon itself the extraordinarily conservative hue of *dharma* as such. In the century since Baṅkimcandra's canonization of the *saṃnyāsī* rebellion this has at once retarded the pace of Indian social reform while giving independent India an enviable stability in an age of creeping, but inevitable modernization.

III. A Contagion of Chaos: The North Indian Rebellion of 1857

The north Indian rebellion of 1857–59—known to the British as the Sepoy Mutiny—might well be the most thoroughly documented but least understood revolutionary movement of the nineteenth century. In spite of the extent of the primary and secondary literature, there is no consensus concerning the nature of the revolt. Here, even more than ordinarily, scholarship reflects ideology. Apologists for the British tend to depict the revolt as essentially military. Indian nationalists tend to depict the revolt as an organized movement of national resistance. Scholars concerned with the history of the "third world" have seen the revolt as one in a series of peasant insurgencies responding to imperialist oppression. I shall not attempt to arbitrate between these perspectives, all of which can teach us something. Rather, after briefly reviewing the main chronology of the revolt, I shall outline its central features and shall attempt to elucidate what it tells us about the role of traditional religion in apparently revolutionary movements in India.[34]

In the years following the defeat of the Marathas in 1819, the East India Company managed to absorb one Indian principality after another. By 1857 the British were the new masters of the Indian subcontinent. With a force of only 271,000 (228,000 native troops; 43,000 Europeans) they ruled a realm of some two hundred million inhabitants.[35]

The revolt of the native troops in the Company's army began in the Winter of 1857. Rumors concerning the use of animal fat—repugnant to both Hindus and Muslims—to grease the cartridges for the army's new Enfield rifles began circulating as early as January. Disturbances in March led to the disbanding of several native regiments. On May tenth, the garrison at Meerut revolted. The troops marched on Delhi. They occupied it on the eleventh, and proclaimed the last of the Mughals, Bahadur Shah, once again Emperor. As news of the fall of Delhi spread, other mutinies followed. By June, British authority had disappeared from vast areas of central India. The rebel triumph was short-lived. British forces reoccupied Delhi in September. In March 1858 they re-took the cities of Lucknow, Jhansi, Bareilly and Gwalior. Although fighting continued for another year, by June 1858 it was clear that the British had reasserted their paramountcy over India.[36]

Putting aside ideological concerns, R. C. Majumdar correctly discerns the underlying pattern of the revolt:

> In general [the mutinies] followed the pattern set at Mirat. The sepoys killed the officers and other Europeans on whom they could lay their hands, in many cases sparing neither women nor children. They also released the prisoners from jail, plundered the treasury, burnt government offices, and then either set out for Delhi, or joined some local chiefs, or roamed at large, seeking to enrich themselves by indiscriminate plunder of both Indians and Europeans.[37]

In a typical locality the revolt went through three phases: first, there was a "spontaneous" mutiny of native soldiers displeased with the way they were treated by their British officers; second, this mutiny acquired a nativist character in which both Europeans and their property were destroyed; third, joined by any number of disaffected elements in the population, the mutineers degenerated into looters preying on Indians even more than on Europeans.[38]

The first and third "phases" in this progression are not surprising. The successful mutiny of a town's sepoy garrison was tacitly taken as a signal that ordinary social restraints had been abrogated; in that situation one could indulge in transgressive behavior. In Majumdar's words:

> The success of the mutineers at various places, and the massacre or flight of the local British officials . . . led the people . . . to believe that the British *raj* had ceased to exist. No visible symbol was left of its authority . . . and there was almost a complete political vacuum. . . .[39]

To put this in the idiom of Hindu myth, just as it was to be expected that the dharmic order of society would come to an end in the dissolution following the *kaliyuga,* so it was to be expected that every dynasty would periodically come to an end in a period of moral chaos. So one British officer outside of Delhi reported:

> [In one of the rooms] a native, from his appearance a soldier, was haranguing the men and saying that every power or government existed its alloted time, and that it was nothing extraordinary that that of the English had come to an end, according to what had been predicted in their native books.[40]

As a movement of "retainers" which tended to degenerate into free-lance banditry, the Revolt of 1857 thus fits perfectly into the "feudal" pattern of periodic chaos accompanying the decline of a regional dynasty. It is precisely its chaotic, disorganized, spontaneous character that marks it as traditional, as pre-modern in character. The factor which distinguishes it as *in part* a modern, anti-colonial movement was its nativism, and this nativistic streak was its most obviously religious component.

The tale of official British hostility to the religious traditions of India is well known. The forty years after the legitimation of Christian missionary activity in 1813 saw both a series of technological innovations (the railway, the telegraph, steam engines, the first cotton mill, the beginning of the great trunk roads), and a series of direct attempts to subvert indigenous social traditions. *Satī* (the "voluntary" immolation of widows), the slave trade and infanticide were prohibited; "thugee" was attacked; the remarriage of widows was legitimised; English education was made available to Indians.

On the common level, the typical British officer saw India as:

> a detestable country [whose] people were savages; its food inedible; its climate horrible; the whole damned place . . . full of revolting insects that ate huge holes in new, expensive uniforms, of soggy peaches that tasted like turnips and cantankerous camels that smelled like drains.[41]

The leading Evangelicals made no bones of their contempt for the traditional religious system. Charles Grant, a prominent Company servant, opined:

> We cannot avoid recognizing in the people of Hindostan a race of men lamentably degenerate and base; retaining but a feeble sense of moral obligation; yet obstinate in their disregard of what they know to be right.

Macaulay, in his famous *Minute on Education,* remarked that no Orientalist "could deny that a single shelf of a good European library was worth the whole native literature of India and Arabia." In 1836 he prophesied that within thirty years "there would not be a single idolator among the respectable classes of Bengal."[42] It was no paranoia for the common Indian—Hindu or Muslim—to imagine that the British were out to transform native life. It's no wonder that by 1857, there was considerable estrangement between the British and the Indian populations.

In the eighteenth century, relations between Indians and Europeans had often been close. Fraternization was common and the Company tried not to interfere in local affairs. By 1857 the situation had changed. Greed, missionary earnestness, and plain old-fashioned racism all contributed to a new attitude, transforming Indians into the "subject race" of a "benevolent," morally and technologically superior power. By 1857 the psychological and cultural stress of colonial occupation was clear. This more or less guaranteed that in a time of crisis some Indians would turn nativist. Hence, the revolt of 1857, to the extent that it was directed against the British, was less an attempt to appropriate Western goods for Indians than an inchoate, disorganized drive to efface evidence of Western culture. (In one telling example the very milestones which had been laid down along a highway were smashed or tossed into the fields.)[43] Nor is it surprising that the revolt of 1857 was a prolonged violent encounter marked by rage, brutality, and mutual incomprehension.

The revolt of 1857 was not a modern revolution. It was a traditional outbreak with certain modern dimensions. Speaking broadly, it had three causes.

The first was political: the century and a half between the death of Aurangzeb and the Mutiny saw the disintegration of the Mughal Empire, fratricidal conflict between the Indian successor states,[44] the expansion of the East India Company, and the dispossession of many local and regional elites. This led to an unraveling of traditional polity and, at the first sign of British weakness, to widespread if disorganized attempts to restore the traditional political order. These restorative impulses contributed to the eradication of British administration in vast areas of north and central India. They were not strong enough to provide an alternative administration.[45]

The second cause of the revolt was economic: whatever one's ultimate assessment of the impact of British policy on the Indian economy, there can be no doubt that it precipitated a general dislocation of the traditional economic order.[46] The rule of the Company saw heavy taxation of the peasantry, the decline of certain industries and handicrafts, the introduction of plantation agriculture and the reorganization of the system of land tenure. This produced a large number of disgruntled, downwardly mobile individuals drawn from all classes: "nobles," landlords, petty bureaucrats, merchants, artisans, shopkeepers and peasants. By 1857 there was a large body of discontented people with an economic grievance willing to take advantage of any lapse in British authority.

The third and most significant cause of the revolt was psychological. The Western presence in India challenged the entire traditional culture, a culture in which, as in all traditional societies, religion played a leading role. The West brought with it the whole panoply of Enlightenment values and mores: philosophical scepticism; economic, political and social individualism; competitiveness; and what from a traditional Indian perspective still appears to be an astonishingly licentious attitude toward sexual behavior. Especially as articulated by the Evangelicals, Western values were correctly understood as calling into question the whole complex of traditional Indian life. That this aggressive cultural invasion came armed with a superior technology made it all the more threatening. Hence the nativism of the Revolt of 1857: the attempt in many localities to efface every evidence of Western culture—factories, churches, schools, telegraphs, railways, and most appropriately, government records.

What was the role of traditional religion in the revolt of 1857? To the extent that the revolt was a "passionate protest against the relentless penetration of the west"[47] the religious element in it must have been central. Even Gough—who has cogently argued that scholars overemphasize the religious element in Indian communal violence while underemphasizing class conflict—describes it as "a holy war, so announced repeatedly by rulers and religious leaders."[48] But this is insufficiently precise: the religious factor in Indian revolutionary movements can only be assessed if the internal complexity of the subcontinent's religious life is kept in mind.

From my perspective as a student of traditional Hindu polytheism and theology, the main point is this: Because of its very nature the dharmic society legitimates several different sorts of revolutionary and anti-revolutionary behavior:

(1) In the first instance it legitimates violent, popular outbreaks when the authority of regional hierarchies break down.[49] The very manner in which the revolt of 1857 spread reveals something of the intense stress on which it fed. Two metaphors dominate the accounts, that of contagion and conflagration. The revolt spread like a disease or like a fire. In other words, it struck many observers as spreading irrationally, magically.[50] In this sense one might compare the social disorder which it engendered to the festival of Holi on which all India "enjoys" a ritual reversal of social roles.

(2) Islam and certain strands in traditional Hinduism further legitimate local "millenarian" protest movements under the leadership of "shamanic" holy men. There is, for example, the case of the Maulavi Ahmadulla of Fyzabad who preached *jihad* against the British and was proclaimed "Caliph" *(khalifat ullah)*.[51]

(3) On the other hand, the dharmic vision provides no precedent for coordinating or pursuing these outbreaks over any length of time. The narrative mythic traditions, oral or written, led people to expect periodic outbursts of repressed emotion, of the hatred and resentment which was certainly there, but also led them to expect these outbreaks to be temporary, without lasting effect.

(4) Even more significantly, in its myths, rituals and laws the dharmic society inculcates a fear of chaos so deep as to dispose much of the population to an instinctive defense of the social order. I in no way mean to revive the old stereotype that the Hindu tra-

dition renders Indians passive and fatalistic. I do judge that the dharmic society, in the end, works against the sort of sustained, ideological anarchy which often characterizes successful revolutions.

(5) The traditional religious order provides, in addition, an extraordinary safety value. *Saṃnyāsa,* institutionalized renunciation, seems to have provided many individuals with a ready means for dealing with stress, whether it was brought on by traditional caste oppression, new economic inequality, or the psychological deprivation engendered by the colonial situation.

(6) Finally, traditional Hinduism prepares people for the possibility that when there is a breakdown of the traditional, self-functioning, self-correcting order relief shall come about magically, through the intervention of a charismatic guru who will reestablish the dharma.[52] Thus it is not entirely surprising that within 60 years of the ineffective outbreak of 1857, the Indian masses responded to a charismatic nativist such as Mohandās K. Gāndhi.

IV. Satyāgraha in Context: Three Faces of Mahātma Gāndhi

Shortly before his death, Mohandās Gāndhi was asked by a foreign journalist: "How would you meet the atom bomb . . . with nonviolence"? He replied:

> I will not go underground, I will not go into shelter. I will come out in the open and let the pilot see I have not a trace of evil against him. The pilot will not see our faces at his great height, I know. But that longing in our hearts—that he will not come to harm—would reach up to him and his eyes would be opened.[53]

It is tempting to respond cynically to such an utterance, to deplore Gāndhi's retarded sense of *realpolitik.* Such a response would be a mistake. As the success of Richard Attenborough's film indicates, Gāndhi—lone apostle of engaged quietism—will not go away.

Gāndhi's importance as a world political and spiritual leader is underscored if one contrasts him with two of his contemporaries. Gāndhi first came to dominate the campaign for Indian independence during the Non-Cooperation movement of 1920–1922, at the very time Lenin was establishing the Soviet system in Russia and Mussolini was establishing Fascism in Italy. In all three cases a charismatic leader was attempting to found a regime of a new sort on the basis of his instinctive rapport with the common people. Indeed, Gāndhi came to personify the Indian freedom movement because of his ability to mobilize the Indian masses by appealing to their political and religious aspirations. His most distinctive contribution to the movement, the concept of nonviolent noncooperation, was at once political and spiritual. According to Gāndhi, India merited independence only if it were won by the conscious use of that technique of victimless confrontation which he dubbed *satyāgraha,* a technique designed to produce a spiritual conversion in oneself *and* in ones "opponent."[54] Like Lenin and Mussolini—unlike another contemporary, Woodrow Wilson—Gāndhi stood outside the tradition of liberal democracy. But, unlike Lenin and Mussolini, Gāndhi proposed a polity based on inner transformation of character. Thus, to reach a final assessment of the relationship between traditional religious ideology and modern revolution in India, one must come to terms with Gāndhi.

The first thing that any student of Gāndhi should confess is that the Mahatma is a more complex figure than meets the eye.[55] In order to evaluate the spiritual component of Gāndhi's contribution to the freedom movement, I shall focus on what I call his three faces, or guises: Gāndhi the seeker, Gāndhi the passionate conservative, and Gāndhi the magician.

(1) It was Gāndhi's fate to make of his inner ambiguities a public program. This is the main lesson of Erikson's meticulous study of Gāndhi the man.[56] Throughout his career, Gāndhi stubbornly refused to distinguish between self, family and society. A single ethic was to hold good in all circumstances. In this Gāndhi accurately reflects both the dharmic and *saṃnyāsic* traditions according to which ethical principles are ultimately unvarying, even though the manner in which they are put into play is infinite. Gāndhi is, at the same time, setting himself up for a confrontation with modern, Western civilization according to which ethical principles have increasingly been seen as "situational," that is, relative.

As Erikson stresses, and as many have noted, for much of his life Gāndhi suffered from recurring insecurity rooted in an intensely ambivalent relationship with his parents. Many of the characteristic traits of Gāndhi the seeker are undoubtedly expressions of this ambivalence. One of the first things a Western observer is likely to note, in reflecting on Gāndhi's personhood, is his lifelong struggle to come to terms with embodiment and sexuality. Gāndhi expressed his chagrin over being embodied in a characteristically Indian fashion, in terms of impurity. As Erikson notes, for Gāndhi "to remain unblemished" was "*the* overweening emotional necessity."[57]

Another psychologically striking trait is Gāndhi's androgynous ideal. His utterances are replete with metaphors of motherhood. It seems clear that he strived to be both mother and father to all with whom he came into serious contact.[58] Erikson's discussion of Gāndhi's "recruitment" of his inner circle of disciples is revealing. What Erikson doesn't realize is that Gāndhi conforms perfectly to the pattern by which gurus typically relate to their disciples. In both cases patterns of familial identification and courtship are adapted to an ostensibly non-familial, asexual relationship.[59]

Thirdly, one notices that Gāndhi was persistently restless. It is not only his moving to England and South Africa (for which, by the way, he was officially outcast). After returning to India he wandered from place to place with a sort of regular irregularity. Again, Gāndhi the seeker is conforming to traditional spiritual practice. Among the things which a renouncer renounces is a permanent home: his mission is to be his home.

Gāndhi the human being dealt with his insecurities by transforming himself into Gāndhi the politician and Gāndhi the Mahātma. He did this exactly as one would expect. As a Western educated traditionalist Gāndhi had a compelling need to justify his very existence. "I must reduce myself to zero,"[60] he wrote. He attempted this self-justification through simplicity, the refusal to do harm *(ahiṃsā),* chastity *(brahmacarya),* and an utterly scrupulous adherance *(āgraha)* to truth *(satya).* The result for Gāndhi the seeker was loneliness of a special kind. With one foot he stood with the great troubled yogis of the past. With the other he stood as a political prophet, an indispensably modern guru, "the only available person who [could] handle" the task.[61]

(2) The tendency to beatify Gāndhi—a tendency he hardly discouraged—has often led Westerners to imagine that he was an ethereal, impractical man. Nothing could be less true. He was a wiley, intuitive politician, fully the equal of the Machiavellis of his day. Before assessing Gāndhi as a religious figure, it is important to consider the role he played in Indian politics. The evaluation of Gāndhi the politician is very much a live issue in India today. There is extensive partisan literature, but no consensus as to his

political goals, competence or effectiveness. While the last word on the question is far from said, it is important to understand that a *prima facie* case can be made for conceiving of Gāndhi as a brilliant conservative strategist. Although this calls into question the commonly held conviction that, at heart, Gāndhi was a social revolutionary, it seems clear that a consistent upholder of the dharmic vision of society would have to be instinctively conservative. That this position is by no means to be despised I shall later suggest.

The simplest way to document the conservative strand in Gāndhi's thought is by reference to his outspoken anti-modernism.[62] To be sure, Gāndhi is so complex and his writing so voluminous that generalizations are difficult. It is true that Gāndhi was deeply influenced by certain Western figures, Tolstoy and Thoreau among them. Nonetheless, an anti-industrial diatribe is central to the Gāndhian vision. It cannot be wished away. The most popular of Gāndhi's books in the West has always been the *Autobiography*. This is a remarkable document, and comparison with the *Confessions* of Augustine and Rousseau is legitimate. The *Autobiography*, nonetheless, portrays only one of Gāndhi's masks, that of Gāndhi the seeker. To glimpse Gāndhi the passionate conservative, one must read *Hind Svarāj*.[63]

In *Hind Svarāj* Gāndhi argues that Indian civilization is morally superior to the pseudo-civilization of the West:

> The tendency of the Indian civilization is to elevate the moral being, that of the Western civilization is to propogate immorality. The latter is godless, the former is based on a belief in God. So understanding and so believing, it behoves every lover of India to cling to the old Indian civilization even as a child clings to the mother's breast.

The sins of the west are "self-indulgence" and enslavement to the machine. The West is found wanting because it is not the land of *dharma:*

> Civilization is that mode of conduct which points out to man the path of duty. Performance of duty and observance of morality are convertible terms. To observe morality is to attain mastery over our mind and our passions. So doing, we know ourselves. The Gujarati equivalent for civilization means "good conduct."[64]

With such a thesis *Hind Svarāj* is as much an example of anti-colonialist nativism as was the indiscriminate destruction of European artifacts during the Revolt of 1857. One should not be shocked that Gāndhi once said, "I hold that economic progress . . . is antagonistic to real progress," nor that he was willing to dismiss the Western, modern "notion of justice" as "Satanic."[65] It should not be forgotten that as the son and grandson of Bania officials, Gāndhi was a scion of the Indian elite. Given his background, his personality, and his ideology, his political position is understandable. One would expect him to move heaven and earth to see that any religious "revolution" which *he* launched did not turn into a social revolution.

A case for considering Gāndhi's role in the freedom movement as conservative is outlined by Omvedt.[66] Her thesis is that:

> the social function of Gāndhian nonviolence in Indian history has been to allow India to achieve a political revolution (formal independence) without having a social revolution. Gāndhi's control of the movement was directed not only at achieving independence from Britain, but also at pacification of the Indian revolution itself.[67]

Omvedt offers three main arguments. In my own terms: (a) Gāndhi advocated the reform rather than the abolition of the caste system. He thus played the role of progressive traditionalist and this in general had the effect of strengthening the significance of hierarchy within Indian society. (b) Gāndhi acted consistently to prevent agrarian and urban revolt from getting out of hand, most dramatically when he called off the Non-Cooperation Campaign after the police were attacked at Chauri Chaura in 1922. This had the effect of containing any sort of popular uprising which threatened to result in class warfare. (c) Gāndhi, along with the bulk of India's elite, gave no support whatsoever to free-lance and spontaneous rebellions which broke out more frequently than one is led to believe. He thus repudiated the potentially successful mutiny of the Royal Indian Navy in 1946, and fought the efforts of "Untouchables" to organize as an independent pressure group.

Omvedt attributes Gāndhi's conservatism to his class origins, his being "the friend of capitalists and Brahmans." She points out that "Gāndhi's fear of violence was in large part a fear of the chaos he perceived as threatening the structure of Indian society and the position of the Indian elite if mass energies were not controlled." This is surely so, and yet it is a half-truth. Gāndhi's fear of chaos can hardly be explained solely in terms of class struggle. After all, it is Gāndhi who launched the Quit India Campaign with the remark, "Leave India to God or to anarchy."[68] From the psychological perspective which we have learned from Erikson it seems certain that Gāndhi the politician both feared and courted anarchy. For social anarchy, the unbridled play of bodily passion provided the ultimate stage upon which Gāndhi the magician could perform.

(3) The central Gāndhian technique for bringing about authentic religious and political change was *satyāgraha,* "truth-force," "soul-force," literally, "adhering firmly to that which is."[69] Under Gāndhi's direction *satyāgraha* meant an organized campaign to right a wrong. Such a campaign typically involved preparation, the issuing of an ultimatum, and relevant forms of non-cooperation or civil disobediance.[70]

How is one to understand *satyāgraha?* In the broad perspective of Indian cultural history, and in terms of its effects, one cannot take Gāndhi's own descriptions at face value. He explains what he hoped to accomplish through *satyāgraha.* We must ask what *satyāgraha* really amounted to.

The protestations of Gāndhi and his followers notwithstanding, it seems to me that fasting was of the essence of *satyāgraha*—after all, Gāndhi "fasted to the death" some seventeen times.[71] This means that, in the end, *satyāgraha* is a form of meditative compulsion, an inspired modern adaptation of the *vrata,* the traditional Hindu ritual of taking a vow in order to compel an unruly universe to behave as one thinks it ought. In this context taking a vow is a supreme act of will and is understood to be effective by virtue of the power one has accumulated through heroic acts of self-restraint (*tapas,* "inner heat").

Tapas was one of the characteristic activities of a *saṃnyāsī* and Gāndhi speaks of *tapas* often: "Real suffering bravely borne melts even a heart of stone. Such is the potency of suffering or *tapas.* And there lies the key to *satyāgraha.*"[72] In applying these Vedic concepts in a new way Gāndhi was drawing upon an ancient psycho-ritual complex according to which one may win rewards commensurate with the perfection of ones self-denial. In Erikson's words, "to take active charge of senseless suffering by deliberately choosing to court meaningful suffering can be experienced as an exhilarating mastery over fate within a new ritualization."[73] Understood critically the use of *tapas* to gain one's will strikes one as a technique for shaming the universe, an audacious form of cosmic blackmail—as when an unruly three year old holds his breath until his parents capitulate to some demand.

In India, the innumerable mythic precedents must be kept in

mind. I choose one for the purpose of illustration, the story of king Bhagīratha compelling the gods to allow the river Ganges to descend from the heavens to the earth:

> When the story opens the earth is suffering from an intense drought caused by the sage Agastya who had—for perfectly good reasons—swallowed the oceans. King Bhagīratha needed water to perform rituals for his ancestors. "He decided to force his will upon the celestial powers and compel them to release the heavenly Ganges itself." In order to do this he went to Gokarṇa, a site holy to the god Śiva. "Here, for a thousand years, he devoted himself to fierce penances. With unflinching determination he accumulated superhuman energy." Eventually the god Brahmā, "attracted by this ascetic fervor," appeared and promised Bhagīratha a boon. Bhagīratha requested that the celestial river Ganges be allowed to descend to the earth. Brahmā replied that only the god Śiva had the power to grant that request and he advised Bhagīratha to continue his austerities. Then "Bhagīratha . . . betook himself to the Himālayas, and there spent another penitential year, fasting, existing on dry leaves, finally on merely water and air, standing on one foot erect, both arms uplifted, will-power concentrated on the god." Eventually Śiva was moved and "acquiesced."[74]

Obviously Gāndhi did not indulge in such flamboyent physical austerities. Yet—when push comes to shove—*satyāgraha* is traditional *tapas* internalized. In *satyāgraha* Gāndhi has carried forward the process of psychologizing *tapas* which had been begun in the Indian meditative and Yogic traditions.

Proponents of Gāndhian *satyāgraha* can rightly point out that to this traditional psycho-ritual complex Gāndhi added a vital, modern ethical dimension. Certainly that was his intention . . . and yet one has to wonder whether, in actuality, the ethical intention ever made much difference. Gāndhi and the Hindu mythic tradition are in perfect agreement. As Heinrich Zimmer observed, the myth of Bhagīratha glorified the "omnipotence of ascetic willpower." In 1918 Gāndhi wrote: "From the ancient culture of India, I have gleaned a truth which, even if it is mastered by few persons here at the moment, would give these few a mastery over the world."[75] Just so the *Matsya Purāṇa:* "Desired objects are obtained by asceticism and there is nothing impossible for an ascetic."[76]

Gāndhian *satyāgraha* should be understood in the context of a range of non-violent but coercive tactics used in modern India to compel the capitulation of an opponent.[77] Among these, *satyāgraha* is doubtless the most challenging but the least used. In that sense Indian society is not Gāndhian in temper. Must one conclude that Gāndhi was a failure? After all, Gāndhi did not singlehandedly gain independence for India—the threat of violence and the altered power situation in the world in 1945 did that. Nór could Gāndhi singlehandedly prevent the communal rioting that accompanied the partition of the Raj. And he himself was assasinated.

But we need not judge Gāndhi the man by the same magical standards of perfection that Gāndhi the magician set for himself. The fate of many third-world countries since independence highlight Gāndhi's achievement. He succeeded in being midwife to a society which for nearly forty years has remained reasonably stable, both modernizing and traditional in spite of the many internal and external obstacles it has faced. Part of the credit for this should surely go to what strikes me as the center of the Gāndhian legacy: a style of being at once religious and political, speaking at once in the language of the elite and of the masses. Let us call this dharmic conservatism, a way to be conservative without becoming obscurantist.

Using the terms I have borrowed from Philip Rieff, Gāndhi's *satyāgraha* amounted to the adaptation of *saṃnyāsa*—the paradigmatic vehicle of ostensibly transgressive change in traditional India—to the condition of modern Indian nationalism. As a modern *saṃnyāsī* Gāndhi individually transgressed some of the interdicts of dharmic society (cleaning latrines, mingling with Untouchables). He carried out other interdicts more intensively than ordinary Hindus. He thus made the thrill of vicarious transgression available to his followers in the very name of the highest interdicts.

Just as institutionalized *saṃnyāsa* represented the triumph of social order over the force of that anarchic religious individualism which might have appeared to threaten traditional India, so institutionalized *satyagraha* represented the triumph of social order over the force of that revolutionary extremism which might have appeared to threaten modern India. Like its traditional prototype, *satyāgraha* was radical in appearance but profoundly conservative in effect. In so adapting a traditional social mechanism to the modern age Gāndhi demonstrated the creative potential of the Hindu tradition. Indeed, as a dharmic conservative, Gāndhi might well be characterized as the unsung conservative hero of the Indian revolution which never was.

V. Conclusion: Changeless Change, Disordered Order: Continuities in Hindu Society

Philip Rieff has defined revolution as:

> a significant discontinuity in the moral demand system, an interchange in the relation of interdictory-remissive controls, by which men may well do what they have not done before—and do not as they have done . . . Revolutions [he adds] may be defined as reversals—violent or non-violent—of significant behavioral controls.[78]

If one accepted this as a working definition, one would have to conclude that there has never been a revolution in India, and no sign that one is impending.

The psychologist Sudhir Kakar reaches much the same conclusion. Social change in modern India, he observes, has been for the bulk of the population, gradual and bearable. He describes India as:

> . . . one of the "last bastions of the Mother" in an increasingly instrumental, technocratic and rational age.
>
> [He concludes] . . . that a psychological revolutionary situation in India can only come about if large sections of Hindu society question the usefulness if not the existence of 'ultimate' reality, bring up to awareness its parameters in Hindu infancy and firmly reject many of its social and cultural manifestations as vestiges of an archaic, personal, and historical past.[79]

Kakar realizes that such a fundamental psychological revolution would mean the disintegration of a coherent, religious culture. He does not predict that such a revolution in values is likely to take place. He worries how India shall cope with gradual, accelerating, piecemeal industrialization without such a revolution. My reflection on these matters leads me to concur. Revolution in any fundamental sense in India is unlikely. So far, modernization has proceeded without social disintegration—although there is a very intense fear of chaos. Whether this balance of change and order can continue indefinitely is difficult to say, but I see no reason to presuppose that it cannot.

NOTES

1. I wish to acknowledge the generous support of Judith Pitney, Hal Williams and Lonnie Kliever, and of Southern Methodist University which allowed me to spend a month in India during the period I was working on this paper.

It is impossible for me to acknowledge by name all of the many friends in India who assisted me. For particular help I must thank Drs. Pradeep Mehendiratta and Venugopala Rao of the AIIS; Dr. Navjivan Rastogi of Lucknow University; Dr. Sunthar Visuvalingam of BHU; Mr. Gautam Vohra of the *Times of India;* and for their gracious hospitality, John Taber and Marianne Kramer. I am especially grateful for the assistance of Mrs. Marilyn Duncan of SMU's Fondren Library and Ms. Dorothy Reddington of Cornell University in obtaining bibliographical items unavailable in Dallas.

2. I use the term "sacred order" in the sense of the social theorist Philip Rieff. I am not using the term "sacred" as it is conventionally used by "Historians of Religion."
3. In spite of its equivocal nature the contrast between the "traditional" and the "modern" remains an important conceptual tool helping one compare and contrast the scientific and industrial civilization of the West with our own earlier civilization and non-Western civilizations. In characterizing India as still "traditional" I intend neither a negative nor a positive judgment.
4. I am *not* using the word "myth" in the popular sense of "something false," but in a technical sense referring to a "narrative which makes one or more spiritual points indirectly."
5. It has become common for western scholars to interpret *dharma* as having a cosmological referent, as a term for the cosmic order taken as a whole. Tempting as this is, it is not supported by the texts. The traditional usage of the term is clearly social: See, Wilhelm Halbfass, *Indien und Europa, Perspiktiven ihrer geistige Begegnung* (Basel: Schwabe Verlag, 1981), ch. 17 "Dharma im selbstverständnis des traditionellen und des modernen Hinduismus," pp. 358–402.
6. Western attempts to understand the system of *dharma* reflect different ideological presuppositions. It seems to me that the theoretical and descriptive work of the French sociologist Louis Dumont and the Indian psychotherapist Sudhir Kakar illumine the implicit ideology—the underlying conceptual structure—of traditional Indian society with peculiar clarity. See Dumont, *Homo Hierarchicus, The Caste System and Its Implications* (Chicago: Univ. Chicago Press, 1979, rev. ed.), and *Religion/Politics and History in India, Collected Papers in Indian Sociology* (Paris: Mouton, 1970); Dumont's work has been subject to much discussion. See, J. F. Richards and Ralph Nicholas, eds., "Symposium: The Contribution of Louis Dumont," *J. of Asian Studies* 35:4 (1976), pp. 579–650. Kakar, *The Inner World, A Psycho-analytic Study of Childhood and Society in India* (Delhi: Oxford Univ. Press, 1978), and *Shamans, Mystics and Doctors, A Psychological Inquiry Into India and Its Healing Traditions* (NY: Knopf, 1982).
7. The contrast between the West as individualistic and India as "collectivist" might seem to be a Western prejudice: our refusal to recognize as individuals, persons whose traditional values are radically different from our own. Note in this regard that pre-modern India produced neither spiritual autobiographies, nor confessions, nor diaries. See Dumont (1979), pp. 231ff; also "The Individual as an Impediment to Sociological Comparison and Indian History" (1970, pp. 133–150); and "The Modern Conception of the Individual, Notes on Its Genesis," *Contributions to Indian Sociology* 8 (1965), pp. 13–61.

8. Wealth is a significant secondary determinant of status. The extent to which it modifies status as determined by degree of impurity varied from time to time, and today varies according to both region and the relative position of a group in the caste hierarchy. Note especially the existence of a "dominant land-owning caste." See, M.N. Srinivas, "The Social System of A Mysore Village," pp. 1–35 in McKim Marriott, ed., *Village India, Studies in the Little Community* (Chicago: Univ. Chicago Press, 1969 [1955]). The main point is that while economic factors may distort caste ranking based on purity, they rarely if ever call the system as a whole into question.

9. The symbolic distinction between pure and impure should not be confused with an ethical distinction between good and evil. In contrast, the distinction between purity and impurity is a symbolic way of indirectly expressing concern with certain primal, threatening aspects of the human condition. On the notion of impurity see the discussion in Dumont (1979).

10. The ranking of each group in the caste hierarchy depends on the balance of specific impurities with which that group is associated. A Hindu community is *never* ranked according to a single criterion. Status is always determined by the "average" assessment of a group on a number of criteria. Among the most typical sources of pollution: (a) any bodily secretion, in particular, excrement or saliva; (b) anything having to do with birth or death; anything concerned with the taking of life, in particular the slaughter of cows or the handling of carrion. Finally, there is a catchall criterion: because pollution is by definition contagious, association with an impure person is itself a potent source of impurity.

11. "Toward a Theory of Culture: With Special Reference to the Psychoanalytic Case," pp. 97–108 in T.J. Nossiter, *et al.*, eds., *Imagination and Precision in the Social Sciences: Essays in Memory of Peter Nettl* (NY: Humanities Press, 1972), p. 99.

12. "By What Authority? Post-Freudian Reflections on the Repression of the Repressive as Modern Culture," pp. 225–55 in J.P. Diggins and M.E. Kann, eds., *The Problem of Authority in America* (Philadelphia: Temple Univ. Press, 1981), p. 227.

13. This account is a digest of W. Norman Brown, "The Rigvedic Equivalent for Hell," "The Creation Myth of the Rg Veda," and "Theories of Creation in the Rg Veda," pp. 14–19, 20–33, 40–52 in Rosane Rocher, ed. *India and Indology, Selected Essays of W. Norman Brown* (Delhi: Motilal Bansidass, 1978).

14. For a lively account of the contrast between *sat* and *asat* see the first of the articles by W. Norman Brown, "The Rigvedic Equivalent for Hell," cited above.

15. The assumption is that the local elites recognized (in some sense) Brahman supremacy and in turn were legitimized as "human," that is, as fitting somewhere in the classificatory scheme of communities.

16. The oral tradition worked both ways: there are many examples—even today—of lineage myths being "invented" to justify the increased status of a newly powerful group (e.g., a new dynasty), or to attempt to justify the desired status of a group with social aspirations.

17. In North India, the system of communal interdependence was formalized as the *jajmāni* system, a complex of hereditary and obligatory duties (services and payments in kind) between "patrons" *(jajmāns)* and their "clients."
18. In fact one just cannot distinguish between Hinduism (a foreign loanword in any case), Jainism and Buddhism as if they were organized religions. Only with Islam does one get the notion of religious exclusivism in anything like the sense to which we are accustomed.
19. By now considerable evidence has been collected to show that monarchs actively intervened to enhance the harmoniousness or the efficiency of the caste system. One way that they did this was by making grants to communities of Brahmans, to temples, or to one or another religious "foundation."
20. See Bernard Cohn, "Regions Subjective and Objective: Their Relation to the Study of Modern Indian History and Society," pp. 5–37 in Robert I. Crane, ed., *Regions and Regionalism in South Asia* (Durham, N.C.: Comm. on South Asian Studies, Duke Univ., 1966). If this regional hypothesis is correct, it means that tensions between the "center" and the states shall remain a problem in India for the foreseeable future. One should not, however, overlook counter-vailing forces of unification.
21. This and subsequent quotations from *Ānandamaṭh* are taken from the excerpts in Wm. Theo. de Bary, ed., *Sources of Indian Tradition,* vol. II (NY: Columbia Univ. Press, 1958), pp. 155–65. I have not had access to the Bengali text and have refrained from modernizing the English.
22. The title *Ānandamaṭh* has been translated literally as "The Abbey of Bliss," but this is misleading. It means rather, the hermitage or monastery (i.e., *āśram*) of the Ānandas.
23. In Bengali the name of this author who lived from 1838 to 1894 is Ban kimcandra Caṭṭopādhyāy. I shall follow the Bengali convention of referring to him as Baṅkimcandra.
24. The Extremists spurned gradualism, derided social reform and were generally unconcerned with Hindu-Muslim relations. They tolerated and sometimes advocated terrorism. Their opponents were known as the Moderates. The conflict between the Extremists and the Moderates is typified by the contrast between their leaders, the two most important figures in the Nationalist Movement prior to Gāndhi: Bal Gangadhar Tilak and Gopal Krishna Gokhale, respectively, both of whom were Marāṭhī *Citpāvan* Brahmans. See Stanley A. Wolpert, *Tilak and Gokhale: Revolution and Reform in the Making of Modern India* (Berkeley: Univ. California Press, 1962). Wolpert's thesis that Gāndhi succeeded because he blended the social progressivism and non-violence of the Moderates with the militance and religious aura of the Extremists is consistent with the interpretation in this essay.
25. It should be noted that in Bengali and the other vernaculars of modern India the word chosen to translate the peculiar English term religion was *dharma.*
26. Such is the judgment of Dušan Zbavitel who contends that Baṅkimcandra's patriotism "was an excuse for the author to distort history, to introduce supernatural phenomena, anachronisms, and so on" (*Bengali Literature* [=HIL

vol. IX, part II, fasc. 3] (Wiesbaden: Harrassowitz, 1976) p. 241). Of course, it is precisely those factors which Zbavitel criticizes that accounts for *Ānandamaṭh's* enormous success in its own terms.

27. "The Fighting Ascetics of India," *Bull. of the John Rylands Library* (Manchester), vol. 9 (1925), p. 448.

28. My account of the so-called *saṃnyāsī* revolt is based largely on David N. Lorenzen, "Warrior Ascetics in Indian History," *J. of the Amer. Oriental Society* 98:1 (1978) 61–75. Lorenzen adroitly surveys the rather scattered secondary literature and suggests avenues for further research.

29. This and the following quotations are from Lorenzen, pp. 72–75.

30. One should probably not make too much of the fact that this aspect of the "rebellion" was led by *fakīrs* (Muslim ascetics) rather than *saṃnyāsīs* (Hindu ascetics). On the popular level, one hardly finds a strict distinction between Hindu and Muslim "renouncers." It would not, moreover, be surprising if the various "orders" of Hindu "warrior ascetics" spent as much time fighting each other as they did fighting the Muslims. After all, as the evidence Lorenzen marshals suggests, many of the warrior ascetics were armed in order to defend local territorial and economic interests.

31. Although Indian economic history is beyond the scope of this paper, one might observe that some of the *saṃnyāsīs* had become successful traders and money lenders. They had apparently developed an extensive trading network and were in an advantageous position for accumulating capital. Might one argue that the British retarded the development of Indian capitalism by the forced transfer of funds from the mercantile *saṃnyāsīs* to the land-based *zamindars?*

32. To be sure, there is evidence that the British attempted to block pilgrimages to certain nominally Muslim holy places in northern and central Bengal (see the discussion of J.M. Ghosh's *Saṃnyāsī and Fakīr Raiders in Bengal* in Lorenzen, pp. 72f.). Obviously this attempt would have generated "religious" resentment, but at this period and in this context it is unlikely that it was perceived as Western interference in or persecution of native religion. For one thing what was principally at issue appears to have been the "revenue" generated along the pilgrimage route and during the fairs held at the holy places. Moreover, the category religion had not yet established itself in the Bengali consciousness.

33. The period of the *saṃnyāsī* rebellion largely preceded the outbreak of the French Revolution in 1789. The modern sense of the word "revolution" was, therefore, still in the process of development, and it may be doubted whether many British traders and officials in India conceived of the *saṃnyāsī* rebellion as the precursor of a revolutionary movement.

34. For a readable yet well documented popular account woven from contemporary documents see Christopher Hibbert, *The Great Mutiny: India 1857* (NY: Viking Press, 1978; Penguin, 1980). Various theories concerning the Revolt are summarized in Ainslie T. Embree, *1857 in India: Mutiny or War of Independence?* (Boston: D. C. Heath, 1963) and in Sashi Bhusan Chaudhuri, *English Historical Writings On the Indian Mutiny, 1857–59* (Calcutta: World

Press, 1979). Representative works include: S. B. Chaudhuri, *Civil Rebellion in the Indian Mutinies, 1857–59)* (Calcutta: World Press, 1957); R. C. Majumdar, *The Sepoy Mutiny and the Revolt of 1857* (Calcutta: KLM, 2nd ed., 1963); and Surendra Nath Sen, *Eighteen Fifty Seven* (New Delhi: Publications Division, GOI, 1957).

35. Joseph Schwartzberg, ed., *A Historical Atlas of South Asia* (Chicago: Univ. Chicago Press, 1978), plate VII.B.3b; Stanley Wolpert, *A New History of India* (NY: Oxford Univ. Press, 1977), p. 234.

36. The revolt failed because vast areas of the subcontinent (the entire Deccan and deep South) were unaffected; because many regions and communities—notably the Punjab and the Sikhs, sided with the British; because the rebels had no central organization whatsoever; and because the revolt tended to make possible the sort of class warfare which was bound to frighten the elite into supporting the British.

37. *British Paramountcy and Indian Renaissance,* pt. I [=R.C. Majumdar, ed., *The History and Culture of the Indian People,* vol IX] (Bombay: Bharatiya Vidya Bhavan, 2nd ed., 1970), pp. 476ff.

38. It is to be stressed that this scheme is a conscious oversimplification. Local variations were enormous: in some instances, e.g., in Delhi, local (indigenous) administration continued to operate; in other instances, e.g., in the case of Nana Sāhib in Kanpur, an attempt was made to reestablish it; in a few instances a popular outbreak preceded the revolt of the troops; nor is it to be suggested that all of those who fought the British became brigands.

39. Majumdar, p. 497.

40. Hibbert, p. 97, citing: N. A. Chick, *Annals of the Indian Rebellion,* David Hutchinson, ed., (London: 1974) and Colonel Edward Vibart, *The Sepoy Mutiny as Seen by a Subaltern From Delhi to Lucknow* (London: 1898).

41. Hibbert, p. 34, based on a pastische of sources.

42. The quotation from Charles Grant is cited in Stuart Cary Welch, *Room for Wonder, Indian Painting During the British Period, 1760–1880* (NY: The American Federation of Arts/Rizzoli International, 1978), p. 183; the quotation from Macaulay's *Minute* is cited in de Bary, p. 45; the second quotation from Macaulay is cited in Welch, p. 185.

43. Hibbert, p. 204.

44. The principal successor states were that of the Peshwa (i.e., the Marathas), those of the Nawabs of Oudh and Bengal, and the Sikh kingdom in the Punjab.

45. One of the reasons the Revolt did not cohere into a successful, reactionary revolution was the fragmentation of the traditional powers who were in fact more oppossed to each other then each of them was to the British. I am following the classificatory scheme proposed by Kathleen Gough, "Indian Peasant Uprisings," *Bull. of Concerned Asian Scholars* 8:3 (1976), pp. 2–18. Gough distinguishes (1) restorative movements, (2) religious movements for communal liberation, (3) social banditry (a phrase of Eric Hobsbawm), (4) terrorist action, and (5) mass insurrections for the redress of particular grievances.

46. There is no consensus concerning the impact of colonization on the Indian economy. Ideological commitments often influence analysis. I have tried to describe the British impact on the economy in such a way as to side step the debates over the "de-industrialization of India," and the "introduction" of private ownership of land and of capitalism. See Morris D. Morris, "Values as an Obstacle to Economic Growth in South Asia: An Historical Survey," *The J. of Economic History,* XXVII:4 (1967), pp. 588–607; this important essay is reprinted in Thomas D. Metcalf, ed., *Modern India: An Interpretive Anthology* (NY: Macmillan, 1971), pp. 187ff.; also, Morris D. Morris, ed., *The Indian Economy in the Nineteenth Century: A Symposium* (New Delhi: Indian Economic and Social History Association/School of Economics, 1969). The theories of "oriental despotism" and of the "Asiatic mode of production" have been largely discredited.

47. The words are Percival Spear's. They are cited in Hibbert, p. 392.

48. Gough, p. 7. There were such proclamations, but it is still difficult to determine their extent.

49. Western scholars have sometimes ignored the existence of radical and subversive popular movements in India. We are indebted to a number of scholars for giving them the attention they merit. See, in addition to the essay by Gough mentioned above, Kathleen Gough and Hari P. Sharma, eds., *Imperialism and Revolution in South Asia* (NY: Monthly Review Press, 1973); Robin Blackburn, ed., *Explosion in a Subcontinent, India, Pakistan, Bangladesh and Ceylon* (Baltimore: Penguin Books, 1975). For a solid, non-ideological analysis of peasant rebellion focusing on the mid 19th century, see Eric Stokes, *The Peasant and the Raj: Studies in Agrarian Society and Peasant Rebellion in Colonial India* (Cambridge: Cambridge Univ. Press, 1978); on Stokes see Thomas R. Metcalf's review article, *J. of Asian Studies* 39:1 (1979), pp. 111–19. To appraise the leftist perspective on revolutionary currents in Indian society one should start with the dispatches Marx wrote for the *New York Daily Tribune* in the 1850's: Karl Marx and Friedrich Engels, *The First Indian War of Independence, 1857–1859* (Moscow: Progress Publishers, 1959); for an impassioned, if unfortunately sloppy, leftist portrayal of life in India's villages see, Robert Bohm, *Notes On India* (Boston: South End Press, 1982).

50. If one accepts the argument that the revolt was not organized, then these metaphors may be taken as accurate. At least in part, the revolt spread by rumor and imitation from one district to adjacent districts. In this it might profitably be compared with the spread of witchcraft persecutions during the "Great Witch Hunt" of the 17th century, and with the outbursts of popular discontent that periodically rippled through English and French societies in the 18th and 19th centuries. Of course rumor *also* worked to spread British misconceptions of the revolt. Consider the famous case of the mysterious, traveling chapatties, the common flat bread of North India which some of the British believed was used to send messages secretly from village to village!

51. R. C. Majumdar, *British Paramountcy and Indian Renaissance,* part I [*The History and Culture of the Indian People* vol. 9] (Bombay: Bhartiya Vidya Bhavan, 1963), p. 499, and Hibbert, p. 370ff.; the existence of "messianic" elements and "revitalization movements" in the Hindu tradition merits further study.

There is Stephen Fuchs, *Rebellious Prophets: A Study of Messianic Movements in Indian Religions* (NY: Asia, 1965).

52. The precedent for this is not, I think, the *avatāras* of Viṣṇu who by and large do *not* function that way, but "sacred" kings who protect *dharma,* and the leaders of certain of the *bhakti* (devotional) movements. The possible influence of Christian and Muslim mythology merits study.

53. Erik H. Erikson, *Gāndhi's Truth, On the Origins of Militant Nonviolence* (NY: W.W. Norton, 1969), p. 430. Erikson attributes the story to an essay by Pyarelal Nayar, Gāndhi's biographer, which appeared in *The Statesman* in 1954.

54. Gāndhi was fifty-one years old in 1920. He had developed his techniques of non-violent resistance in South Africa before returning to India in 1915. The agitation for Indian independence peaked in four waves: (a) the *Swadeshi* Movement following the partition of Bengal in 1905, (b) the Non-cooperation Program which followed the Jallianwala Bagh (Amritser) massacre of 1919; (c) the Civil Disobediance Campaign which began with the Salt March of 1930, and (d) the Quit India Campaign of 1942. Gāndhi led three of the four.

55. The literature on Gāndhi is large—there are said to be over 400 biographies alone—but critically uninspiring. In addition to Erikson's study, I have found the following works most helpful: Joan V. Bondurant, *Conquest of Violence, The Gāndhian Philosophy of Conflict* (Berkeley: Univ. California Press, rev. ed., 1965); Gail Omvedt, "Gandhi and the Pacification of the Indian National Revolution," *Bull. of Concerned Asian Scholars* 5:1 (1973), pp. 2–8; Lloyd I. and Susanne Hoeber Rudolph, "The Traditional Roots of Charisma: Gandhi," part two (pp. 155–249) in *The Modernity of Tradition, Political Development in India* (Chicago: Univ. Chicago Press, 1967). For a guide to the literature see, Mark Jurgensmeyer, "The Gandhi Revival—A Review Article," *J. of Asian Studies* 43:2 (1984), pp. 293–98.

56. I have drawn extensively on Erikson's work which quotes lavishly from Gāndhi's voluminous writings—the *Collected Works* now number over 80 volumes! I, however, wish to stress that my conclusions about Gāndhi differ from those of Erikson and the other authors cited above in a number of ways. Any errors of judgment I make should not be attributed to them.

57. Erikson, p. 117; Erikson's analysis of Gāndhi's sexuality, pp. 229–54, especially pp. 234–37, repay careful reading.

58. There is the well known case of the Mahatma's affection for his orphaned niece Manu. In the Rudolphs words, "In his old age, he liked to think of himself as a mother to his grandniece, Manu, the girl who shared his bed as a daughter might her mother's and who had lost a mother" (p. 215). Manu wrote a memoir entitled *Bapu—My Mother; bāpu* is a Hindi word for "father." In this book she relates that Gāndhi once said to her "Have I not become your mother? I have been father to many, but only to you am I a mother" (quoted p. 215, n. 63). Contrast Gāndhi's use of the metaphor of being a mother and father with the imperial conceit that the Raj was both mother and father *(māmbāp)* to India, a theme in Paul Scott's *Raj Quartet.*

59. Erikson, pp. 309–21. See especially the comments on marriage, p. 312.

60. Erikson, p. 59.

61. Erikson, p. 170; cf. the statements quoted on p. 139, "He who would be friends with God must remain alone or make the whole world his friend," and p. 388, "I am the one man who can today preserve the peace in India as no other man can."

62. There have been Indian critics of Gāndhian anti-modernism all along. Standing in this tradition is *India: A Wounded Civilization* (NY: Random House, 1976) by V.S. Naipaul, a descendant of the Indian diaspora. Naipaul is especially critical of Gāndhianism as represented by Vinoba Bhave.

63. This work, written in 1909, still reflects the disillusionment of Gāndhi's life in London and, to a lesser extent, in South Africa. The title means "Indian Home Rule."

64. The translation is from the excerpt included in DeBary, pp. 251–67; pp. 257 and 255.

65. Cited in Erikson, pp. 281 and 340.

66. Ironically Omvedt seems to take it for granted that any right thinking person would agree that a social revolution in India (like the one in China) would be a good thing. She assumes that the fact that Gāndhi prevented such a revolution will make one think less of Gāndhi. Apparently it hasn't occurred to her that the opposite might be the case, nor that one can deeply regret both the condition of the Indian village proletariat and the fact of caste oppression without thinking that a violent, social revolution would make things better.

67. Omvedt, p. 3b. Space precludes a full analysis of Omvedt's argument here; in general my religious analysis of Gāndhi complements her socio-political analysis.

68. In fact, Gāndhi does not seem to have uttered those precise words. R.C. Majumdar cites two versions of the full passage, the first of which is, "Leave India in God's hands, in modern parlance, to anarchy, and that anarchy may lead to internecine warfare for a time or to unrestrained dacoities. From these a true India will rise in place of the false one we see" (R.C. Majumdar, ed., *The Struggle for Freedom* [= *The History and Culture of the Indian People*, vol. 11], (Bombay: Bhartiya Vidya Bhavan, 1969), pp. 644ff.

69. Joan Bondurant's study of *satyāgraha* (see above), written in the late 1950's, remains a model of prudent, sensitive exegesis. Bondurant avoids hagiography and over-simplification. Her portrayal of *satyāgraha* as "at once a mode of action and a method of enquiry" (p. v.) successfully clarifies Gāndhi's *intention*. Her detailed analysis of five *satyāgraha* campaigns (pp. 45–104) provides a basis for evaluating its *effect*, at least during Gāndhi's lifetime. Her discussion of *durāgraha*, "symbolic violence," negative resistence, makes clear that the campaigns of civil disobediance we have seen in the West since the Civil Rights Movement have *not* been Gāndhian. Nonetheless, I do not share Bondurant's final appraisal of *satyāgraha*. See especially ch. 5, "Conservative or Anarchist? A Note on Gāndhi and Political Philosophy," pp. 146–188.

70. See Bondurant, ch. 3, "*Satyāgraha* as Applied Socio-political Action," pp. 36ff.

71. Erikson, p. 351. This figure apparently excludes fasting for personal spiritual purification.
72. This is from Gāndhi's *Satyāgraha In South Africa,* Erikson, p. 183.
73. Erikson, p. 335.
74. Variants of this myth are found in many Hindu texts. I have adapted this account from Heinrich Zimmer, *Myths and Symbols in Indian Art and Civilization* (Joseph Campbell, ed., NY: Harper Torchbooks, 1962 [1946], pp. 113ff.).
75. From the 15th leaflet issued during the Ahmedabad labor *satyāgraha;* cited in Erikson, p. 356.
76. *Matsya Purāṇa* 154:290, cited in Stella Kramrisch, *The Presence of Śiva* (Princeton: Princeton Univ. Press, 1981), p. 351.
77. An enumeration of these is beyond the scope of this paper. The most famous is the *hartal,* a shopkeeper's strike. To the best of my knowledge no one has yet investigated the use of these coercive techniques in pre-modern India. Lorenzen, p. 66, notes an instance in the 11th C. when a group of Brahmans use hunger strikes in order to deal with a prime minister they disliked; conversely, it is reported that Bahadur Shah threatened to kill himself in a vain attempt to control the mutinous sepoys inside the Red Fort. See, E. Washburn Hopkins, "On the Hindu Custom of Dying to Redress a Grievance," *J. of the Amer. Oriental Society* 21, (1900), pp. 146–59.
78. Rieff, (1972) pp. 100ff.
79. Kakar, (1978) p. 187.

3

Religion, Ideology and Revolution: The Problematical Case of Post–1979 Iran

BRUCE B. LAWRENCE

I: Prolegomena on Religion, Ideology and Revolution

Prolegomenon I: A General Assessment

The three terms aggregated for this volume—Religion, Ideology, Revolution—evoke different images. They also suggest variant constituencies, foci and outcomes. Yet they do share certain irreducible features. To look at how they intersect in any given context, especially in the context of post-1979 Iran, it is valuable to begin by noting what they have in common from the viewpoint of Western intellectual and social history.

First, all three presume a level of abstraction from innate human experience. Neither Religion nor Ideology nor Revolution convey basic emotions, gender distinctions or life cycle occurrences. They are not a primary datum for biology or other natural sciences, even though two of them (Ideology and Revolution) have been invoked as interpretive categories by historians of science, as the discussion below of Thomas Kuhn makes clear.

Second, all three derive from culture rather than from nature. They are cultural foci, situating individual men and women within larger social units while at the same time imposing generalized social constraints on a spectrum of human clusters, from the larger (civilizational and national) to the smaller (regional and local) to the smallest (tribal or familial). The double focus for each is: individual motivation and conduct on the one hand, and social or corporate exchange, on the other.

Important as these commonalities are, the principal concern of this paper will be the differences that separate Religion from both Ideology and Revolution, and also separate each of them from the other. They do not enjoy equivalent roles in the history of Western culture nor do they receive equal emphasis in contemporary thought. We will argue that there is paradoxically an inverse relationship between lexical antiquity and current-day priority. Religion is the oldest of the three, traceable as a self-conscious analytical category to the 1st century B.C. Roman orators. Cicero and Lucretius (W.C. Smith 1962:24–26). In a sense, Religion is the parent of the other two: Ideology being the stepchild (some would say, "ugly or mischievous" stepchild) and Revolution the fosterchild (restless, contentious and seldom grateful).

Indeed, compared to Religion, both Ideology and Revolution are babes in the annals of Western intellectual history, having made their appearance in the Enlightenment, and until very recently being limited to places touched by the Enlightenment: Europe, England, America, Russia. Other cultures, the famous dyad of Orientals and Primitives, were thought to have inferior (pagan, polytheist, or fanatical) religions but they were not even capable of engendering Ideology, much less fomenting Revolution.

Within the Western domain of cultural hubris, more tacit then explicit in its presuppositions as well as its judgments, Ideology projects a larger role than Revolution. To understand the peculiar perception we have of both its "parent" (Religion) and its "sibling" (Revolution), we must look closely at Ideology. Coined by the French philosopher Destutt de Tracy at the end of the 18th century, Ideology was intended to be a new science, a way of discovering "objective" truth behind the theological facade which masks the subjective manipulations characteristic of the institutional Church, that once authoritative bastion of Christendom. The intent of Ideology was, quite simply, to displace the authority of Religion—both as an analytical category and as an epistemological certitude. The image of the free-thinking individual who elected to be a rational man of conscience was counterposed to the parody of mendacious bishops, creedally blind clergy and ritually numb laity. Secular forces, emerging in a progressive society, would outstrip the complacent Church in ministering to human needs: the psychiatrist's couch, for instance, would replace the confessional booth (see Foucault 1980:115–131), just as science would dispel the myths of angels, demons, other worlds and, of course, God.

It is necessary to underscore the anti-religious intent of de Tracy's Enlightenment mind because it infused much of the later, post-Enlightenment usage of the term Ideology. Marx went so far as to make the parent into an offspring of its child, recasting Religion into an Ideology. In that way, he could both acknowledge its psychological tenacity among the ignorant masses (of no concern to de Tracy) and also revalorize its institutional forms as mere epiphenomenal projections of class conflict and economic interest. Latter-day disciples of Marx are less bold, but historically more correct, than their master when they argue, as does D. Bell, following K. Mannheim, that "ideology is a secular religion," (Bell 1960:400). By this reasoning, Ideology may be said to tap the same emotional reserve as Religion but it channels the energies of its believers into this world rather than the next; cadres of ideologues see politics not metaphysics as the window to their salvation.

While Ideology and Religion have had an almost *Oedipal* relationship in the history of ideas, Revolution has appeared as a belated offspring of their protracted conflict. The first Revolution may have been the garden conspiracy of Genesis 3, but neither it nor subsequent revolutions became a subject for extended theoretical speculation until after the French Revolution. It was the success of Bastille Day and the Marxist-Leninist revolutions of the early 20th century that drew attention to Revolution as a subcategory of Ideology and one among many outcomes of ideological fervor.

Yet for students of Ideology, Revolution is not the sole or even the major expression of their intellectual trust. Conservatives and reformers abound. So do nihilists. The latter, unlike revolutionaries, are not content to transform the status quo; they want to destroy society, whether as dropouts, terrorists or hooligans.

In effect, Ideology takes cognizance of Revolution but only as a subcategory, a kind of fosterchild, to use the family metaphor once again. Ideology remains prior to and superior to Revolution, both as analytical category and as referential context. Revolution, for example, is inextricable from politics. Yet ideologies can and do claim several contexts. There are ideologies of progress, science and modernization: they rank alongside those of nationalism, communism and naziism in shaping and reshaping the world in which we live. While the latter are clearly political, the former extend beyond politics, suffusing every aspect of modern-day societies—economic, intellectual, cultural and religious.

Yet, despite the claims of ideologues, it is not ideologies but rather revolutions which have been termed "the locomotives of history." To the extent that revolutions have implemented certain ideologies while denying or impeding others, at the same time that they have also outpaced the influence of (organized) religions, it could be argued that the dominant, riveting category of this paper is Revolution. The fosterchild has usurped the movable throne of intellectual preference, and become the new parent, at least for this generation!

Had there not been a revolution in Pahlavi Iran in 1978–79, would there now be any concern for a paper on Iran? Who would care to read an analysis of Iran in which Ideology and Religion were related to one another but not to Revolution? No one. It is the intrusion of Revolution as an actual occurrence that calls attention to both Ideology and Religion and that requires their investigation as potential catalysts of Revolution.

In summary, the purpose of our first prolegomenon is to call attention to the historical complexity and symbolic asymmetry of the three terms synergized in this volume. While Revolution is the most dramatic, at times mesmerizing category, Religion is the oldest and most familiar. Yet it has been eclipsed in contemporary Western thought, and even now in its partial revival is subordinated to Ideology. Latent Marxist influences have assured that Ideology will continue to serve as the linchpin, the mediating category between Religion and Revolution. Though all three do not necessarily converge, when they do, it is Ideology that provides the catalyst for a powerful aggregation, initiating an impetus for change that is likely to prove irresistible. In the contemporary world, Religion cannot have a direct relationship to Revolution; it is always mediated by proponents of Revolution through Ideological, that is to say, propagandistic channels.

At the outset it is crucial to remember the intrinsic independence of these terms, as well as their possible, but contingent, dependence. Religion can and did function for a long time without relating to either Ideology or Revolution as "explicit categories." Ideology now exists apart from either of the other two, but Revolution does not: by its very nature it depends on Ideologies and ideologues, and at those points, in those moments where all three intersect, it is Ideology that bridges, even as it modifies and fuses, the symbolic power of Religion with the activist intent of revolutionaries

Prolegomenon II: The Methodological Divide between Humanists and Social Scientists

We do not begin this task *de novo*. Much has been thought, said and written on all three of the terms which confront us in this volume, and also on recent events in Iran. Before turning our attention to Iran, we must not only describe the history but also evaluate the significance of each term in our composite theme: Religion, Ideology, and Revolution.

Their history mirrors, as I have suggested, the influx of post-Enlightenment (specifically Marxist categories), into the entire intellectual fabric of Western society during the past 200 years. One result has been the profound, often bitter disagreement between humanist and social scientist as to the appropriateness of studying each within the academy. The humanist feels as comfortable with Religion as he feels ill at ease with Ideology and Revolution. Yet Religion for the humanist is primarily a product of high culture, to be discovered through the exegesis of literary texts and the historical investigation of urban institutions. The social scientist, by contrast, feels comfortable with Ideology and Revolution; when drawn to the investigation of Religion, he seeks out a very different brand of Religion than the one selected by the humanist.

For the social scientist, Religion is part of the primal data of human experience. It has to be discovered anew, reported, examined and analysed at every level of contemporary society. Its evidence is oral as much as textual; rural as well as urban. It involves heretics along with the "orthodox"; laity and illiterates side by side with priests and ritual specialists. Primitive cultic patterns have to be uncovered and then compared with classical/medieval/modern histories. In each instance, the investigator has to probe the tacit dimensions, what people do without knowing they do it, as well as the explicit categories, what they claim to be doing, whether talking among themselves or to outsiders.

It is a very irreverent and idiosyncratic kind of Religion that the social scientist seeks, at least from the humanist perspective. It is Religion stripped of faith claims or theological baggage. It is Religion arrayed with all the other evidence of social organization. Yet the persistence with which social scientists pursue their brand of religious data intensifies the cleavage between them and the humanists. After all, why could not social scientists have left Religion to the humanists and pursued subjects closer to their "scientific" mind set, such as Ideology and Revolution? Certainly, Ideology and Revolution seem more basic to an understanding of the dynamics of contemporary society than does Religion. And are not social scientists preoccupied with politics, its idioms, its actors, its outcomes?

Logic would seem to favor the humanist protest, but the accidents of biographical history have ironically predisposed social scientists to be more concerned with Religion than with either Ideology or Revolution. It is in the biography of founding fathers that lies the clue to comprehending the baffling proclivity of social scientists to religious phenomena. The pioneering figures of sociology/anthropology were Max Weber and Emile Durkheim. They have been at once revered and cited but also qualified and challenged by later social scientists. Both men became preoccupied, albeit for divergent motives in dissimilar contexts, with concerns that were irreducibly religious. The vast corpus of their writings reflects these same religious concerns. The index of their continuing influence, and also of the priority accorded Religion above Ideology and Revolution, may be seen in the disproportionate space allocated to each in the major reference work for social scientists, *The International Encyclopaedia of the Social Sciences* (hereafter abbreviated as *IESS:* see Sills 1968). There we find a single-authored seven page article on Revolution (W. Laqueur), a double-authored twenty page article on Ideology (E. Shils, H.M. Johnson), but a multiple-authored fifty-five page series of four articles on Religion. The first, on Religion itself, is divided into three subcategories: Anthropology (C. Geertz), Sociology (R. Bellah) and Psychology (J. Dittes). It is followed by a second article on Religious Observance, a third on Religious Organization and a fourth on Religious Specialists, the last also directing attention to the variant perspectives of Anthropology and Sociology. To all this must be added articles elsewhere on independent religious traditions, founding figures, seminal thinkers, major exponents, *etc.*

Despite the massive array of social scientific investigation into Religion, the *IESS* offers a description but no definition of Religion, or for that matter, Ideology or Revolution. The argument often advocated—sometimes by humanists as well as by social scientists—is that definitions bind and delimit, while descriptions merely set out movable boundaries. We contend, however, that the complexity of our subject matter requires at least provisional definitions of each term, in order to make sense not only of their historical development but also their contemporary interaction. At the least one might say that:

- A Religion is a range of beliefs and practices encompassing the human life cycle but pertaining especially to rites of passage or moments of transition, namely: birth, puberty, marriage and death. It is in such moments that individuals believe that they experience a transtemporal solidarity within their own community, reinforcing their corporate identity, and at the same time setting them apart (consciously or unconsciously, intentionally or inadvertently) from other individuals and communities whose beliefs and practices differ from their own. For many religions and their adherents, all beliefs and activities which they perceive as religious have a single or multiple, but in every case transcendent and ultimate, referent to which they ascribe the material origin of the universe as well as their individual location within it.

- An Ideology is a cluster of interests advocated by specific groups in pursuit of commonly held goals that derive from and relate to precise contexts, with specifiable, determinate boundaries both temporal and spatial. No transcendent referent is needed or desired. As E. Shils states, "No great ideology has ever regarded the disciplined pursuit of truth as part of its obligations. Indeed, ideologies do not credit the independent cognitive powers or strivings of men" (see Shils 1968:73). Ideologies then are inherently inimical to both philosophy and theology, not only in their traditional formulations and expressions but also in the persistent attraction they hold for modern men and women in the late 20th century.
- A Revolution is that attempt to transform the basic character of a society which often occurs only after a protracted struggle between opposing groups, with the victorious out-group becoming the new in-group and claiming not only to replace the modes of governance but also to revise foundational goals and to reshape major institutions in the post-revolutionary era.

All three definitions would benefit from extended comment on antecedents and also intentions. But for the purposes of this paper, two elaborations will suffice. One is short and it concerns the cleavage between Religion and Ideology. The other is necessarily long since its intent is to offer a revisionist interpretation of the limits to Revolution and revolutionary change.

You will note that in the above definitions, Religion often includes a transcendent referent, while Ideology emphatically denies its utility. The difference is as fundamental as it is pervasive. No matter how we particularize differences within and between the major monotheistic traditions—Judaism, Christianity and Islam—each presupposes a transcendent referent. It is not an added, tacked on dimension; it is the foundation of all the rest. The transcendent is viewed as both source and culmination of the entire human domain. Yet Ideology, by its very nature, postulates the autonomy of the human domain; it relates all actors and factors to what is knowable, testable and doable. A transcendent referent, far from being postulated or desired, is systematically excluded.

The inevitable tension between Religion and Ideology as competing truth claims needs to be aired, and occasionally erupts in unexpected settings. A Muslim scholar listened with rapt attention to a very long peroration on Islamic ideology at a recent conference. As soon as the speaker was done, his hand shot up and he jumped to his feet exclaiming to the speaker (who also happened to be a Muslim): "Do you not feel, at the very least, a slight friction between the adjective 'Islamic' and the noun to which you apply it, 'Ideology'?!" If we have correctly reflected the nuance of distinction between the two, every person of a professing religious community should feel a similar friction when discourse on Ideology shifts to his own sacred symbols. Ideology is too pervasive to be disbarred, yet it is too dangerous to be allowed to remain unqualified.

Revolution presents a further set of tacit problems that are infrequently teased out and openly faced. The most fundamental problem about Revolution deals not with its causes or its occurrence but with its aftermath: "Is there any such thing as a fully successful revolution, one which produces a disjuncture from the pre-revolutionary state of affairs (and affairs of state) as complete as its leaders and spokesmen (the ideologues, if you will) claim on its behalf?" The evidence would seem to be mixed, and human experience suggests that seeming discontinuities may indeed mask lingering, persistent continuities.

It is to reduce the inflated claims often made on behalf of Revolution (not only by its ideologues but also by its students) that we need a third and final prolegomenon before turning our attention to the Iranian context.

Prolegomenon III: Revolution—the Long and Hard View

It was Hans Mol who once remarked that "the utility of most concepts . . . depends on the frame of reference in which they are used" (Mol 1976:22). He was speaking about the sociology of Religion but he could have been speaking about the sociology of Revolution, since the notion of what we mean by Revolution depends finally for its utility on how broad our frame of reference is within the span of human history. I propose to look at two kinds of events: those which are, at least to some observors, indisputably more significant than revolutions, and those which are adjudged to be considerably less significant.

The second kind would seem to be easier to identify; they can be described as house revolts, *coup d'etats,* uprisings, protest movements, or insurrections. Yet all these terms imply retrospective judgments of attempts at political change which many of their advocates would have claimed, and often did claim, as "revolutionary." The outsider/insider, emic/etic controversy is not easy to solve at any level on any topic (Geertz 1983:55–70), but we will sidestep it here by assuming that the Iranian Revolution of 1978–79 can stand the test of time and avoid being downgraded to what one historian has predicted it will become: a mere variant of the aridisolatic tyranny common to all Iranian polities since the 6th century BC (Katouzian (1983:276–77).

But the first category of events needs to be further examined. How do we understand the limits of the Islamic Republic of Iran, even if it becomes a successful, longterm revolution? That question relates to the larger question: how do we cap the mushrooming ambivalence of the word "Revolution" as it applies to a variety of contexts beyond the Muslim world and Iran?

Of those concepts which suggest a scope and depth of change exceeding the connotation of Revolution, three come to mind: (1) the axial era popularized by the German philosopher Karl Jaspers; (2) the contemporary, as distinct from the modern, phase of global history advocated by the Oxford historian Geoffrey Barraclough; and (3) the paradigm shift described by the M.I.T. historian qua philosopher of science, Thomas Kuhn. The inclusion of Kuhn raises special questions because the phrase which he coined "paradigm shift" appeared in a book entitled, *The Structure of Scientific Revolutions* (Kuhn 1962). Yet as we shall see, the thesis of that book challenges, indirectly as well as directly, the very manner in which we think about Revolution and Revolutions.

The first two concepts are temporal. Their authors ask us to reconsider what time frames we would deem adequate in gauging both the changes that have brought our world into being and also the way that we view those changes. Jaspers' global thesis synthesizes with compelling clarity what others had been saying piecemeal but not advocating as a thesis for centuries. Something so astonishing occurred in several regions of the world during the first millenium B.C. that we have to speak of that time as axial:

> An axis of world history, if such a thing exists, would have to be discovered empirically, as a fact capable of being accepted by all men, Christians included. This axis would be situated at the point in history which gave birth to everything which, since then, man has been able to be, the point most overwhelmingly fruitful in fashioning humanity; its character would have to be, if not empirically cogent and evident, yet so convincing to empirical insight as to give rise to a common frame of historical self-comprehension for all peoples—for the West, for Asia, and for all men on earth, without regard to particular articles of faith. It would seem that this axis of history is to be found in the period around 500 B.C., in the spiritual process that occurred between 800 and 200 B.C. It is there that we meet with the most deepcut dividing line in history. Man, as we know him today, came into being. For short we may style this the "Axial Period," (Jaspers 1955:1).

Jaspers' choice of centuries is bolstered by the concurrence within the same time span of numerous major breakthroughs. At one level, these eruptions are spiritual, moral and intellectual. In Palestine the rise of Prophetic Judaism; in Persia the ascent of Zoroastrianism; in India the transition from the Vedas to the Upanishads, with the emergence of Buddhism, Jainism and other sects; in China the preachings of Kung-fu-tzu and Lao-tsu, auguring the Confucian, Taoist and classical Chinese tradition, while in Greece the appearance of Homer and Hesiod signalling the age of pre-Socratic and classical philosophy—all occurred within the synchronic time frame labeled the Axial Period. In the recorded history of the civilized world, the so-called Afro-Asian *oikumeme,* there has never been a period when human reflections and spiritual aspirations were so crystallized and redirected simultaneously in different cultural traditions. Yet the change was also marked in other, non-religious spheres of society. Civilization always entails complexity and in addition to "the spread of common cultural patterns and political empire over vast areas and in a manner that embraced large masses of people," we also find in the Axial Period "spectacular advances in material technology (particularly agriculture), writing, the rise of cities, universal kingship and bureaucracy (or "palace organization"), law codes, large-scale military organization, systematization of religion, priesthoods and the spread of common mythologies." (Schwartz 1975:2.)

What matters for our purposes are less the fine points of Jaspers' thesis than the fact that it sets forth the basis for ali subsequent thought about man in society, whether one looks to Western, Indian, Chinese or Islamitic civilization. Though at the time inspired by "the consciousness of small groups of philosophers and wise men who may have had a very small impact on their immediate environment," one can say from the vantage point of two millenia that "once these transcendent movements emerge they become independent variables which are involved in intricate and often convoluted ways with the subsequent history of human culture in all the higher civilizations." (Schwartz 1975:5.)

Striking by its absence from Jaspers' vocabulary is the word 'revolution'. What he describes as a series of breakthroughs or radically new developments were for him markings or stages in an evolutionary process, both biological and historical. Evolution supplants Revolution as his major organizing concept, but it is Religion which plays a spectacular and central role in historical evolution, not only giving rise to the Axial Period but also sustaining and perpetuating its legacy.

Ideology is mentioned only in passing by Jaspers. It is defined, then dismissed as a self-limiting, negative concept:

> An ideology (he declares) is a complex of ideas or notions which represents itself to the thinker as an absolute truth for the interpretation of the world and his situation within it; it leads the thinker to accomplish an act of self-deception for the purpose of justification, obfuscation [or] evasion, in some sense or other to his own advantage . . . Bestowal of the epithet ideology upon a way of thinking is to reproach it with untruth & untruthfulness and therefore constitutes the most violent attack. (Jaspers 1955:132)

Despite the evils of ideologies and the contests for power they cloak and accelerate, Jaspers is optimistic about the basis for a world order emerging beyond the present chaos and confrontation. In the 1980s, unlike the late 1940s and early 1950s, Jaspers sounds like an evolutionary positivist: can one still hope to harness the instrumentalities of science and technology to a spiritual worldview as comprehensive and progressive as that of the Axial Period?

G. Barraclough would probably demur. He examines a different, much smaller time frame than Jaspers. Looking at but one tangent of the Afro-Asian *Oikumene,* the modern West, he underscores the uniqueness of the problems which characterize the contemporary era. Despite his more modest scope and less optimistic tone, Barraclough, like Jaspers, introduces a perspective that challenges the ultimacy of any one revolution, even as it raises questions about whether Revolution itself is a meaningful category of historical analysis.

During the period 1955–60, argues Barraclough, we collectively moved into a new chapter of world history, primarily because changes that had begun with Stalin's death in 1953 finally crystallized and produced a momentous shift in patterns and possibilities for all human life. For Barraclough that shift was as drastic as the one which began in the 15th and 16th centuries and, accelerating by the end of the 19th century, marked the transition from the medieval to the modern world. In his view, recent history is marked by three stages of uneven duration and unequal importance: the medieval (1450–1890), the modern (1890–1955), and the contemporary (1955–). Although he enters the caveat that there are no precise dates to the most recent period, since "contemporary history begins when the problems which are actual in the world today first take visible shape," (Barraclough 1964:20), he clearly believes that the contemporary period is the most important because of three coincident developments which preceded it: the ascent, then descent of European colonial power; the redefinition of global power on a US-USSR axis; and finally the looming threat of large scale thermonuclear disaster.

Ominous in themselves, these features of the modern world have accelerated in their global impact because of three further trends that have only begun to emerge since 1955 or more precisely, 1960:

1. Communism and capitalism evened out as world systems. The number of countries whose population had become communist equaled those that could be labeled capitalist or at least non-communist. One consequence of this trend was to end the ideological era: ideologues could flog the supposed superiority of their respective outlooks, but it was empirical (read: economic, political and military) gains not propagandistic platforms that measured the success of capitalism and communism as alternative systems.
2. Newly emergent Asian and African countries formed self-consciously anti-Western coalitions. Reacting to their inferior ranking as Third World, they experienced massive internal upheavals as they tried to fit the "nation state" rubric onto the patchwork territories alloted them by the major powers in the post-colonial era. Often what resulted were military

dictatorships, yet the power concentrated in them brought a heightened sense of cohesion to regional blocs in Latin America, Asia and Africa, and also imparted a new urgency to their role in international relations.

3. Further breakthroughs in scientific research and technological application produced at once a far greater potential for human development and also a more awesome prospect of world-wide destruction. The nuclear nerves of the superpowers might become jangled, or a human accident might unleash a fury that could neither be recalled from the offending side nor absorbed without a retaliatory response from those offended. Nuclear holocaust, in short, became a far more dreaded spectre than even "moderns" had anticipated.

Barraclough's attempt to bifurcate the contemporary from the modern era of global history may not be sustainable, and there is nothing original in any of the depictions or judgments he has put forth. Unlike Jaspers, he omits both Ideology and Religion from his canvas of concerns, the former because it allegedly vanished as a substantive factor in international relations after Stalin, the latter because it ceased to register any significant impact on public affairs after the Enlightenment.

Yet Barraclough merits inclusion in our study if only because he provides a valuable overview to the revolutionary process in so-called Third World countries: he not only draws attention to the colonial context—he also tries to assess its durative impact. Colonization did not disappear with the achievement of political independence. Economic and psychological dependence of the colonized on the colonizer persisted, often evoking a level of violent opposition gradually accelerating, instead of decelerating, after 1960.

Though Barraclough does not apply his thesis directly to Iran, it still has high explanatory value when looking at both the global and regional contexts into which all Iranian events must be situated. Iran has never escaped the grips of an ongoing colonial legacy which has fueled the Janus-like appeal to religious loyalty and revolutionary action. We will examine the components and outcomes of that anti-colonialist mindset after looking briefly at the third and final demurrer from revolution, Thomas Kuhn.

Kuhn's book, *Structure of Scientific Revolutions* (1962), has been recently described, without hyperbole, as "having had a wider academic influence than any other single book of the last twenty years" (Gutting 1980:v). Far more narrow than Jaspers' or Barraclough's theses, Kuhn's work "seeks explicitly to explain the success (as distinct from the truth) of science" (Hollinger 1980:217). In fact, Kuhn sees the ultimate object of science to be puzzle-solving rather than truth-seeking. Precisely because he downplays the importance of truth in the scientific method, Kuhn's is a very unsettling book; it shelves without refuting the notion of scientific objectivity or value-free exploration of natural laws. Kuhn is not an intellectual anarchist, as is I. Lakatos or P. Feyerbend, with whom he is often compared, yet the far flung evidence which he arrays with deft literary skills points to the conclusion that every scientific breakthrough or discovery (or revolution), in fact, results from a five-stage cyclical process: (1) being situated in a secure tradition, (2) looking at novelty and experiencing confusion, (3) encountering disagreement over whether to resist innovation or encourage it, and if the latter, in what direction, (4) then coalescing around a candidate (a theorem, a procedure, *etc.*) that might become (5) another secure tradition (Hollinger 1980:199). In effect, he is describing a process of change which he restricts to scientific communities but with suggestive parallels to other (some would say, all) human communities. The real Kuhnian debate, therefore, has been: to what extent can one extrapolate from his thesis, the heart of which is the paradigm shift (at stage 4), a process that has wider, non-scientific applicability yet equally defensible validity?

Kuhn's book is crucial for our investigation into Revolution because of its fault-line, or at least the fault-line which has been perceived by his most linguistically minded critics. It lies in his very use of the word "revolution", or its equivalent "paradigm shift". Kuhn stresses that once the shift has occurred, there results a new order incommensurable with the old one that has been superceded. Yet at the same time, he tries to account for continuity by saying that such shifts or revolutions are themselves "episodes in scientific development," and that "progress" is achieved through them. In effect, Kuhn subjects his thesis to an old variant of the familiar theme "trying to have your cake and eat it too." He wants to explain how science succeeds from the viewpoint of the participants at the moment when they succeed, but also to show in retrospect how their "revolution" embodies elements of continuity which they scarcely would recognize, or if they recognized, could not bring themselves to admit.

All this suggests that Kuhn is deeply indebted to the political realm for his analogue "revolution". Yet he seems unaware of the ambivalent fluctuation of that term among political theorists. Marx himself shifted from his early view that Revolution must entail violence to a later position that each Revolution is "an epochal change which is considered to be separable from any specific kind of political event or political behavior; it is defined by its outcomes, not by its means of realization" (Vernon 1980:269). Locke held the opposite view, namely, that a Revolution is but "a political expedient, a temporary suspension of legality resorted to by practical men who have exhausted all the alternatives, and its object is to restore legality as quickly as possible. It is not an historical construct but a political category." For Locke the maintenance of community stability is always the foremost desideratum of political organization and action. Hence there is only a nominal (not an essential) difference between revolutionary and evolutionary change: what is called a political revolution may be—indeed, should be—an instrument of political evolution.

Kuhn's scientists seem to act much more like Lockean than Marxist revolutionaries, which, of course, brings us to the nub of our conundrum: do we define Revolution by the canon of its participants or by some canon which must always be retrospective and therefore at odds with the narrowly existential orientation of self-styled revolutionaries? In the provisional definition offered above, we tried to combine both emphases. It is unfortunate that the early Marx postulation of violence as indispensable to revolutionary action has diverted attention away from the later Marx' emphasis on outcome, as well as the Lockean perspective just cited.

If the French Revolution was the classic modern revolution, sparking interest in both Ideology and Revolution that neither had known before Bastille Day, then it is also the French Revolution that makes clear the need to separate motives from outcomes when looking at any revolution:

> Political historians and political scientists have quite often suggested that the self-definitions of revolutionaries are in part deluded. At least since Tocqueville, and even more since Albert Sorel's great study of the continuity between the Old Regime and revolutionary France, they have pointed to *The Envelope of Longer-Term Constraints and Dispositions Which Survive Political Violence*. . . . (We must) always separate from each other two pictures of revolution which are distinct. A political revolution (minimally defined) is an act of violence through which power is un-

constitutionally transferred; such an event is connected only contingently, and may not be connected at all, with the sort of drastic and across-the-board change for which we also use the word "revolution". *This* revolution is very likely to take place over a fairly lengthy and also indefinite period of time; it is very likely to consist in connections and implications which are invisible to or imperfectly grasped by those who live through it, and in general it is something much more readily accessible to the reflective backward glance of the historian. At any rate it is not encompassed by the practical resolves of revolutionary actors, for it is not within their power to determine how much will change, how, and to what longer-term effect, as a result of their action . . . It was partly for this reason that Albert Sorel's more notorious cousin, George, declared that all revolutionaries were moved by myths, for what they will turn out to have done is not defined by what they think they are doing. (Vernon 1980:259–60)

It is appropriate to conclude our long—and also hard—view of Revolution with a quotation distinguishing revolutionary claims from evolutionary changes. We have examined three theorists who either qualify or dismiss the validity of Revolution as a diachronic category in historical analysis. In the perspective of Jaspers, no Revolutions, (whether pre-modern Western like the French or contemporary Third World like the Iranian), alter the fundamental directions of the Axial Period. For Barraclough, on the other hand, revolutions of the Third World do matter but not in comparison with their Western predecessors (English, French, Russian, *etc.*) Rather, their nature and influence is determined by synchronic, spatial and also psychological factors. Spawned in the contemporary period, they erupt in formerly colonialized regions as delayed reactions to the deeprooted hostility which colonial rule has engendered. Kuhn, finally, would agree that revolutions recur in several spheres, scientific and technical as well as political and social. Yet he is compelled to admit (with the help of his critics) that the viewpoint of revolutionaries accents a disjuncture between their context and their predecessors; a disjuncture often unsustainable from a longer, broader view of the socio-political process such as an outside observer or historian is prone to take.

All these tangents are helpful in considering the Iranian Revolution: Jaspers forces us to look at broader contextual changes than are implied by political revolution; Barraclough draws our attention to two invaluable distinctions (a) between First and Third Worlds and (b) between colonization as past history and as contemporary mindset; while Kuhn questions the rhetoric of both participants and analysts who would accent the uniqueness of any revolution. His challenge to those who read the second part of this essay is clear; no one with the short retrospect of six years (1985–1979) should conflate the claims advocated with outcomes yet to be determined, or ignore persistent continuity with elements that are intrinsically, irradicably Iranian.

II: The Iranian Revolution in Comparative Perspective

In the first two Prolegomena we tried to prioritize and then define the three concepts that this volume is addressing. We concluded, on the one hand, that Revolution was the *leitmotif* to which Religion related through the mediation of Ideology, but on the other hand, that Revolution itself was susceptible to multiple evaluations as an analytical category explaining historical change. Hence in the third and final Prolegomenon, we offered three analytical categories which seem to surpass Revolution in their explanatory scope. Especially the Kuhnian paradigm shift, which applies to scientific as well as political transformations, allows us to reconsider Revolution for the actual change it realizes, as distinct from the claims to change its ideologues promote.

Yet when we turn our attention to the Iranian Revolution as a specific case in point for testing all the hypotheses and qualifications introduced in the Prolegomena, we are faced with an initial problem of multiple proportions. How do we make sense of this revolution on a comparative scale? With which revolutions do we compare it? And what importance do we attach to participants' ideological claims, as distinct from external observations and analyses? A brief list of contextual markings may help us broach the defiant perplexity known as Iran:

1. The revolution of 1978–79 was a Third World Revolution, exhibiting several of the features that Barraclough scored as characteristic of the contemporary period in global history. It was a local happening, yet it was precipitated by transregional factors, not the least being Iran's marginalization in world economy and politics until the 1960s and even more the 1970s, when increased oil prices and subsequent mismanagement of the income they provided sparked an economic crisis in Pahlavi Iran. Numerous groups, not only the clerical elite, were affected by these events. Dissatisfaction focused on the autocratic leader but also on the external, col-

onizing forces with which he associated himself. The Iranian word for this extreme dependency on foreign income, foreign military aid, foreign political adventurism and also foreign lifestyles is *gharbzādegī*, "excess of the west" or as some would have it, "Westoxification." Rightly or wrongly, it labels the Shah as transmitter and perpetuator of the colonial past which Iranians of nearly all classes so deeply resented. In Barraclough's view, the simmering protest against colonial controls accelerated after the achievement of political independence and was redirected against the fifth column within each country, in this case, those individuals and groups perceived to be foreigners with Iranian faces and names, chief among whom was Mohammed Reza Shah.

2. The 1978–79 revolution was not only Third World, it was Shi'i-Iranian, Iranian-Shi'i. The two markings are inextricable; there is no neat division of religious from national, or national from religious, in the consciousness of most Iranians. For the enemy within to be opposed there had to be a moral, specifically Shi'i criterion against which he could be measured and found wanting. It is erroneous to suggest, as many have, that the Shah was vilified because the majority of Iranians were Shi'i rather than Sunni Muslims and therefore had a deep distrust of, or outright aversion to, political power, especially when exercised by an autocratic monarch. The accomodation between Shahs and their Iranian Shi'i subjects goes back to the early 16th century and the founding of the Safavi Empire, a vast and successful bureaucratic, military patronage state. The crisscrossing of religious-political authority and the constant need of even the most powerful monarchs to claim religious legitimation, ensured that the Shah would project himself as "God's Shadow on Earth." From the Safavi period, Iranian rulers had arrogated to themselves the multivalent title "God's Shadow on Earth." Even though some have remarked that "Mohammed Reza Shah seems to have given little more than ritually dutiful attention to this aspect of his role" (see Willner 1984:82), he never disavowed it. Yet in the minds of his Iranian subjects there remained an implicit, irradicable question mark: is it possible for *dīn* & *dunyā*, (the demands of religion and the lures of worldliness), to be reconciled? How does the ruler resist the latter while promoting the former? Do the clergy,

as repositories of Islam but even more as custodians of hope for the illiterate masses, deem him to be *sultān ādil* or *sultān jā'ir*—a just ruler or a despot? Until 1979, there was no expectation, nor is there any religious literature to support the view, either that monarchy is unequivocally unIslamic or that a cleric should rule in place of the Shah. Rather, the hope was that the Shah—if not this Shah, then another Shah or his equivalent—could be made accountable to the standards of justice, which also meant at least the appearance of rejecting, rather than promoting, colonial or western influence in Iran.

3. There is a further, essential caveat to enter at the beginning of our investigation of the 1978–79 Revolution. Not only was it Third World & Iranian-Shi'i but it was unexpected. Advocates as well as adversaries were not prepared to have it succeed, American social scientists have been especially baffled by its occurrence. Some of them may share the quasi-Marxist, anti-colonial rhetorical posture of the Iranian clergy who spearheaded the revolution and have been its principal beneficiaries. Yet most social scientists are not sympathetic with the religious claims that these same Iranian clerics make on behalf of their revolution. Some have even gone to extraordinary lengths to "prove" that the 1978–79 revolution was not, in fact, a religious revolution (see Green 1982:122–34 & Keddie 1981:258–72).

The media, also caught unawares by the 1978–79 Revolution, have tended to go in the opposite direction, caricaturing the Ayatollah Khomeini as a ruthless religious fanatic, comparable only to Qaddafi of Libya (who ironically, along with Asad of Syria, is his only fullfledged Muslim ally) and imputing a religious motivation to all the claims and activities of Khomeini supporters.

To make sense of the 1978–79 Revolution, one must bracket out, at least initially, preconceptions about aggregate topics like Islam, Shi'ism, Holy War, *etc.*, and instead focus: (1) on the number and the nature of the revolutions that have occurred in modern Iran, (2) on the particular events which comprise the 1978–79 Revolution, and finally (3) on the comparison of this revolution with other revolutions that have taken place beyond Iran, specifically including American revolutions.

Most Americans do not realize, and the media have made no attempt to help us remember, that Iran has experienced three revolutions in this century. The first two explain a great deal about the climate in which the third erupted. The first was the Constitutional Revolution of 1905–11. It, too, was a revolution against the Shah, though he was then a Qajar rather than a Pahlavi Shah. It, too, was sparked by a protest against foreign (then British, now American) influence, involving tobacco rather than oil. It also had the support of at least some segments of the Iranian clergy. Yet the principal agenda for that revolution was its advocates' insistence on the implementation of a uniquely Western democratic instrumentality, namely, a constitution. Hence the name the "Constitutional Revolution."

It failed. The reasons were several, but they are less important than the occurrence of this revolution and its persistence for nearly six years. Many Iranians talk of that revolution as if it had happened yesterday, and even those who do not share the goals of the Islamic Republic of Iran compare its origins with the Constitutional Revolution of 1905–1911 (see Keddie 1983b & also Katouzian 1983).

Yet the other, the second Iranian revolution of this century is absent from the minds of most Iranians; it is also neglected in scholarly as well as popular analyses of Iran (for an exception see Saikal 1980:ch.III). This was the so-called "White Revolution," heralded by the late Shah in January 1963. As its name may suggest, it was to be a revolution without violence, which would upgrade or modernize the state of Iran's economy (especially the agricultural sector), during the remainder of the 20th century. It, like the Constitutional Revolution, was a failed experiment, yet it deserves comment because it much more closely corresponds to the kind of scientific revolution of which Kuhn speaks or the communications revolution of which we hear so much these days (see, e.g., Gouldner 1976).

Once we accept the existence of three revolutions (not merely one) in modern Iranian history, how do we begin to describe this revolution? Some would go back to the 7th century, and look at what has been termed the Kerbala paradigm (see Fischer 1980: passim). That phrase refers to the massacre of the Prophet Muhammad's grandson Husayn by a rival Muslim leader on 10 Muharram 680, and marks the historical separation of the Shi'i community from the rest of the Muslim world. Others would say, however, that Iran is not irrevocably stamped as a 12er Shi'i nation until the emergence of the Safavi state in the 16th century, and therefore, that is an appropriate point for looking at the genesis of the 1978–79 Revolution.

Neither of these arguments will seem convincing to most Americans. They would prefer a more recent, seemingly objective, listing of the events that led up to and followed from the 1978–79 Revolution. Such a list would include:

- June 1963—anti-government demonstrations sparked by the arrest of Khomeini.
- November 1964—Khomeini exiled, first to Turkey, then to Iraq and finally (1978) to Paris.
- January 1979—the Shah departs Iran
- February 1979—Khomeini returns to Iran
- 4 November 1979—American Embassy invaded by Iranian dissidents: the 14 month hostage crisis begins, with Walter Cronkite doing a daily countdown.
- December 1979—the Constitution of the Islamic Republic of Iran is ratified by popular referendum.
- January 1980—Bani Sadr is elected the First President of the Islamic Republic of Iran.
- July 1980—the Shah dies in exile and is buried in Egypt.
- September 1980—the Iran-Iraq war begins with the Iraqi invasion of Khuzistan.
- 20 January 1981—the American hostages are released
- June 1981—Bani Sadr is dismissed as Commander-in-Chief of the Iranian Armed Forces and later goes into exile in Paris.
- Summer 1981—bombings by underground opposition (Mujahedin-i Khalq) kill several top officials of the Islamic Republic of Iran, including Khomeini's likely successor Beheshti.
- December 1982—83 member assembly of experts designated to select Khomeini's successor.

As satisfying as that list might be to an American audience, it would be heatedly contested by others, even those who oppose the current regime in Iran. A very active and visible women's group, for instance, has felt oppressed and excluded by the 1978–79 revolution. A listing of their version of significant events that comprise what for them has been a retrograde revolution, would include the following:

- 1935–36—Reza Shah compels women to drop the veil in public places.
- 7 January 1937—declared as Women's day by the Shah.

- 1938—women are admitted to Tehran University.
- 1958—High Council of Women is organized and later (1966), replaced by Women's Organization of Iran, with branches in all major cities.
- 26 January 1963—A six-point reform program labeled the White Revolution is introduced. Two of its crucial provisions are: land reform and women's suffrage.
- 1967—women are accepted into the judiciary and drafted into the police and army.
- 1967—Family Protection Law passed, modified in 1975 to provide for mutual consent in divorce.

(Having rolled forward, the wheel of women's rights then rolls back.)

- February 1979—Family Protection Law suspended.
- March 1979—women no longer appointed judges; public veiling required; women barred from competing in international sports.
- May 1979—coeducation banned.
- March 1980—First Islamic Constituent Assembly elected: 2 women among 217 representatives.
- April 1980—universities closed indefinitely.
- May-July 1981—further steps to implement compulsory veiling, including the firing of unveiled women from public jobs.
- July 1981—Parliament ratifies Bill of Retribution, especially hard on women offenders.

This list, like the preceding one, could be expanded. Its purpose will have been served, however, if it conveys how pernicious has been the effect of the 1978–79 Revolution for Iranian women who identify with the women's rights movement. Though it is a list with which Americans can empathize, it will appear to most as an ancillary list, fundamentally less important than the first list which concerned those events auguring a dramatic, public transference of internal political power and international realignment.

Yet the larger problem which we Americans face in post-1979 Iran is not the choice between our version or women activists' version of the revolution's chronology—intriguing as those differences may be—but rather the lack of any appropriate parallels to the three Iranian revolutions in our own national experience.

The inclusion of the White Revolution in our profile of 20th century Iranian Revolutions may help us to recapture a sense of the distance between our own experience as American citizens of the modern, now contemporary, world and the quite different experience of Iranians as marginal aliens to the modern, and also the contemporary, world.

Let us attempt some blunt historic parallels. The Iranians—who are as vastly different among themselves as we Americans, but who for the purposes of this discussion will be reduced, simplified and labeled as "Iranians"—experienced a Constitutional Revolution in the first decade of this century. It bears comparison with our own revolution of 1776, which in the 1780s also produced a constitution. But if one speaks of the rearrangement and distribution of economic and political power, then the "real" revolution in America may have been capitalist instead of constitutional; it may have taken place in 1860–64 instead of 1776 (B. Moore 1976:111–155). By either reckoning, we are still faced with the fact that at some date prior to the modern era there did take place in America two revolutions: one constitutional, the other capitalist, and by even the most rigorous historical canon, both may be said to have succeeded; for did not the capitalist revolution presuppose, even as it developed beyond, the constitutional revolution of the preceding century? The same may be said of our "white" revolution. It would have been impossible without the earlier revolutions—constitutional and capitalist. The "white" revolution comes close to being what Barraclough depicts as the momentous scientific breakthroughs and technological applications unique to the contemporary period in world history. Though the change they initiated was gradual and non-violent, their combined effect created a fissure within American/Western society between the technological and literary subcultures, as C.P. Snow augured, with a resulting longterm impact that may prove to be as durative as that of precipitate, often violent political revolutions.

We are left then with still another list: the names of two different types of revolutions experienced in the United States and in Iran. They are uneven. Though sharing certain formal characteristics, the two sets of revolutions miss at the most crucial junctures. The constitutional, capitalist and white revolutions of America are clearly part of the evolving political-economic profile which distinguishes America among the community of nations. The capitalist revolution has no Iranian counterpart, while the constitutional and white revolutions which did take place in Iran were not linked to one another nor did they mount a sustained, cumulative change, either within Iranian society or in the larger global domain.

Yet our comparison up to this point omits one crucial piece of evidence: we have not yet considered, the "Third" Iranian revolution of the 20th century. It is neither constitutional nor white but Islamic. As such, it has no precedent within Iranian history, yet at the same time it has no parallel—either past, present, or remotely conceivable in the future—within the United States of America. It underscores a gap in our self-perceived national identity: can we claim to be an intensely religious nation of whatever stripe in comparison with Iran? It is a delicate question, one which some would parry by pointing to the force of civil religion in 20th century America. But civil religion is a surrogate national religion, as Bellah, Handy and May have pointed out, and even its proponents would not hold it up as the likely pretext for a violent, wrenching revolution of the kind Iranians experienced in 1979. The opposite, in fact, seems to be the case. We Americans have not experienced, nor do we have the capacity to experience, a religious revolution such as we are now witnessing in Iran. What we have had, in its stead, are but partial revivals and reawakenings among circumscribed groups, occurring for limited times in specific locales. They have not been generalizable to several regions nor embraced by several classes nor sustained for a sufficient length of time to qualify as a religious revolution. That term, like the experience it connotes, is a non-starter in American social history.

Our comparison of revolutions indicates more graphically than any chronicling of history could, the structural differences between American and Iranian societies but also the perceptual divide between Iranians and Americans. At the very least, they have underscored why we are so persistently, intrinsically unable to understand Iran—either the last five years or the preceding eighty-five years. In Iran, unlike the USA, not only is religious motivation and symbolism much closer to the national identity and continuous experience of dominant groups but that very depth of religiosity pits the majority of Iranians against the Westernizers in their midst, the Shah and the elites who supported him, as well as the Westernizers beyond, both the USSR and the USA.

Despite the communications revolution, there persists what might be called a worldview gradient, separating peoples and nations more dramatically (often with tragic consequence) than do geography, politics, economics or religion. Revolutions, if we study them carefully, can be instructive. We differ from Iranians because of our revolutions which succeeded while theirs failed (the constitutional and white), but even more because of the one revolution which we had and they didn't (capitalist) *and* the one revolution which they undertook and (apparently) won while we did not even recognize its possibility, so distant was a religious revolution from us.

The further and major question to consider is what revolutions have occurred beyond Iran with which the latest (the Islamic Revolution), can be gainfully compared? Unfortunately, the answer most often given is *jejune*: Western Orientalists tirelessly point to the French and Russian revolutions (see B. Lewis 1983), while non-Iranian Muslim scholars point to the counter-example of the Turkish Revolution of the 1920s, which seemed to presage a tide of secularism for the heartland of the Muslim world (see Waheed az-Zaman 1984). Other revolutions that have been or could be cited are: the Polish and Afghan, neither of which has been successful, though both share aspects of resistance, protest and violence evident in the Iranian case; and also the Algerian Revolution of the 1960s together with the Libyan Revolution of 1969. The latter especially merits comparison with Iran as a further case study in the relationship of ideology and charisma to revolutionary aims.

What needs to be recognized at another level, however, is the inappropriateness of all these other revolutions—pre-modern and modern, capitalist, communist and Third World—to the Iranian experience "from the Iranian perspective." Before trying to compare, we have to recognize that for the participants themselves no comparison is possible or acceptable. On the occasion of the Fourth Anniversary of the Islamic Revolution, one of its ideologues wrote a book in which he declared:

> If what had occurred in Iran was merely a reform and not a revolution, then such a movement could have proceeded without confronting any difficulties. However, any change which is in contradiction to the interests of the world oppressors is a revolution and not a reform. What has taken place in Iran is a revolution in its real sense; a Revolution which is unparalleled in the world and unprecedented among the revolutions of contemporary history. It can be proudly stated that nothing matches it except the movement of the divine prophets. In the same way that the divine prophets' movements were for the purpose of destroying the existing oppressive systems and creating new systems based upon divine precepts, this revolution came to destroy the existing anti-human values in today's world and to restore the divine human values to humanity. Naturally, such a phenomenon cannot be termed "reform". This is a revolution,

in fact the most profound revolution in human history after the movements of the divine prophets. (Muhajeri 1982:151–52).

One can follow the logic of such an ideological declaration, and begin to chart the further consequences of the Islamic Revolution in Iran for other states in the region, for non-Muslim neighbors (especially the USSR), for the western alliance, and for the world. Many have undertaken to do just that in a fantasy chase that one scholar has aptly dubbed the "circus media symbolism" (Fischer 1980:239).

A more serious and plausible stance is to examine again the question that we posed in looking at Kuhn's "paradigm shift." Do you accept the insiders' statements of what constitutes a successful revolution, or do you look elsewhere for other models, leading to broader analyses, with more sober conclusions? The latter option seems preferable. While it is true that almost no political revolution ever became recognized *ex post facto* as a revolution unless its proponents first labeled it as such, it is also true that many alleged revolutions have been subsequently downgraded and classified as something less than revolutions, including, as we have seen, our own American revolution, to which many historians now refer simply as "the American War of Independence." A comparable example within recent Iranian history is the *Mosaddeq interregnum,* 1951–53, a severe challenge to the Shah that was ended only with outside (read CIA) support for Mosaddeq's overthrow. Yet had Mosaddeq succeeded, he and not Khomeini, would be remembered as the architect of a revolution that ended Pahlavi rule and began another chapter in Iranian history.

Deeper questions, also harking back to Kuhn, now surface. What constitutes a successful political revolution? Does a revolution that signifies merely political change qualify as a revolution in the fullest connotation of that term? As it turns out, the two questions are inseparable. B. Turner, looking at the critical transformations which have characterized western societies, notes that in each case the presence and the services of an autonomous, commercial middle class were required to make the transition from feudal/religious to industrial/secular culture. That class has been lacking in Middle Eastern societies; its absence has produced the "No Revolutions" thesis which dominates much writing on the pre-modern and modern Middle East. It is an Orientalist argument, but it also has its Marxist counterpart, namely, that these societies, precisely because they have not undergone genuine "Social" revolutions, have experienced in the transition from colonial rule to post-colonial independence "merely political *coups d'etats* and palace revolutions" (Turner 1978:66 and also Cohan 1975:214).

Yet most self-proclaimed revolutionaries assert their intent to change more than the form and figures of the existing polity; their ideology includes a platform for the total restructuring of the economic, judicial and administrative instruments as well as the symbolic profile and political leadership of the post-revolutionary society. That was the claim in Iran in 1978–79. It may simply be too early to take a careful, accurate stock of the relationship between revolutionary ideals and operational realities, i.e., to assess the adequacy of those engaged in this revolution to live up to their own high sounding ideological platitudes. But let us try.

The Italian journalist Elaine Sciolino has raised the same question we are asking: did Iran experience a true revolution? She attempts to answer her own question by looking at a range of empirical evidence that relates to the structural features of Iranian society. She is alert to the crucial distinction between descriptive and explanatory analyses. The former throws up a wealth of factual data to "prove" that what has happened and continues to happen is "revolutionary." The latter examines the underlying continuities between the ancien regime and the revolutionary government, often in a manner reminiscent of Sorel's treatment of the French Revolution discussed above.

By this latter canon, the verdict on Iran's most recent revolution must remain moot. If one examines two crucial indices, for instance, the mode of political representation and sources of revenue, there has been little change since the Pahlavi period. The state has been called an Islamic Republic, yet it does not function as a democracy. There is a single party *majlis* (parliament), with courts, mosques, schools and land law functioning under a hierarchically monitored ideology as rigid as that which prevailed prior to 1978. The income which allows the new government to function domestically and also to carry out a costly foreign war with its neighbor, Iraq, continues to derive from the west-oriented segment of the economy. Since the fall of the shah, the actual percentage of foreign exchange revenues deriving from the oil sector has, in fact, increased and it now constitutes 80% of Iran's export earnings.

New revolutionary institutions have been established, but many of them shadow institutions remaining from the ancien regime, with only the personnel circulating. Particularly at the provincial level, almost the same procedures are followed today as were in place six years ago. The court system has not been reorganized. In the absence of an Islamic Retribution Bill (ratified in 1981 but not yet enacted), individual revolutionary courts and firing squads acting as neighborhood committees continue to operate. On the crucial issue of land reform, little has been done since the time of the Shah.

Land reform is indeed the most evident single issue for gauging how difficult it is to implement a genuine social revolution in Iran. Ironically, the *majlis* (composed of 270 elected members, all of them, including the two women, Khomeini loyalists) and the twelve member council of guardians (an appointed body even closer to Khomeini than the *majlis* and with veto power over legislation coming from the *majlis*) have been in sharp disagreement on just this point. The former engages in sharp, heated "public" debates that would rival those of the Knesset in Israel, while the latter operates only in secret, albeit in direct consultation with Khomeini. The former has loudly advocated rapid socialization of the entire economy, including land. Social justice—a Shi'i populist theme as we earlier noted—is its shibboleth. The latter has quietly held out for individual rights, retention of private property (with scriptural support from the Qur'an) and also free trade (not restricting it to the Muslim bloc as the *Majlis* has advocated). In effect, there is a continuing ideological contest, with practical points of conflagration, between the *majlis* and the council of guardians. Only the undisputed authority of the Imam (as Khomeini is affectionately and fearfully known) holds together the Iranian government on these issues.

Yet other revolutions have survived both internal advocacy conflicts and seeming ideological contradictions within the social fabric of their constituents. While one may call attention to what has not happened yet in Iran, as Sciolino (1983) does with deft attention to detail, it is also possible to stress what has changed, especially in the formation of an opposition to the Shah (who as recently as six years ago looked militarily & politically invincible to most observors) and also in the prosecution of a successful uprising against him and his regime.

Theda Skocpol, whose book, *States and Social Revolutions* (Cambridge:1979) has been hailed as the finest revisionist approach to the study of revolutions since Crane Brinton's *The Anatomy of*

Revolution (1938), disagrees with Sciolino's analysis of the Iranian revolution primarily because her emphasis is on the changes that occurred prior to 1978 and also in the immediate aftermath of Khomeini's triumphal return to Iran. Defining social revolutions as "rapid, basic transformations of a country's state and class structures, and of its dominant ideology" (Skocpol 1982:265), she points to the failure of the Shah's "White Revolution" as the decisive setback for his ideology of Mimetic Progress, which then created a vacuum filled by the counter-ideology of Islamic Revival. The White Revolution gave way to the Islamic Revolution but also prepared for it.

The Shah's managerial myopia was his undoing, in Skocpol's view: instead of meshing his polity with his constituents, he created a rentier state, increasingly addicted to revenues from exports of oil and natural gas. He related the state to the rest of Iranian society through expenditures rather than tax levies. It was a monstrous policy misjudgment that proved to be fatal:

> The Shah did not rule through, or in alliance with, any independent social class. During the 1960s he launched a "White Revolution" to buy out landlords, redistribute land to wealthier peasants, and extend bureaucratic state control into the villages. Poor planning left much of the agrarian economy impoverished, however, forcing millions of poorer peasants to migrate to the towns and cities. Urban Iran grew to become almost 50% of the population before the (Islamic) Revolution, and all urban strata relied heavily for privileges, employment and services on burgeoning state expenditures. (Skocpol 1982:269).

In other words, the Shah's failed revolution created not only a platform of grievances but also a grieving constituency—urban-immigrant, disenfranchised, angry peasants—for the subsequent Islamic Revolution. Still, for that latter revolution to succeed, it needed a mobilizing ideology and an energizing charismatic leader. In 12er Shi'a Islam, it found the ideology; in Khomeini, the leader.

Here is a point-by-point case exemplification of the thesis we put forth in the Second Prolegomenon, namely, that Religion mediated through Ideology could contribute to the outbreak of a political revolution. But other ancillary conditions are also needed. In the case of Iran it was not only Shi'i Islam mediated through Khomeini's revisionist ideology (e.g., monarchy is unIslamic: a cleric can/should rule in his stead, *etc.*) but also the coincidence of antecedent structural flaws in a too-rapidly industrializing rentier state that was badly mismanaged by an autocratic ruler. Religion, ideologically refocused, served as a catalyst, but not a sufficient cause, for the 1978–79 revolution:

> Shi'a Islam was both organizationally and culturally crucial to the making of the Iranian revolution against the Shah. Radicalized clerics, loosely following the Ayatollah Khomeini, disseminated political ideas challenging the Shah. Then the networks, the social forms, and the central myths of Shi'a Islam helped to coordinate urban mass resistance to give it the moral will to persist in the face of attempts at armed repression. . . . [For] if a historical conjuncture arises in which a vulnerable state faces oppositionally inclined social groups possessing solidarity, autonomy, and independent economic resources (as the clergy did through the bazaari connection), then the sorts of moral symbols and forms of social communication offered by Shi'a Islam in Iran can sustain the self-conscious making of a revolution. (Skocpol 1982:275).

Sadly, the comparative insights of Skocpol's essay fail to yield a post-revolutionary assessment of the 1978–79 cataclysm. Having highlighted the structural flaws created by the Shah and exploited to their advantage by the Shi'i clergy (though not all of them initially were confrontational, see Floor 1983), Skocpol does not explore the extent to which these same flaws were remedied, or even recognized, in the subsequent institutional realignments of the new government.

It is worth emphasizing that Skocpol's approach is the reverse of Sciolino's. As we saw, the latter tries to look back on the claims of the revolution and square those with what has happened in Iran since 1979. Yet Skocpol, like many others, is mainly fascinated with the onset and early success of this revolution and how it corresponds with other recent revolutions, either conforming to or deviating from a general causal theory of revolutions. In the last paragraph she does venture to suggest that: "of course, events in Iran may outrun the Shi'a revolutionary leadership. . . . For when the oil runs out, or if international demand goes severely slack for a prolonged period, then the material basis for an unproductive revolutionary utopia will be gone. Iranian history will then reach a watershed perhaps even more momentous than the revolutionary events of the present time." (Skocpol 1982:280).

This last statement underscores the weakness of the many social scientific studies of revolution. They are all retrospective, and hence unable to cope with current contingencies or to predict future possibilities. J. Goldstone, summarizing all such theories, wryly noted that:

> The study of revolutions remains like the study of earthquakes. When one occurs, scholars try to make sense of the myriad of data that have been collected, and build theories to account for the next one. Gradually, we gain a fuller understanding of them; but the next one that occurs still surprises us. Our knowledge of revolutions, like that of earthquakes, is still limited. We can detail the patterns in those that have occurred, and we can list some of the conditions conducive to them; but better understanding of exactly when they are likely to occur still lies in the future. (Goldstone 1982:205).

That severely restrained conclusion, with its minimal explanatory yield, can be expanded in the case of Iran. As Eqbal Ahmad suggests in a superb commentary on Skocpol's article, the crucial stage in the Iranian revolution has not yet been reached. It is internal rather than external in focus. In strict administrative and political terms, little reorganization of the state has so far occurred, and so "unless there is a second revolution in Iran (likely) or the country disintegrates from the ongoing revolutionary chaos (unlikely!), Iran will witness the restoration of a Pahlevi-type state with the Shah" (Ahmad 1982:300).

That diagnosis contains a prescription for further stages to the internal transformation of Iran beyond what has already taken place or even been firmly projected by the current clerical leadership. Yet it is, as Ahmed indicates, a likely event, however hazy its contours remain at present. One element that is too often neglected is the demographic dimension of this next level of revolution. It has been aptly pointed out by Fischer. He stresses "the necessary conjunction of the revolutionary process with the demographic explosion in Iran. The options for which kind of revolution will eventuate are as multiple as the actors participating, or waiting to participate, in the continuing drama of Iran. All options are open, none are yet certain." (Fischer 1980:239).

Still, the option voiced by Sciolino and expanded by Ahmad, seems most likely; that a second revolution will occur but only after Khomeini's demise, and it will result in a regime that is fiercely Islamic, avowedly revolutionary (though still ambivalent on major economic issues like land reform and income redistribution) and consistently repressive of all segments within Iranian society which continue to oppose its policies. At the same time it will be boldly aggressive in seeking to desseminate its views beyond Iran, globally as well as regionally. The furthest influence of this revolution will not be open to scholarly assessment for at least another decade, but we can be certain that 12er Shi'a Islam recycled as a radicalized clerical ideology will be a major component of that assessment.

References

Ahmad, Eqbal, 1982, "Comments on Skocpol". Theory and Society 1:293–300.

Arjomand, S. A., 1984, From Nationalism to Revolutionary Islam. Albany.

Barraclough, Geoffrey, 1964, An Introduction to Contemporary History. New York.

Bayat, Mangol, 1983, "The Iranian Revolution of 1978–79: Fundamentalist or Modernist?" Middle East Journal 37/1:30–42.

Bell, Daniel, 1960, The End of Ideology. New York.

Cohan, A. S., 1975, Theories of Revolution. New York.

Feuer, Lewis S., 1975, Ideology & the Ideologists. New York.

Fischer, Michael M. J., 1980, Iran: From Religious Dispute to Revolution. Cambridge.

Floor, Willem M., 1983, "The Revolutionary Character of the Ulama: Wishful Thinking or Reality" in Keddie 1983a:73–92.

Foucault, Michel, 1980, The History of Sexuality. New York.

Geertz, Clifford, 1983, Local Knowledge. New York.

Goldstone, Jack A., 1982, "The Comparative & Historical Study of Revolutions" Annual Review of Sociology 8:187–207.

Gouldner, Alvin W., 1978, The Dialectic of Ideology & Technology. New York.

Green, Jerrold, D., 1982, Revolution in Iran. New York.

Gutting, Gary, 1980, Editor, Paradigms & Revolutions. Notre Dame.

Hollinger, David, 1980, "T. S. Kuhn's Theory of Science & Its Implications for History" in Gutting 1980:105–22.

Jaspers, Karl, 1953, The Origin & Goal of History. London.

Johnson, Harry M., 1968, "Ideology & the Social Systems" in Sills 1968 vol. 7:76–85.

Katouzian, Homa, 1983, "The Aridisolatic Society" International Journal of Middle East Studies 5:259–81.

Keddie, Nikki R., 1981 Editor, Roots of Revolution. New Haven 1983a, Editor, Religion & Politics in Iran. New Haven. 1983b, "The Iranian Revolution in Comparative Perspective" American Historical Review 88/3:579–98.

Kuhn, Thomas, 1962, The Structure of Scientific Revolutions Chicago.

Laqueur, Walter, 1968, "Revolution" in Sills 1968:vo. 13:500–507

Larrain, Jorge, 1979, The Concept of Ideology. Athens, Georgia.

Lewis, Bernard, 1983, "The Revolt of Islam" New York Review of Books 30 June:35–38.

Mannheim, Karl, 1936 (1955), Ideology & Utopia. New York.

Mol, Hans, 1976, Identity & the Sacred. Oxford.

Moore, Barrington, Jr., 1966, Social Origins of Dictatorship and Democracy Boston.

Muhajeri, Masih, 1982, Islamic Revolution: Future Path of the Nations Tehran.

Saikal, Amin, 1980, The Rise and Fall of the Shah. Princeton.
Schwartz, Benjamin I., 1975, "The Age of Transcendence" Daedalus 104/2:1–7.
Sciolino, Elaine, 1983, "Iran's Durable Revolution" Foreign Affairs 61:893–920.
Shils, Edward, 1968, "The Concept and Function of Ideology" in Sills 1968:vol. 7:66–76.
Sills, David L., 1968, Editor. International Encyclopaedia of the Social Sciences 18 volumes. New York.
Skocpol, Theda, 1979, States and Social Revolutions. New York. 1982, "Rentier State & Shi'a Islam in the Iranian Revolution" Theory and Society 11:265–83.
Smith, W. Cantwell, 1962, The Meaning and End of Religion. New York.
Tabari, Azar & Yeganah, Nahid, 1982, Compilers. In the Shadow of Islam: The Women's Movement in Iran. London.
Turner, Bryan, 1978, Marx and the End of Orientalism. London.
Vernon, Richard, 1980, "Politics as Metaphor: Cardinal Newman and Professor Kuhn" in Gutting 1980:246–67.
Voegelin, Eric, 1975, From Enlightenment to Revolution. Durham, North Carolina.
Weil, Eric, 1975, "What is a breakthrough in History?" Daedalus 104/2:21–36.
Willner, Ann Ruth, 1984, The Spellbinders: Charismatic Political Leadership. New Haven.
az-Zaman Waheed, 1984, "Islamization in Pakistan Some Recent Developments" Unpublished paper delivered at Conference on Contemporary Pakistan, 25–27 October. Columbia University.

4

Ideology In Rural Struggle: Contradictions of Popular Movements in Highland Peru

WILLIAM W. STEIN

Introduction

Peru was shocked on January 30, 1983, when the mass media reported on the recovery of the bodies of eight journalists who had been clubbed and hacked to death in the remote Andean community of Uchuraccay, located in the Ayacucho region (Guzmán Figueroa, et al. 1983, Vargas Llosa 1983, Amnesty International 1983:27–43, Salcedo 1984, Landa 1984). The group had left the city of Ayacucho a few days before with the object of verifying reports that seven alleged *Sendero Luminoso* (Shining Path) guerrillas had been killed in an ambush by people from Huaychao, a peasant community near Uchuraccay. The Sendero is a "dogmatically Maoist" (McClintock 1983a:19) faction which originated in the city of Ayacucho; it is influenced by the thought of both Mao Tse-Tung and Che Guevara on the waging of armed struggle against cities from the countryside (Davies 1984). It declared war against the Peruvian government in 1980 and, thereby, brought about the government's declaration of martial law in seven southern Peruvian provinces in December 1982 (Barton 1983). These events were called to the attention of North Americans by the publication, in English, of an account of the Uchuraccay tragedy in *The New York Times Magazine* by the internationally acclaimed Peruvian novelist, Mario Vargas Llosa (1983:20), who commented on the impact of the Huaychao killings on the country: "What a relief! The peasants weren't identifying with the guerrillas, after all—they were fighting them! And that meant that Sendero Luminoso could not last much longer. If only other villages would follow Huaychao's example and kill the dynamiters of power pylons and the executioners of mayors." The murdered journalists, however, had refused to believe that peasants were responsible but, instead, blamed the police and paramilitary forces; they were en route to

Huaychao to seek the truth. This was the assessment of the Peruvian left, in general, and should be understood in the context of the slogan urging an alliance of the proletariat and the peasantry, which represents not only a key element of proletarian revolutionary doctrine and program but is a strategy of class struggle which, necessarily, must be pursued in societies where peasant masses represent a numerically important sector of the population. Nevertheless, it is also possible to question the possibility of such an alliance, with a vision conditioned by a different ideology,[1] as is evident in the suggestion by the Peruvian jurist, De Trazegnies Granda (1983:139), that the slaughtered journalists' belief was "due to an ideological vision of reality," i.e., a proletarian revolutionary one, which could not "admit that peasants would place themselves aggressively against those they should see as social liberators."

This contradiction will be examined in this essay, but it must be considered in the larger context of Peruvian popular movements in which rural populations have been major components, that is, rural movements with non-rural components and urban ones which have attempted to forge alliances between urban classes or sectors and rural masses which, before the middle of this century, made up four-fifths of the country's inhabitants. In any complex society which is largely rural, an urban sector that wishes to assert its rule, and its right to rule, must enlist allies from the rural part. The rural and urban parts of such a society are mutually interdependent to the extent that no single sector is capable of that assertion by itself. More than that, since these parts are linked by social networks through which they are fastened to each other, interpenetrate each other, and reproduce each other, there really can be no such thing as a social movement involving only one part. Furthermore, since ideology and consciousness are functions of the particular insertions of the varied social sectors of a complex society—that is, their social condition is both a determiner of and determined by their vision of reality—it follows that the same social movement or event will be interpreted in different ways by the different sectors, and the same symbols will have different meanings. Upon examination, these differences appear as ideological oppositions and clashing forms of consciousness, obstacles to the achievement of the goals of social movement.

Long before the articulation of proletarian revolutionary doctrine, different sectors of complex societies were aware of needs for social alliances in movements directed toward such varied goals as revindications of property rights, relief from oppression, assertions of self-determination, demands for social justice and claims to the legitimate rule of states. Marx and Engels, advocates of the proletarian cause, and writing in 1850 on France and Germany of the time, developed ideas which were to take on a deeper significance, and to be applied to a wider range of rural situations, with time and the development of this trend of thought. Marx (MECW 10:71, 134) concluded that the French peasantry, whose attachment to the land amounted to "property fanaticism," was "absolutely incapable of any revolutionary initiative." Engels (MECW 10:21–22) is to be credited with first proposing an "alliance of the working men in the towns and the peasantry of the country," because "no government, except on acting in the interest of the working men of the towns will free [the peasants] from the misery and starvation into which . . . they are falling deeper and deeper every day." In an assessment of sixteenth century revolutionary action by the German peasantry, Engels (ibid.:432) acknowledged that the "tenacity and stamina with which the peasants . . . surmounted all the obstacles arising from their scattered way of life . . . and with which they renewed their conspiracies over and over after countless dispersions, defeats, and executions of their leaders . . . is truly admirable." Nevertheless, he (ibid.:481) added, "local and provincial disunity . . . ruined the whole movement." He (ibid.:410) stated that these peasants "were unable to make revolution on their own. . . . Their only chance of winning lay in an alliance with other estates."

The view of the peasantry as a nugatory revolutionary force in itself was further developed by Marx (MECW 11:187), in a famous passage on the French peasant masses of the nineteenth century in *The Eighteenth Brumaire of Louis Bonaparte*, written in 1852, which compared these small holders with "a sack of potatoes." They lived "in similar conditions but without entering into manifold relations with one another." They were isolated by their mode of production which separated "their mode of life, their interests and their culture from those of other classes, and put them in hostile opposition to the latter." Yet, because there was "merely a local interconnection" among them, "and the identity of their interests" formed "no community, no national bond and no political organization," they were not a class and they could not assert their class interests: "They cannot represent themselves, they must be represented." The Mexican political economist, Bartra (1978:51–

53, 75–76), comments on Marx's statement: because peasants consist of "a multitude of private interests . . . without their own political superstructure," their mode of production must always have "a secondary and subordinate character"; a peasantry lacks a class system because "in its interior there arises no dominant class which can subdue the whole society."

Because peasants—rural small producers who, in Wolf's (1966:10) words, are integrated into larger societies through "an asymmetrical structural relationship between producers of surplus and controllers"—are not able to make revolution on their own does not mean that they are "unrevolutionary" in any abstract sense. Peasant populations tend to be well aware of the oppressive "asymmetries" which keep them poor and dependent, and actively seek allies from non-peasant sectors of their societies; similarly, non-peasants (i.e., various urban classes) are aware of the utility, for their purposes, of alliances with peasants. What is to be noted in this essay is that all these different social sectors bring different ideologies and different forms of consciousness into such alliances, that not all participants in resulting movements are aware of the different meanings that are attached to the same symbols, that shared symbols can be manipulated by those sectors which are more aware of these differences, and, finally, that these differences affect the outcome of social movements when participants oppose each other's goals. On the basis of these conceptions, four Peruvian social movements have been selected for discussion: the Túpac Amaru Rebellion of 1780–81, the Atusparia Uprising of 1885, the Andahuaylas land invasions of 1974, and the current Sendero Luminoso popular war.

For these purposes a difficult historiographic problem must be faced and understood: the fact that the history of social movements with large rural components is written by urban people. Deustua (1983:224) notes, with regard to the history of a nineteenth century movement in southern Peru, that the logic of the events is obscure because "reconstruction of what happened can only be achieved from the perspective of the dominant social groups (landlords, political authorities, local bosses and so on), because they were the only ones who had access to the means of communication, information and writing. The reconstruction of peasant movements, from the point of view of the peasants themselves, is a much more complex task which requires access to oral tradition." We need, thus, to go behind history's back. Deustua (ibid.:225) adds, moreover, that we are also obliged to connect the history of peasant movements with "rural history, the history of Peruvian agrarian structure, the existence of internal regional markets which make up national space, and the evolution of more general economic cycles and fluctuations," as well as "other phenomena which occur totally on the margin of the rural world, but whose repercussions may be felt in it."

Because of Peru's large rural population, its rural history is a subject of great national interest—although this has not always been the case.[2] It is written and debated by urban people who represent many different ideological trends, and so it is not surprising that the peasantry's significance in national life is a matter of divergent opinion. The debate is intense among proletarian revolutionaries who understand that neither they nor peasants can hope to secure relief from oppression and exploitation alone, but that both sectors must struggle together, led by proletarians who can place class interests over individual interests. The question of the exact nature of articulation in the worker-peasant alliance is a strategic ideological element open to a variety of interpretations. In a recent discussion by several Peruvians, representing different trends of proletarian revolutionary thought, a representative of the Peruvian Communist Party, Gustavo Espinoza (in Lauer 1977:88–89) deplores the contemporary movement which "renounces the old and classic conception of the working-class as the most revolutionary and sees . . . the most revolutionary force in the peasantry," concluding that "all that is needed to make revolution is to form a group of insurgents," send it to the hinterland, "and begin to shoot"; this trend really operates marginally in relation to the masses, "replacing the working-class," and engaging in "interminable polemics about the nature of the society." In contrast, Ricardo Letts (in Lauer 1977:120), representing the Revolutionary vanguard, a Maoist party, maintains that "the peasantry is a force of the greatest importance for the revolutionary transformation of the country, the principal democratic force" in terms of "the nature of its location within the society, its contradictions with the dominant class, and by its specific character which comes from its numbers as the national majority."

García Sayán (1982:212), a Peruvian social scientist who has examined the details of several modern rural movements and compared them with revolutionary movements in other countries, questions any characterization of the peasantry "as an autonomous transforming force." Modern experience shows that "for peasant rebellions to change into successful revolutions it is necessary for peasants to have leaders from other classes." Where "peasants have been an important force," they have not brought their actions to a successful conclusion "in an isolated way" but with non-peasant allies in political and military organizations. Where they have been "restricted to rebellions without getting away from their own banners and leaders, they have achieved modification of the countryside, or some parts of it, but they have not taken control of the State, the cities or strategic non-agricultural resources."

Rural history is filled with the tragic record of aborted movement, failed revolt, blunted purpose and social disintegration, not to overlook harsh judgment, punitive retaliation, and suppression and distortion of rural visions of such events by non-peasant social sectors, even including former allies. This can lead to the dismal view of the peasantry as simply an inadequate social sector, symbolized by the use of the word "peasant!" as an epithet—in Peru, the words "*indio*" ("Indian") and "*indiada*" ("Indian crowd") mean approximately the same.[3] Is there something "wrong" with peasants? Is it their attachment to the land, their material or spiritual poverty, their primitive world view, or their inability to transcend local interests that prevents their assertion of human dignity? Bak and Benecke (1984:10) raise a corollary question in emphasizing peasant religiosity: the image of "the often so called reactionary, counter-revolutionary or restorative character of rural revolts in general, and of movements informed by religious ideologies in particular." The problematic lies in explaining "the alliance of poor peasants, rural laborers and even miners with religion and with clergy, without being, therefore, forced to label men and women fighting against oppression and unfreedom as reactionaries."

We are well advised to avoid blaming the victims of oppression for that oppression. In the case of Peru, Spalding (1984:278–279) critiques conventional explanations for the failure of rural revolts: the "isolation of the peasantry from the wider society, the lack of a tradition of coordination and organization among isolated household farmers, [and] the mutual suspicion of neighbors born of the isolation and competition that is an omnipresent part of existence for the peasant farmer." She notes, in opposition to this view, that Andean communities have not been based upon isolated household units, nor have they been "isolated and cut off from the [metropoli] that [have] dominated [them] and absorbed [their] production."[4] Rural defeats, rather, are to be explained in terms of the historical experiences which "distorted traditional social groups and gave them new orientations," and which, while giving "all of the members of native Andean society an enemy and a focus for their frustration and their anger," also "introduced division and suspicions that, in the end, could not be overcome." Such a social context is fertile ground for the development of networks based on clientelism with local power derived from the asymmetrical reciprocities of town patrons and their rural followers, in which the "brokerage"[5] services of local hereditary rulers (called *kurakas* in the Central Andes), under the colonial system of indirect rule, have been replaced by those of the *gamonal* (the local or regional boss), in modern times. Such a society is also receptive to the ideology of resignation preached by representatives of a Church enlisted in the political pursuits of the ruling sectors of both colonial and republican states. Conveniently for a servile social order, as Spalding (ibid.:251) observes, "the usual position taken by official religion in fulfilling its role of enlisting the exploited as active participants in their own exploitation"—although it may be pointed out that religious ideology can and has been utilized in support of liberation, as, for example, in Klaiber's (1982) documentation of Túpac Amaru II's use of Old Testament images in defense of his movement. It may also be noted that in the Andes, specifically, where conquerors and conquered came historically from physically different populations, the ideology of the value of European connection, a racist doctrine, found a compatible target in the *mestizos*,[6] persons with real or alleged genetic heritage from both European and native Peruvian sources, who endeavor, Spalding (1984:254) says, "to be more European than those [with] the easy security of lineage and established ancestry" in the ruling sector, and where "in any crisis those people who identified themselves as members of European society stood together against the 'other,' whatever or whomever that might be."

Popular revolts in Peru have not succeeded in bringing about social change; indeed, more change in the country can be explained in terms of the influence of socio-economic events in the world surrounding it. Nevertheless, Peruvian history is the chronicle of an unceasing rural (and urban) struggle against the oppression that has characterized Peruvian history from 1532, the year that Peruvians were first subjected to foreign invasion and domination. The number of rural protests, uprisings, strikes, and other assertions of human rights in the face of what amounts to nothing less than piracy, illegal expropriation, genocide, ethnocide and other terrible abuses carried on by the invaders and succeeding generations of the elite sectors of the society, is uncountable and will probably never be known in full. A recent, admittedly non-representative and non-random, sample by Guzmán and Vargas (1981), drawn from newspapers published during the period between 1956 and 1964 only, presents a listing of 837 large and small movements. Although there is no evidence of uniformity of social unrest for every decade of every century—for example, Lazo García and Tord M. (1978:115) record that 27% of all social conflicts they were able to record for the period between 1713 and 1807 were uprisings, the rate of occurrence of which tended constantly to increase during the century, intensifying and concentrating in the second half—there can be no doubt that Peruvians have been anything but passive victims. The selection of the four movements to be presented here is a function of historians' interest in specific events, available documentation, and my reading and research.

I: The Túpac Amaru Rebellion, 1780–81

Espinoza Soriano (1981:169) says that 1780 was "a typical year of the Andean eighteenth century, . . . a period of social and political convulsions generated as a response to the increase in fiscal charges, tributes, and the generalized exploitation to the detriment of Indians and other *estaments,* including injury to mestizos and creoles." O'Phelan (1977a:113, 1979:91) views Túpac Amaru's movement as one which was "inserted into a complex of minor revolts [as] a culmination of them"; it "materialized the insistent protests which had been taking place since the beginning of the 1770's." Túpac Amaru was a *kuraka,* that is, a member of the regional elite which traced its descent to the prehispanic nobility. It was a privileged sector whose function was to keep order and collect taxes. He was born José Gabriel Condorcanqui, in 1738 in a town in the Cuzco region, but later took the surname of Túpac Amaru from his ancestor Felipe Túpac Amaru, the last Inca ruler who was executed in Cuzco by Viceroy Toledo in 1572. Túpac Amaru II began the revolt on November 4, 1780, when after lunching with the regional *corregidor*—a tax farmer appointed by the Spanish Crown—he took the latter prisoner, placed him on trial for fiscal abuses, and hanged him on November 10. An army of thousands was formed and large parts of southern Peru were liberated from the Spanish colonial system for several months. Eventually, colonial authorities sent reinforcements to the region, while Túpac Amaru had difficulties which included excommunication by the Bishop of Cuzco, failure to take the city of Cuzco, active opposition by a number of other kurakas with their own peasant followings, and dissention among his own forces. He was captured on April 6, 1781, tortured to extract a confession, subjected to a month-long trial, and executed (along with his wife, sons, other relatives and other leaders of the revolt), on May 18 of that year (Valcárcel 1947, Lewin 1957, Fisher 1966, Flores Galindo 1976a, Sivirichi Tapia 1979, Golte 1980, Szemiński 1983).

O'Phelan (1976:192) makes the useful distinction between revolts "which break out of productive activity itself" and "those which originate in the circulation of production," that is, struggles over productive resources as opposed to struggles over the distribution of what has been produced—although, as she (O'Phelan 1983:82) has more recently noted, the compartmentalization is by no means complete since, in the eighteenth century (and, one might add, in the two succeeding centuries) peasants have taken advantage of rebellions and other forms of social unrest to assert their claims to lands usurped by others. Thus, while Túpac Amaru's movement is known by historians as an "anti-fiscal revolt," it was actually more complex than that. It began with a challenge to the colonial system of *repartimiento,* the forced sale of commodities by *corregidores* in their rural domains, designed, according to Golte (1980:14–15), to break "the self-subsistence of peasant producers who had to accept the goods distributed and were necessarily obliged to sell their produce or their labor power in order to pay for the 'commodities' which had been distributed to them." The "*repartos*" contained some goods, such as cloth or mules—provided recipients were fortunate enough to be given healthy ones—which were useful; however, they also contained useless items, such as books in foreign languages, out-of-fashion apparel, overstocks for which there was no demand, and other assorted commodified garbage, sold to rural people at prices significantly above their rates in the market. Golte (ibid.:108, 118) points out that the system was not a simple abuse of power by *corregidores* but, rather, "it was an economic mechanism, in the functioning of which a large number of the dominant groups of colonial society were involved"; increases in the "*repartos*" can be related to "the growing accumulation of capital on the part of the merchants and commercial houses of Lima." Thus, as Flores Galindo (1981:261) observes, "some medium and small provincial merchants," who were also *kurakas,* "were disputing the reduced regional market with the big Lima merchants"; this illustrates how "a mercantile dispute could rapidly turn into an anti-colonial conflict and become, given the alliance between merchants and bureaucrats, a class struggle." Túpac Amaru was one of those provincial merchants with whom the *repartimiento,* in O'Phelan's (1976:130) words, "was competing," and whom "it was displacing."

Flores Galindo (1976b:272) points out that Túpac Amaru "was neither poor nor Indian in a strict sense." He owned coca fields, mines and 350 mules which made him a relatively large trader and transporter. His early education was in the hands of priests; he attended a Jesuit secondary school in Cuzco; and he read Latin easily, spoke correct Spanish, and was fluent in Quechua (Lewin 1957:386, Flores Galindo 1976b:272). According to Lewin (1957:387–390), it was likely that he, like other educated provincial people of the eighteenth century, had read Garcilaso de la Vega's *Los Comentarios Reales de los Incas* ("Royal Commentaries of the Incas"), a chronicle of prehispanic times written by a member of the first generation of *mestizos,* and was conscious of his own descent from the Inca rulers of ancient Peru. Túpac Amaru was in no way a peasant; the term "regional gentry" would be quite appropriate to describe his social background. Stern (1982:167) describes this "growing sector of *ladino* Indians" of colonial times as wealthy people who "bought and used the accouterments of cultured Spanish folk. They wore fine clothes (made in Europe), travelled on horse and saddle, bought furniture, jewelry and trinkets for their homes, enjoyed wine with meals, and owned Spanish firearms and swords. The successful (or pretentious) appropriated the Spanish titulature of Don or Doña, and acquired urban predilections." Stern (ibid.:169) also notes "a striking enthusiasm on the part of wealthy Indians" for Christianity. In contrast with peasants who "submitted to a thin overlay of Christian ritual," the gentry "developed close bonds with Christian gods and their representatives on earth." While, for some, this was a practical matter of social and economic betterment, for others it was "far more than a superficial overlay" and "Christian religion expressed relationships and aspirations which deeply touched their lives."

We are touching here on a basic ideological cleavage between the towns and the countryside, that is, between urban and rural religion. Castelli (1978:202) points out that in prehispanic times the deities for agrarian peoples of the Andes were essentially regulators of nature. In the syncretistic religion of post-conquest times, continuities appear to be linked to the continuation of agrarian existence. Urbano (1982:66–67), speaking of contemporary peasants, says "Andean mythical discourse . . . is not foreign to Christian traditions implanted by Spanish Catholicism of past centuries." A culture hero may "act and speak with actions and words which, at times, are reminiscent of Judeo-Christian actions." But there are also "other Andean oral traditions or mythical cycles in which the heros are mountains, forests, rivers, lakes, ponds and other Andean spaces. In reality, the live space of the Andes is as important, or more so, for mythical cycles than heros or personages described as persons. In this connection, mythical cycles related to the origins of Andean communities or settlements are particularly important. . . . [M]any of those cycles, constructed with materials of diverse origin, both Christian and Andean, constitute an excellent example of the logical capacity to organize the world and things as a function of Andean characteristics and the 'rationality' that governs daily life." Marzal (1971:367–368) observes that in the Andes "religion is one of the principal foundations of peasant society," but notes that the Christianization of this peasantry was one "not so much of individuals but above all of native society." In a more concrete study of one peasant community, Marzal (1977:232–233) finds that for rural people religious ritual has quite practical application: peasants "give more importance to the celebration of the rite than to personal religious faith, and so they take on the obligation of 'passing the *fiesta*' or they take part in rituals . . . without understanding their real significance. They also give more emphasis to the utilitarian character than to the celebration of rituals and so most of their religious rituals are 'to obtain something' from God. Moreover, when they resort to the priest they carry on a relationship with him that seems more like one of 'client-religious services professional' than of one belonging to a community of believers, and therefore each person wants his 'own ritual' . . . more than a communitarian celebration. Finally, it appears that . . . religion is more useful in order to resolve material problems of life than to assure ethical behavior or to question personal conduct." Custred (1973:79–80) characterizes Andean ritual as "an analogue of the things peasants must do to survive," that is, to engage in the production of subsistence and in social life. Peasants do not require an understanding of the meaning of a rite, in order to make it work, "any more than it is necessary for the operator of a machine to understand the working of the machinery he deals with." The "really effective rationale for the ritual efficiency" depends upon "the associative value of the symbolism with basic peasant experience."

Túpac Amaru's forces were made up of both peasants and non-peasants; people from different worlds with different visions of reality. There is no reason to challenge Flores Galindo's (1981:255) application of the term "popular revolution" to the movement, for there was massive participation by peasants and urban artisans who formed the bulk of an army of five thousand men. However, the movement was not directed by these but by *mestizos* and *creoles* whose numbers, according to O'Phelan (1979:99–100), were "numerically less significant," but whose participation was "more determinative," despite such ambiguities as "*mestizos*" who fought with slings, i.e., peasant weapons, and needed interpreters to testify during the official investigation of the movement after it had been defeated. Indeed, in her work on several popular movements of the eighteenth century in northern Peru, O'Phelan (1976:186) questions the notion of the possibility of a "purely" peasant revolt. The peasantry, as Choy (1976:264) says, was "the most powerful force . . . but not the most revolutionary one, because it was not the directing class which would give direction to changes."

O'Phelan (1979:106–107) speaks of the "favorable conditions for an alliance" created by increased fiscal pressures on the peasantry, the threat of the extension of tribute to *mestizos* and Black *estaments,* and the possibility, even, of including *creoles* in the "*repartos.*" However, while town and country were linked in the revolt, Kapsoli (1983:13) suggests that a real class alliance did not exist, because "when the peasant population passed beyond Túpac Amaru's control and acted violently against *creole* and *mestizo* interests" the latter ceased to give their support. Golte (1980:18) notes that the leaders of the movement were from the *mestizo petite bourgeoisie* and the *kurakas,* so that when the peasants, unaware of the nature of the alliance, extended the struggle beyond the *corregidores* and their retainers they were struggling against the very social groups from which their leaders came. Szemiński (1976:218–221) observes that the different sectors had different goals, according to their insertion in the social formation: the peasantry was interested in having the several forms of taxation to which they were subjected reduced; the *kurakas* wanted their sphere of influence in the countryside increased, and the peninsular (i.e., population originating in Spain) administrative apparatus abolished; other *estaments,* such as the artisans and small merchants, hoped to have the fiscal system modified to favor their peasant clients; and the *creole* landlords wished to displace peninsular people in both administration and commerce. Valcércel (1947:118) proposes, in addition, that the masses were moved not only by their wish to shake off oppression but also by the desire for vengeance and loot. With such a heterogeneous aggregation of self-serving and mutually conflicting interests, it is little wonder that the alliances fell apart. Cornblitt (1976:178) points out that most of the native Andean aristocracy refused to recognize Túpac Amaru's royal descent and fought against the rebellion; however, Hünefeldt (1980:361–362) notes, the seventeen *kurakas* of Cuzco, who remained faithful to the Crown, and who provisioned the city while Túpac Amaru had it under siege, had business interests there which transcended any other form of solidarity they might have felt. The elite sector of Cuzco, which Túpac Amaru hoped to attract to his cause, feared the possibility of social revolution more than it did Spanish domination; this explains both his alleged "vacillation" in laying siege to the city as well as the city's failure to aid the rebellion (Cornblitt 1976:176–177, Choy 1976:263, Szemiński 1976:247, Golte 1980:190).

Flores Galindo (1976b:278–283) states that just as there were two languages used in the revolt, Spanish and Quechua, there were two ideologies as well: one was the "program that everybody knows, the abolition of forced labor and forced sales, cancellation of duties and fees, the creation of the Cuzco court, and so forth" which was "directed at the *creoles, mestizos, kurakas,* and Indian nobles" who "could read Túpac Amaru's proclamations and letters"; and the other was the program directed at the masses, "using a language with messianic roots . . . manifested in the use of traditional musical instruments, the use of flags with 'the arms of the Inca Kings,' and especially in the use of the name Inca." This is why the diverse, even contradictory, characterizations of the revolt *appear* confused though they really were a reflection of the diverse social conditions of the participants: the movement *was* anti-fiscal, socially integrative, messianic, anti-colonial, *and* it contained the "germ of social revolution." The historiographic problem is that surviving documents present well the *creole-mestizo* ideological images of the movement but do not record the ideology which Túpac Amaru and other leaders used in their messages directed at the peasantry. Millones (1979:73–74) says that such messages, obviously, "were in Quechua and most of them had to allude to themes which could stir their audience, with a strong messianic accent, in which social transformations were dramatic, that is, with contours antithetic to discourses and proclamations prepared for *creoles* and *mestizos,* in which the ideological definition of the revolutionary act fluctuated between the well known limits of separatism and reform of the Spanish administration." When Túpac Amaru appeared before the masses, with his rainbow banners as the "Inca King of Peru," it was nothing new, but it was polysemous: in the elite context it fitted into an ideologized view of history; among the masses it "could have had the effect of maintaining the visual and remembered image of the Incas, although there existed no historical memory of them in the western sense of the word." This was a new version of *Tahuantinsuyo,* the Incas' name for their state, in which a different order would exist, "where injustices would be abolished," and which had nothing to do with the "debate over its reformism or separatism."

Rowe (1976:32–34) notes that the moderate nationalists among the elite wanted "a reform of the Viceroyalty which would do away with the abuses of the existing system without destroying it," while the more radical nationalists, influenced by Garcilaso de la Vega's idealized image of the Incas, wanted an "independent Inca state," not, however, "a simple reconstruction" of the ancient one but "a monarchy on the model of the Spanish government . . . with native heads." As fervent Catholics, they also "did not desire to destroy the Church" but, rather, wanted "a Catholic Inca Church" in which members of the native elite would be appointed priests and bishops. The nationalists did not wish, either, "to reject everything they had learned from the Spanish" and "they proposed, at no time, a complete return to the cultural situation of 1532, which was impossible."

The "oral utopia" of the peasant masses had to be quite different from the "written utopia" of the elites (Burga and Flores Galindo 1982:92–93), based as it was on peasant vision. Peasant myths, which are to be found in the Central Andean region from Ecuador to Bolivia, present a cyclic image of succeeding world orders initiated by cataclysms. Silverblatt (1982:38–39) observes that the contrast between order and disorder (or "non-order," "anti-order") is perhaps of equal or greater salience than that between good and evil in Andean cosmology: where the invading Spanish "found the Devil behind every rock," the native people did not conceive of "Evil" incarnated "in a satanic being"; to the contrary, in their vision of the universe, "forces of opposition were conceived which were reciprocal and complementary, both necessary for the reproduction of society." Hocquenghem (1984:157) calls attention to the Andean struggle to recreate order over the past four and a half centuries: "In reality, the order that Indians wanted to reestablish several times was that which allowed the reproduction of their agrarian society. It was based on the respect of an absolute authority, inspired by an authoritarian thought from an inexorable dialectical logic, applied to regulate everything, protect everything, preserve everything, guarantee everything and reproduce everything. In this terribly conservative framework, each person's thought tends to crystalize, freeze and be crushed. Andean order, currently and from the outside, presents itself as repressive; it does away with the individual and denies reality." This is a key, perhaps, to the understanding of otherwise obscure aspects of Andean social movements.

Pease (1973:18) says that in pre-hispanic times the alternating millenia, or world orders, consisted of the conception of four ages separated by periods of chaos in which the world was turned, successively, into stone, water and fire, different forms of destruction brought about by divinities. This seems to have been transformed after the conquest into the more contemporary images of the Ages of God-the-Father, God-the-Son and God-the-Holy-Spirit. According to Urbano (1981:87), the last one, the Age of God-the-Holy-Spirit, is in the future and "coincides with the arrival of paradisiacal times" in which people "will no longer suffer, the high altitudes will produce sub-tropical fruits, valleys will feed flocks from the heights, and all people will live in peace and harmony. All people will have wings." Interestingly, Ossio (1978:244) traces Andean millenarianism to roots in both the Incaic decimal system and Judeo-Christian tradition.

A frequent element of this cyclic image is the Andean culture hero, or messiah (or redeemer), *Inkarrí,* King Inca, who has been beheaded but is growing a new head, and who, when he is complete, will reestablish order in a new world. The figure of Inkarrí may be interpreted as an image of Atahualpa or Túpac Amaru I, the last Inca rulers, although it should be noted that only Túpac

Amaru I was beheaded; Atahualpa was garrotted (González Carré and Rivera Pineda 1983:57–58). Pease (1973:70–71) traces the transformation of the solar hero who founded the city of Cuzco into a messianic, subterranean divinity. Inkarrí, Pease (ibid.:74) notes, is not the sun, but the son of the sun. Urbano (1981:82) adds to this conception the notation that Inkarrí's return is problematic because, being the work of the Christian God, it depends on God's will.[7]

Klaiber (1982:175–176) observes, nevertheless, on the basis of an examination of documentary evidence which, as has been noted, focuses on elite presentations of the movement, that although it is reported that peasants "hailed Túpac Amaru as their 'King and Redeemer,' or even 'Inca Redeemer,' " it is difficult "to establish if [his] movement was 'messianic' or not." Klaiber (ibid.:173–174, 176–178) points out that, as might be expected from a *mestizo* with Túpac Amaru's background, Túpac Amaru "explicitly legitimated his cause with references to the Bible and his Christian faith." Despite his excommunication he never "condemned or repudiated the Church." He did not refer to himself as "Redeemer" but more simply as "Inca King" and a "son of the Church." Moreover, "no direct relation has been established between" the Inkarrí myth and "the figure of Túpac Amaru." Rather, he presented himself as a liberator who relied on the favor of the Christian God." In view of the absence of evidence to the contrary, it is well to keep these considerations in mind. However, even if Túpac Amaru and other leaders did not deliberately manipulate the masses by the use of popular images, it is possible that the masses made their own interpretations of events and of the symbols their leaders presented in messages to the crowds.

II: The Atusparia Uprising, 1885[8]

Despite the century of social change which separates the 1780s from the 1880s—independence from Spanish domination, the guano boom, penetration by foreign capital and the beginning of capitalist development, and the disastrous defeat by Chile in the War of the Pacific, 1879–1883—there are certain resemblances in the social movements of both periods: alliances between urban and rural sectors, the contradictory collaboration of exploiters and those they exploit, and mutually incompatible motives among the different social sectors composing insurrectionary forces, all of which lead to historians' disagreements on whether or not to call a movement anti-fiscal, race war, messianic or revolutionary. The Atusparia movement began on March 3, 1885, when masses of peasants from the mountainous slopes on both sides of the valley city of Huaraz descended to overwhelm its garrison and civil authorities. The peasant army soon swept down the valley to take the other cities and towns, and it soon had the entire region under its control. The central government in Lima hesitated for weeks; finally, it sent an expeditionary force of infantry, cavalry and artillery to impose its order. The peasants, armed with slings, clubs, lances and a few shotguns and rifles, were no match for cannister-shot; and on May 3, during one of the year's most important religious festivals, the government troops drove the insurgents out of Huaraz. After this, the forces on the east flank of the valley accepted amnesty while those on the west flank continued the struggle in the form of guerrilla actions which degenerated into social banditry. Finally, the leader of these last insurgent forces, a miner from the heights on the western side of the valley whose name was Pedro Cochachin, was captured and executed in late September. The movement involved the whole population of a large and densely settled Andean basin and its surrounding regions, about 300,000 townspeople and peasants. It failed to spread beyond this region and these people as a popular movement, but it was clearly linked to the civil war which was going on in Peru at that time. This larger struggle for power and spoils in the postwar crisis was a polarization of those forces and interests which, in order to promote economic recovery, had sought peace with the Chileans, led by the incumbent president, General Miguel Iglesias, and those which wished to continue the fight against the foreign occupation forces, led by the war hero, General Andrés A. Cáceres.[9]

Ideologically, for those Peruvians who were more aware of national interests and aspirations, the Cáceres side represented more than a simple wish to avoid concessions to the Chileans and, if possible, to expel them from the country; it was a populist enlistment of different socio-economic strata with urban and rural bases against land monopoly and domination by the rapidly developing commercial sector of foreign exports. The movement in Ancash, the political subdivision of which Huaraz is the capital, parallels the series of movements in southern Peru, recorded by Spalding (1980:95–96), in which anti-fiscal response on the part of peasants merged with resistance to status loss on the part of smaller landholders and local merchants, and where *both* urban and rural sectors were affected by the decline in local commerce.

The Atusparia movement's name comes from its leader, Pedro Pablo Atusparia, peasant and artisan from a small community near Huaraz, who in 1885 held the leading office in the *varáyoq* organization, a group of around forty peasant officials from several different communities in the political and parochial division of La Restauración, one of the two such fiscal-ritual sections which make up Huaraz district and parish. The *varáyoq* system established by Viceroy Toledo in the sixteenth century was all the local administration that was left to the Peruvian peasantry in the aftermath of Túpac Amaru's revolt when the native Andean elite, already creolized, was forced to merge into the *mestizo-creole* Andean population. *Varáyoq* are appointed annually and are charged with the supervision of communal public works in their respective divisions: the construction and maintenance of roads, bridges, public buildings, churches, shrines and crosses. Until the decay of local power structures, after the middle of the present century, they supervised *corvée* labor performed for the benefit of the urban gentry; and before peasant poll taxes were abolished at the end of the last century they collected these, which were divided between the local administration and the central government. The authority of the *varáyoq* is largely validated in their strategic function in directing hydraulic projects for the irrigation of fields and meadows and, it being literally impossible to separate Andean peasant farming and religion, in their responsibilities for conducting the yearly round of festivals and other rituals.

As an anti-fiscal revolt, the Atusparia uprising is connected to the fiscal crisis Peru was experiencing at the time. President Iglesias, several months earlier, had appointed a new Prefect who arrived in Huaraz and began to devise new methods for increasing revenue. Among these measures were increases in *corvée* service and in poll taxes in the rural sector, as well as licensing fees, occupational certificates and house renumbering charges in the urban sector. He also set about the task of recovering several pieces of state property which had been encroached on by local persons during the wartime confusion. It should be emphasized, here too, that *both* sectors were affected, even if in different ways, and that General Iglesias was an unpopular figure for having led the peace party and having signed the peace treaty with Chile which gave up territory and revenue, in contrast with General Cáceres who had led resistance armies in the hinterland and maintained a populist image among urban people. Among peasants, at least in the Mantaro region, south of Ancash, Cáceres, as recorded in the memoirs of his wife, Antonia Moreno de Cáceres (cited in Kapsoli 1983:163–164), was greeted with dancing and singing, music and showers of flower petals as "the reincarnation of the Inca . . . charged with protecting them from the whites." Could this image of Cáceres have existed for Atusparia and his people? No documentation exists, but it is quite possible.

At some time during the weeks before the revolt in Huaraz broke out, a petition signed by Atusparia and other *varáyoq* with "X's"—they were illiterate peasants—reached the Prefect. It was a politely worded request for reductions in the poll tax and corvée labor so that rural people might attend to their crops; it had to have been prepared by a *mestizo* resident (or residents), of Huaraz. The Prefect, suspecting an alliance of subversive supporters of Cáceres in town with rural people (indeed, instigators of rural unrest, which, actually, is a good hypothesis in the absence of clear documentary evidence), ordered Atusparia's arrest, put him in jail, had him whipped, and had his braids cut off, to make him reveal the names of those who wrote the petition. When the other *varáyoq* appeared to protest this treatment of their leader, they were subjected to it too. Larger numbers of peasants joined a larger protest and, eventually, formed a mass of thousands. After they were fired upon by nervous troops of the Huaraz garrison, they took the city. It is likely that this eventuality was forseen, perhaps even prepared for well in advance, and that both the Prefect and the peasants were maneuvered into the confrontation by the Cáceres party which was numerous in Huaraz.

Klaiber (1977b:94) observes that it "is difficult to understand the native point of view in the republican epoch, principally because their illiterate condition did not allow them to write their own history." We are left with a history of the Atusparia uprising written *by mestizos* and *creoles for mestizos* and *creoles,* in which peasant visions, ideology, and consciousness have been repressed and suppressed. According to a few brief reports in the Lima newspapers of 1885, Atusparia was called "Rey Inca" by his peasant followers. That he is also referred to by those journalists as "a restorer of the ancient empire" is more likely an intrusion of creole ideology. Kapsoli (1984:29–30) records two conceptions, or readings, of the restoration of *Tahuantinsuyo,* the "Inca Empire," in his analysis of materials relating to uprisings in the Puno region in the early 1920s: an official investigating commission was reported in a Puno newspaper as stating that the "thousands of insurgent Indians had . . . the fatal and absurd pretention of wishing to restore the conditions and customs of Tahuantinsuyo." This clearly represents the *mestizo* point of view, which contrasts, and impressively so, with the peasants' point of view, as represented in an Indianist work by Erasmo Roca, also cited by Kapsoli (ibid.): "The Indians have been led to believe that they are going to recover all the lands that belonged to their ancestors and that they are the only ones who have rights over these lands, being descended from the Incas."

The theme of the reestablishment of the Incaic world is also present in Reyna's (1932) book on the Atusparia uprising, an enthusiastic Indianist work based on oral history in Huaraz, but this account goes too far in putting ideas into peasant heads which simply could not have existed there. It is possible that those *mestizos* whose names appear in the historical record, for example, the journalist Luis Felipe Montestruque who functioned as Atusparia's scribe and is alleged to have published a newspaper supporting the movement, and the lawyer Manuel Mosquera who was appointed revolutionary Prefect, disseminated such ideas for elite consumption; however, their messages to the peasantry, to be meaningfully received, would have had to feed into peasant myth. Such people, including other Huaraz residents whose identities are unknown, were agents of Cáceres, and, like Cáceres himself, were *mestizos* who could function in two worlds, the urban *creole-mestizo* one and the rural peasant one; they could also deal with two utopian visions, the urban political reformation under a national hero and the rural millenarian re-creation under a mythical hero.

Klaiber (1977a:68) is impressed by "the allegiance of the [peasants] to traditional Catholicism during periods of revolutionary stress," and notes that in Huaraz "religious fervor even seemed to increase in the midst of rebellion." Atusparia, together with the *mestizo* priest Fidel Olivas Escudero, intervened several times to calm excited crowds bent on destruction, to the extent that ritual observance seemed at times to interfere with the pursuit of the movement's revindicatory objectives. At the end of the first week of the uprising, on Sunday, March 8, Atusparia and another parish priest, Pedro García Villón who is identified by Manuel Reina Loli (personal communication, December 29, 1984) as a Cáceres supporter, organized a thanksgiving mass, conducted with great pomp, with Atusparia seated in the place of honor. Ponte González (1945:95–96) describes Holy Week in Huaraz, under insurgent occupation, as "invested with particular solemnity." He adds: "The processions were rivers of human masses. Never had Huaraz felt such religiosity." Klaiber (1977a:66) views it as "fateful irony that . . . the bloody denouement of the drama was acted out on the other great religious feast day," that of the Lord of Solitude, when "news of the advance of Colonel Callirgos," at the head of the government forces, caused panic. According to a personal communication from Manuel Reina Loli (as noted in Klaiber 1977b:106–107), Atusparia went ahead with the celebration and the annual procession because "he wanted people to have [it] necessarily to calm them as a measure of preparation for the coming battle" and "as a resort to hold back a new sacking of the city." The latter did not occurr; nor did the insurgents put up massive resistance to the entry of the government troops.

Marzal (1983:75) identifies the festival of the Lord of Solitude in Huaraz as one of several Peruvian "great popular devotions" with an "interethnic character," that is, they bring rural and urban people into religious worship in common. The events of 1885 must be interpreted in a context of understanding the meaning of religious celebration, especially its relation to peasant ecology. Peasant ties to the land are more than sentiment; they relate to peasant identity and existence. When Marzal (ibid.:423) states that "the church together with the fiesta of the patron saint is the clearest symbol of the community itself," he is summarizing the interconnection of worship with soil, weather and crop, of people with nature through ritual performance, and of the celebrants' community's specific being on its lands with its moral right to continue being on those lands. González Carré and Rivera Pineda (1983:60) observe that an Andean festival is an intense renewal of people's reciprocal relations with the community and with relatives through mutual assistance in ritual observance. Custred (1980:197) notes that a "ritual is considered by . . . peasants as playing just as important a role in production activities as the role played by the technologies of agriculture and herding." He (ibid.:201) adds that "sacred ritual . . . plays an important role in establishing and maintaining different kinds of social alliances" of peasants with both other peasants and non-peasants. Finally, he (ibid.:203–204) points out that household claims "on land and water resources" are not only reinforced by "a community name, traditional boundary markers and a community level of organization," but that community festivals "parallel and support in the ritual sphere what community organization does in the social and political realms. . . . By organizing and celebrating the recognized feast of a community saint . . . the community is asserting its identity to all concerned through ritual action, while at the same time supporting its own internal organization and its territorial claims." In 1885, when the force of peasant insurgents was approaching one of the valley towns, the townspeople came out to meet it with a religious procession. The peasants stopped, kneeled and prayed. They were disarmed by their inability to make a revolution without reproducing the conditions of their own existence.

The Atusparia movement met defeat, thus, some time before the government forces entered Huaraz. Moreover, its *mestizo* "allies" had already disappeared when their perception of the threat of social revolution seemed far worse than accommodation to the government of President Iglesias. Atusparia was saved from the firing squad by grateful citizens of Huaraz. His co-leader, Pedro Cochachin, who held a commission from General Cáceres, fought on for a while but was ultimately captured by government forces and executed. The government abolished the poll tax; but when Cáceres finally succeeded in replacing Iglesias as president of the country, he succumbed to fiscal crisis and reimposed it. Atusparia died in 1887 and was given a fine funeral by the city of Huaraz.

III: The Andahuaylas Land Invasions, 1974

Burga and Flores Galindo (1980:87) suggest that members of peasant communities "on wanting to recover the land, want also to recover their history." The recovery of land by invasion or seizure, as Hobsbawm (1974:121–123) points out, may take place because it has been alienated illegally, because it does not belong to anybody, or when it belongs to someone else; but in Peru the typical land occupations of this century, especially the large number which have taken place since the late 1950's, are of the first type and based on old titles, claims or other assertions of "immemorial possession" relating to land which the invaders believe to be their own but which has in the past been usurped by others. In such cases, Hobsbawm (ibid.:150–151) adds, there is little evidence that Peruvian peasants have challenged the traditional institution of landlordism; thus, these invasions can not be interpreted as traditional peasant uprisings but, rather, should be viewed as "spontaneous mass assertion[s] of legal rights, stimulated by, but not apparently—except in a few areas—imbued with a modern, or for that matter an ancient, revolutionary ideology."

There are two contemporary sets of social processes that have conditioned land invasions: one consists of the development of communications, the building of roads, the introduction of transistor radios and the diffusion of education, so that former more isolated parts of the hinterland are brought closer to national social economy and peasants have now become literate in Spanish and aware of their civil rights, aided in many cases by the flood of permanent and temporary migrants who, from their urban bases or as repeasantized but worldly-wise members of rural communities, assist in community revindications; the other set of processes consists of the relative decline of agriculture and stock-breeding as compared with other productive sectors, the stagnation of food production—but not agroindustry—in a context of food price control and the subsidy of food imports, and the consequent inability of the landlord sectors to maintain their influence, leading to a new balance of political forces in the 1960s in which land reform laws could be enacted and decreed. As this situation matured, the increase in land invasions constituted land reform from the bottom. Hobsbawm (ibid.:138) says, "if peasants do not have much concrete knowledge about the wider framework which encloses their little worlds, they are acutely conscious of the changes in that wider framework which appear to affect its indestructibility." In some cases these processes and this consciousness have been helped along by ideas and cadres from proletarian revolutionary political parties.[10]

To the extent that land invasions propose change in power structure by displacing landlords they are political movements, but to the extent that they aim at nothing more than the recovery of land they conform to the pre-political model, defined by Quijano (1979:52–53) as those movements which "do not in a direct way plan modification of the deep power structure of the society in which they participate. . . . Generally, they pursue diffusely discernable aims, or concrete goals linked with the actual situation only in a completely segmentary and tangential manner, or indirectly and by implication. In a few of the most advanced cases, when they pass that level, they come to perceive only very limited aspects of the real problem. . . . In any case, they do not come to perceive the specificity of their social interests and to perceive, except in a distorted way under the best circumstances, their social enemies as a sector of different and opposed social interests." He (ibid.) goes on to define a model of interpretation of social reality or ideology, that accompanies such movements, which he calls the "feudal-religious model," which supposes "modes of taking account of a social reality in terms of the relations between people and the divinity, or between people and a 'natural' order of things which cannot be substantively modified." Quijano's (ibid.:107–108) study reveals that peasants have not been able to rise above the pre-political level, except with urban influence; nevertheless, "urban political agitation by itself cannot take complete account of the real situation and of the tendencies which appear in the peasantry." It may be added that professional revolutionaries, that is, people who devote their lives to the cause of social revolution,[11] need patience and understanding if they are successfully to translate their message for the rural sector. The mechanical, forced and uninformed application of proletarian revolutionary ideology in the countryside can only lead to failure. The uncritical resort to the words of Marx, or Engels, or Lenin, or Mao may lead to the wastage of human lives and material resources.

Lenin, who developed and extended the ideas of Marx and Engels by applying them to the Russian agrarian question and, even more concretely, to the forging of an agrarian program for his party at the turn of the last century in his country, presents clear instructions for Russian proletarian revolutionaries: He (Lenin CW 4:242–250) stated that his party should support the peasantry, "insofar as [it] is capable of a revolutionary struggle." Without doubting the "existence of revolutionary elements among the peasantry," but without exaggerating their strength, he added, "it would be senseless to make the peasantry the vehicle of the revolutionary movement." It would be a mistake for a proletarian party, however, to "overlook the revolutionary elements that exist among the peasantry and not afford those elements support." Such support, he warned, was necessarily conditional "because the proletariat cannot and must not, in general, take upon itself the defense of the interests of a class of small property-holders; it can support it only to the extent to which that class is revolutionary." Yet, Lenin was in no way dogmatic: he pointed out that while the support of small property was a reactionary measure, in a social context where the "remnants of feudal dependence" still existed, the small holding "free of all medieval impediments" was progressive.

Lenin (CW 9:98) observed that the peasantry included large numbers of semi-proletarians as well as *petit bourgeois,* which made it "unstable" and compelled proletarians "to rally in a strictly class party." Still, the peasantry's instability was radically different from the bourgeois form: in that historical period, peasants were not as interested "in the absolute preservation of private property as in the confiscation of the landed estates." Thus the peasantry was capable of being an enthusiastic participant in the democratic revolution, "[w]ithout thereby becoming socialist, or ceasing to be [petit] *bourgeois.*" However, Lenin viewed the peasantry as potentially the antagonist of the proletariat. He (CW 11:203–205) called attention to the rural petty producer's dual nature: "A peasant is endowed both with reason and with prejudice; he possesses the revolutionary qualities of a person who is exploited, and the reactionary aspirations of the small proprietor anxious 'to get, but not to give up.' " Proletarian revolutionaries, therefore, should conclude that "such a class of small proprietors cannot be the vehicle for socialism; that socialists can and must support the small proprietor class in its struggle against the landlords solely because this struggle has a bourgeois-democratic significance and can have bourgeois-democratic results; that it is the duty of a socialist not to obscure but to expose the antagonism of interests between the working masses as a whole and these small proprietors, who want to consolidate their own economic position, and who will be hostile to any idea of 'giving up' the land or anything else to the mass of the propertyless and destitute."

In the case of the 1974 land invasions in Andahuaylas, a province in Apurímac Department in southern Peru, in contrast with the earlier movements discussed here, peasants found themselves allied with professional proletarian revolutionaries, who thought of themselves as a "vanguard," but not with urban elites. These peasant occupations of land were in many respects like those of a decade earlier in central and southern Peru described by Handelman (1975) but they were also different insofar as they were reactions to the radical land reform decree of 1969, promulgated by a dictatorial military government which styled itself as "revolutionary," which created "associative enterprises" (i.e., different forms of cooperatives) in place of the prereform haciendas, a situation which was totally unsatisfactory to most poor peasants. The invasions reclaimed the land from the bureaucrats and technocrats who were operating the enterprises as though they were haciendas, and as though little had changed with reform, with profits assigned to the discharge of the agrarian debt (former owners were paid for their estates in agrarian bonds). Sánchez Enríquez (1981:140) states that while this movement involved the whole of Andahuaylas Province, "it did not go beyond being an isolated action, without significant external assistance which would have allowed another outcome," it, nevertheless, "constituted a serious threat to the official agrarian reform program, not only on the provincial but also on the national level." In this "political development in the countryside," he (ibid.:83) adds, the region's rural population achieved "the highest level of political consciousness in its history," not "because of present conditions of exploitation" but because the movement protested "the system of exploitation which was intended to be implemented . . . in rejection of proletarianization and direct domination by capitalism and the State."

The story of FEPCA (the Federación Provincial de Campesinos de Andahuaylas, or Provincian Federation of Andahuaylas Countrypeople) is a short one (Sánchez Enríquez ibid., García Sayán 1982:73–121): it was organized in 1973, carried out its land invasions between July and September of 1974, and was extinguished by the government during that last month. Its leadership was connected with the Vanguardia Revolucionaria (Revolutionary Vanguard) political party: three urban persons, from the *mestizo-creole* population, Lino Quintanilla from Andahuaylas and Félix Loayza from Ayacucho, who spoke Quechua and thus could communicate easily with peasants, and Julio César Mezzich (Salcedo [1984:125] says that Mezzich is currently second in command of Sendero Luminoso; according to McClintock [1983a:22], he is its leader), former medical student and member of a wealthy Lima family, who only spoke Spanish. All were educated and committed professional revolutionaries, but lived as peasants or, rather, as peasant leaders. They tried to understand rural life as best they could, insofar as this is possible for professionals, and to translate their message into terms meaningful to rural people (Sánchez Enríquez 1981:85–87).

FEPCA's program, a radical alternative of self-determination, insisted on the autonomy and independence of the peasantry, the elimination of the hacienda system, collective exploitation of the land, restrictions on the export of capital from the region, and control of agrarian technicians by the peasantry; it rejected the government's agrarian reform laws, the associative enterprise system, and control by government agencies, and it forcefully repudiated the agrarian debt (ibid.:29, 118–120). With regard to this last issue, the agrarian debt, nothing conveys peasant consciousness better than the words of one of the land invaders, a serf from the Hacienda Toxama named Evaristo (quoted in ibid.:166), about the land which had recently been affected by the reform: "The patrón went to Lima several months ago. He lives there very happily, but the house in which he lives and the car he drives, all of that, is the product of our work, our sweat. He has become wealthy by the sweat of our brows. That's enough. We don't want to pay any more for this land. But in spite of that, the government is making us pay the price of the hacienda. That's not fair."

The government's first reaction was to negotiate with the leaders, which led to concessions: acknowledgment by the government of peasant control and acceptance of the agrarian debt by the leaders, their priorities doubtlessly influenced by their interpretation of proletarian revolutionary ideology which emphasizes the seizure of power, as opposed to peasant emphasis on the seizure of the land. This turn in the movement's development, Sánchez Enríquez (ibid.:183–186) says, was "clearly a great step backward in the struggle carried on by FEPCA," but "for the official representatives it constituted an important triumph," and it was perceived as such by the peasants. The leaders, however, were optimistic about their negotiations; the peasants were confused and uncertain. Eventually, the government, through one of its agencies in the region, was able to establish an alliance with the landlords remaining there and the urban population; when this was joined by the repressive apparatus of the central government, FEPCA was eliminated.

FEPCA had other problems. To begin with, the land invasion which had been scheduled for July 15 had to be postponed for three days because the people of one of the communities involved were celebrating an important feast day, a delay which diluted the force of the movement because some of the members of a central planning committee failed to appear, and even when the invasion was taking place, several groups of peasants preferred to keep on dancing and drinking (Sánchez Enríquez ibid.:142–147). Here, because of Sánchez Enríquez's excellent ethnography, we have a more accurate record of the peasant side of a movement that illustrates the clash of different ideologies, different visions of reality and different forms of consciousness, when success depended on the bonding of allies. From the urban point of view of the leaders, filled with the words of Marx, Engels, Lenin and Mao, the peasant celebration must have seemed to be a manifestation of "religious authority," a part of "the whole feudal-patriarchal system and ideology" which binds the people, "particularly the peasants" (Mao 1967:44). For the peasants, the fiesta celebrated their existence, as has been noted earlier. González Carré and Rivera Pineda (1983:36–37) record, in their study of central Peruvian peasants, how a community "could not put aside the cult and the veneration of its sacred patron saint; and therefore when [the people] undertook the recuperation of their lands . . . they went under the guidance of the saint's robes which served them as a standard and emblem." Before any important decision was made, it was the custom in that community to spread out the saint's robe, apportion coca on it for the leaders who would then chew it and examine it for omens of success or failure, while "praying for blessing, protection and help," and then decide to carry out or postpone the venture. Omens were also sought from mountain spirits and from dreams (ibid.:23–24, 37–38). These anthropologists (ibid.:37) conclude: "Ritual permits the reaffirmation of the communal spirit in peasant struggles, the reaffirmation of an Andean Identity which urgently requires a greater understanding and respect in Peru, generally governed by persons who in no way suspect, and understand even less, the complex cultural and historical reality of Andean people."

Not only did the professional revolutionaries, who thought of themselves as the "leading force in [the] revolution," among whose "closest friends" were the peasants (Mao 1967:19), fail to understand the real connection between peasants and their land, the embeddedness of peasant religion in this connection, and the identity of peasant material interest and spirituality, but they had other problems, organizational ones such as the logistics of housing, food supply, attending to the needs of peasant households (e.g., caring for livestock, planting, weeding and harvesting), and occupying constructively the time of a garrison of peasants (Sánchez Enríquez 1981:142–147). García Sayán (1982:208–209) comments: "Like any popular mobilization, peasant mobilization reaches different rhythms and levels according to circumstances. A moment arrives in which it reaches its climax, after which its force decays. In the case of the peasant movement, however, the possibilities of maintaining that 'peak' for an extended time are even more reduced."

Thus, changes in the shape, purpose and composition from one moment to another in a peasant movement, which develop from the conditions of peasant existence and the nature of the larger social formation in which it takes place are problematics for the peasants' non-peasant allies and would-be allies. One of the greatest problems of the Andahuaylas movement was its excessive dependence on three leaders who failed because their professional committment to the revolutionary cause would not allow them to grasp the nature of the rural realities in which they tried to immerse themselves.

IV: The Sendero Luminoso

It would be an error to view the Sendero Luminoso movement apart from other social movements in Peru. General Clemente Noel Moral (quoted in Salcedo 1984:29), military chief of Ayacucho represented it to the press in 1983 as different from the rest: he claimed that the military presence in the region was "combatting the subversion of international communism . . . by means of delinquents, communist murderers whose purpose [is] to implant ideologies contrary to national sovereignty and democracy." (This man who at the time was supervising death squads was hardly an authority on democracy!) President Belaúnde (quoted in ibid.:71), likewise, referred to the *senderistas,* participants in the movement, as "subversive delinquents: only crazy people, criminals or foreign agents [who] could attack democracy." Such views, however, are not simply expressions of paranoid fantasy, as they might appear superficially, but connect with social conditions in Peru which give rise to movements like the Sendero. The Sendero's growth is directly related to the economic crisis of the early 1980's, which has hit hardest at the poorest strata of Peruvian society: an inflation rate which passed 100% between May 1982 and May 1983, accompanied by dropping employment rates, dropping production, and dropping wages. More and more workers are earning less and less money, over half of them receiving less than minimum wages which presently amount to the equivalent of about seventy dollars a month. In 1981, the external debt was 31% of the GNP, in 1982 it rose to 36.6%, and in 1983 to 46.1%; in the latter year, service on it amounted to twelve billion dollars and absorbed half the national budget, in which, for example, expenditures on public health amounted to 3.2% (Mercado 1983:47–48, Quijano 1983:5). González Vigil (1984:25) maintains that the "government's desperate search for a 'scapegoat' for its failures in economic policy and in the confrontation with" the Sendero, is designed "to scare Peruvian progressive and democratic thought and to silence, through fear, the country's critical awareness of the deepening economic crisis." By blaming Peru's internal problems on "international communism," the government is avoiding a confession of its own incompetence and its own dependence on transnational support. In this process, according to Mercado (1983:49), between the Sendero's "executions" and the harshly repressive and punitive measures taken by the government, about 95% of two thousand people killed in this confrontation have not been *senderistas* but "humble rural dwellers into whose homes has been carried the dirtiest war experienced by the fatherland" in a century.

The Sendero's leader is Abimael Guzmán, former professor in the Universidad Nacional San Cristóbal de Huamanga, in Ayacucho, the capital city of one of southern Peru's poorest departments which has been neglected by Peru's rulers and managers: Gutiérrez Aparicio (1984:234) reports that this department, containing 3% of the country's population, received only 0.6% of the total national public investment between 1968 and 1980, and 0.78% in 1981, making it second to last of all political subdivisions in terms of per capita public investment for development. If reports that Guzmán is dead (McClintock 1983a:22) are true, he may well be leader in spirit only. According to the biographical sketch in Salcedo (1984:92–93), he was born in the southern port of Mollendo in 1934, attended secondary school in Arequipa, and defended his degree in philosophy in the university there with a thesis on the Kantian theory of space. Shortly afterward, he received a law degree with a thesis entitled, "The State in Bourgeois Law." When the university in Ayacucho opened in 1959, he was appointed to its faculty. He joined the Communist Party in 1962 but soon, with the Sino-Soviet split, chose the Chinese side. After Mao Tse-Tung died, and the "Gang of Four" lost power, he and his followers "concluded that there no longer existed any genuinely revolutionary country." Millones (1983a:93–96) notes that the Red Banner Peruvian Communist Party, which split from the Communist Party in the 1960's, was itself split in 1970 when the Sendero Luminoso, or Shining Path Peruvian Communist Party, was formed, claiming for itself the "correct" interpretation of the coincidence between the ideas of Mao Tse-Tung and José Carlos Mariátegui.

Guzmán was the leader of this tendency and attracted a large following in the university. McClintock (1983b:7) notes that these students were mostly "from peasant backgrounds and they frequently returned to their villages to talk politics and gain support for Sendero." According to Millones (1983a:93–96), Guzmán tried to learn Quechua but never succeeded; however, most of the people around him were able to communicate with rural people. Sendero recruited both urban and rural participants; some of these, from the notes they have left behind, were barely literate. Mercado (1983:8–11) says that after "purges" in 1979 Sendero broke with other leftist parties, which had attempted to unite for the constitutional convention of that year and the presidential elections of 1980, and in 1980 it declared war on the Peruvian state. The nature of this war is contained in the Maoist concept, "War of the Flea," defined by Taber (1970:29)) in these terms: "Analogically, the guerrilla fights the war of the flea, and his military enemy suffers the dog's disadvantages: too much to defend; too small, ubiquitous and agile an enemy to come to grips with. If the war continues long enough . . . the dog . . . becomes too weakened—in military terms, over-extended; in political terms, too unpopular; in economic terms, too expensive—to defend himself. At this point, the flea, having multiplied to a veritable plague of fleas through a long series of small victories, each drawing its drop of blood, each claiming the reward of a few more captured weapons to arm yet a few more partisans, concentrates his forces for a decisive series of powerful blows."

McClintock (1983a:19) estimates that there are in Sendero "some 3,000 activists who span many parts of Peru and can carry terror right into the capital," who had, by 1983, damaged property with a value of over a billion dollars and were responsible for a death toll of about a thousand people. Sendero has attacked police posts and mines to obtain weapons and dynamite, with which it has blown up public buildings, telephone and electric pylons, bridges and tourist hotels, and even carried out an assault on the Ayacucho jail in which two hundred prisoners were released (Salcedo 1984:93–94, Loveman and Davies 1985:321). Later, Sendero initiated a series of "popular trials and executions" of "policemen, local landowners and government officials, loan sharks, merchants and informants *[sic]*" (Barton 1983:38). According to Cavero (1983:136), it has directed the invasion of haciendas, "not to take immediate possession of them but to destroy them as centers of feudal and semifeudal domination and extra-economic abuses." Salcedo (1984:95) suggests that the terrorist acts against property "were not apparently intended to stir up popular sympathy but only to irritate those in power and to create a climate of generalized panic." Macera (1983:200) observes that "terrorism against things" is an absurd conception, since presumably things cannot feel terror, but adds that it is "a true crime in poor countries, like Peru, to decapitalize [them] through terrorist acts against things." As for terrorism against persons, the reader is referred to Amnesty International's (1983, 1985) letter and briefing, in which some of the details of both Sendero's and the Peruvian government's denials of civil and human rights to people in the affected provinces are listed.

Although Sendero "does not publish, nor seek publicity in other ways" (McClintock 1983b:7), its urban message seems clear. According to McClintock (1983a:21), Sendero aims at world revolution "through a prolonged war in the countryside, eventually encircling the cities." It claims "to have made a unique contribution to Marxist theory in the elaboration of five distinct stages of "armed struggle," which consist of 1) gathering support in the rural sector, 2) assault on the symbols of the bourgeois state, 3) beginning the guerrilla war, 4) expansion of popular support, and 5) collapse of the cities and victory. Its actions include the hanging of dead dogs on lampposts and painting walls with slogans celebrating the "Gang of Four," all directed at the university community but, as Millones (1983a:97) observes, which "would have caused astonishment or indifference as the only reaction" in the countryside. While the "Gang of Four" would mean nothing to peasants, even translated into Quechua, it may be noted that the hanging of dead dogs is polysemous: McClintock (1983a:21) says that this practice may be interpreted "as a repudiation of Chinese leader Deng" or "as a rejection of the 'running dogs' of imperialism"; but it may also signify "a traditional [peasant] warning of a coming attack." The first two meanings would be assigned to it by urban intellectuals, the third by countrypeople. Otherwise, Sendero's rural message, if not deliberately obfuscated, is less clear. Fernández Salvatteci (n.d.:2–18) lists several native Andean injunctions, among other pronouncements, which would all have great appeal in the countryside, that are part of Sendero's line: they advise people to eschew stealing, telling falsehoods, being lazy, being an informer, accumulating wealth, supporting the government, exploiting people, playing foreign music, practicing foreign customs and alcoholism; they prohibit gambling, taking drugs, foreign forms of divination (e.g., palm reading), physical abuse of women, banditry, collaboration with the police, rental of land, accumulation of food plant seeds, arrogance and taking unfair advantage of other people.

In a document with which Sendero broke its silence in early 1982 (reproduced in Mercado 1983:39), and obviously intended for readers of Spanish, Sendero referred to the peasantry as "the principal moving force," under the direction of the proletariat, in a "worker-peasant alliance, the only solid class base possible of all revolutionary fronts." Millones (1983a:98) notes that Sendero strategy, in its attempt to cut off supplies to the cities, is to order peasants to cultivate crops only for their own subsistence, to prohibit local fairs at which rural people exchange their produce, and to blow up bridges used to transport produce. It is difficult to see how such interference with the exchange of goods would win converts among peasants who, in the varied microclimates of their mountain ecology, specialize in different products according to altitude and depend on reciprocities with their neighbors for complete subsistence.

Guzmán Figueroa, et al. (1983:29–30) and De Trazegnies Granda (1983:135) indicate that Sendero had not done much in the more sparsely populated upland Iquicha region in which Uchuraccay, the scene of the 1983 massacre of journalists is located, to attract people to its cause; rather, Sendero used it as a travel route and source of supplies, perhaps even rustling cattle there (although it is true that successful rustlers usually remain unidentified). This has been an irritant to the uplanders, who do not raise the quantity and variety of produce that valley people do. Many of the latter appear to be involved in Sendero. Amnesty International (1983:16, 27; 1985:6) reports the formation of community patrols in the region, possibly with the assistance of regional authorities and military, para-military and police forces, who have instructed them to arrest and kill senderista suspects; it is likely that one such patrol was responsible for the ambush of the journalists.[12] Amnesty International (1985:3) points out that Sendero's style of "execution" is to put its victims through "trials" in public. The fumbling attempts at secrecy, obliteration of victims' identities and mass graves suggest that agencies other than Sendero have been at work in hundreds of killings that have taken place, including those of the journalists. Perhaps, in peasant eyes, Sendero is far the lesser of two horrors. Amnesty International (1983:37) notes that peasant horizontal mobility is also interfered with by government forces; and Quijano (1983:7) suggests that existing rivalries among peasant communities are exploited by the latter forces, that the Sendero guerrillas consist mostly of peasants, and that confrontation between Sendero forces and other peasants are a consequence of armed intervention by the government.

Macera (1983:199, 232) refers to indications of the development of messianic and millenarian movements over the last decade in central and southern highland populations, both rural and urbanized, in which people speak of the imminence of "the third Age or the Kingdom of the Holy Spirit-Inkarrí," a social process "which has been repeating, reiterating and failing since the sixteenth century." Abimael Guzmán (reproduced in Mercado 1983:15), himself, has said: "We have learned to control history, its laws, its contradictions. It is in our hands to resolve everything, forming it with martial deeds; nothing will hold us back. The fate of our enemies is heavy and sealed; the Party is the future, the force, the history, the light of the universe. The Communist Party, pure steel, generated light, imbibing Marxism-Leninism-MaoTse-Tung's thought." These words seem strange to me, disquieting, incomprehensible; but they do not seem to be the words of a "subversive delinquent" who is an "agent" of a malevolent "foreign power."

It is paradoxical that, while literally thousands of suspected senderistas have been arbitrarily slaughtered, the government should have preserved real ones in a special prison. An unidentified journalist, quoted by Jay Mallin (cited in McClintock 1983a:22), visited them and reported: "[T]he prisoners constantly repeated bellicose chants. Soldier-like, they marched, made formations, and saluted. One of their songs was a kind of hymn: it described the seas of agitation and land flooded, then amid the disorder the rising of the sun, and finally the affirmation, 'except for power, everything is an illusion.' It is in the virtual worship of Guzmán, however, that the personality cult aspect and indeed almost messianic character of Sendero Luminoso is most apparent. . . . He is always referred to by his *nom de guerre,* Comrade Gonzalo. Throughout the jail, shouts of 'Long live Comrade Gonzalo!' and 'Gonzalo is armed struggle' were heard. Senderistas called Guzmán the 'Fourth Sword of Marxism,' after Marx, Lenin and Mao. 'The vanguard of world revolution,' they intoned, 'is the thought of Comrade

Gonzalo.' This is reminiscent of the Mao cult in China, of which Deane (1985:107) says that "Mao . . . wound up uttering 'instructions' like an oracle while cadres, in morning exercises, bowed to his portrait and chanted quotations."

If the government's "forces of order," armed with the latest weapons by interested (but hardly "benevolent") foreign powers, and who have been contributing mightily to the disorder (or non-order) which exists in southern Peru, would cease their extermination of almost everyone who is so much as suspected of being "subversive"—hundreds of men, women, and children, innocent and guilty alike—and allow them to testify, we might be in a better position to evaluate the ideology, more likely ideologies, of this movement. It would appear that, as Szemiński and Anisón (1982:210–217, 230) report in their analysis of Ayacucho myths, that the *nakaq* and *pistacos,* beings who are said to slaughter people for their grease, or spinal fluid, which is sold to wealthy manufacturers in Europe and North America who use it to put together space rockets, among other things, in no way represent false consciousness of reality. Andean myths, in this case, represent rather accurately the world of both structural and practical terrorism that surrounds the people.

Conclusion

In this essay, four largely rural Peruvian social movements have been examined, in which the principal contradictions appear in the relations between rural people and their non-rural allies. In the two earlier movements, peasants seem to have been ideologically manipulated by *creoles* and creolized *mestizos,* who themselves were moved by creole utopias of reformism and populism, but who, when they discovered that their urbanized vision had led them to miscalculate the strength of peasant myth, deserted the peasants when peasant pursuit of their own utopian vision of a just social order threatened the reproduction of elite existence. Both Túpac Amaru II and General Cáceres seem to have been perceived by peasants, and perhaps even represented to them, as redeemers who were about to initiate a new age in which the claims of poor people would be revindicated, in a context of peasant myths concerning the establishment of a new order in the universe and Christian conceptions of God. In the two more recent movements, direction also came from the urban sector, not from elites but from persons influenced by proletarian revolutionary ideology which projects the utopian vision of a proletarian dictatorship which will create social justice and redeem humankind by abolishing social classes. These proletarian revolutionaries have offered their myth, consciously or not, and this could not but strike sympathetic chords in peasant consciousness. However, to paraphrase a point that Lenin made on several occasions after the October Revolution, social revolution is made with and by imperfect stuff, formed and deformed in the earlier social formation; in other words, socialist states are not utopias, and socialists are imperfect beings. Proletarian revolutionaries' judgment is not always good. We see this in the leadership of the third movement who, in trading what they conceived as a "victory" in the government's willingness to engage in dialogue for what the peasants saw as "defeat" in their recognition of the agrarian debt, displayed their lack of understanding of the spirituality of peasants' material ties to the land. They may even have viewed possession of the land, as Hobsbawm (1974:124) has expressed it, "as a *petit bourgeois* aberration." Their apparent view of peasant religiosity as an irritating impediment, in striking contrast with the utilization of it by the elite in the second movement to control peasant force and direction, seems to indicate that they were operating under the misconception that their peasant followers had no ideology to start with.[13] In all of this, it may be said, they were unable to put their revolutionary ideology into practice.[14]

By repudiating all other proletarian revolutionary trends, denouncing equally the Soviet Union, the People's Republic of China, Cuba and Albania (Brown 1985:213), Sendero has isolated itself politically. However, it would seem that the movement is not socially isolated but has found a base in the countryside. Its continued existence contrasts impressively with the guerrilla movements of two decades ago (cf. Gott 1971:305–394) and suggests a degree of popular support which the earlier movements lacked. The well documented genocidal campaign of the Belaúnde government forces in the affected provinces, a mass slaughter which is reminiscent of the actions of other military bureaucracies in Central and South America, also suggests that the government is well aware of this popular support, whether or not it is willing to admit the fact, and perceives it, correctly, as a threat that is to be eliminated at any cost. The Peruvian government has successfully used Sendero's terrorism against it by blaming it for acts it has not committed, including offenses against life and property by government forces. It seems clear, moreover, that the government's counter-terrorism operates through alliances established between its apparatus and some of the peasant communities in the region, taking gruesome advantage of inter-community rivalries with peasant death squads, one of which was probably responsible for the Uchuraccay massacre. We are now faced with a situation in which the government's peasants are fighting the Sendero's peasants, a war which can only end in mutual extermination.

Sendero, in its campaign to close off Peru's cities, is basing itself on Mao's strategy in post-1927 China (Mercado 1985:57–61). However, if the Belaúnde government is unpopular, it did not come to power in a fascist coup like Chang's, but it was elected in 1980 by a plurality of voters in a free and honest election. It is not a colonial government, although it is true that Peruvian leftists view Belaúnde as the tool of transnational finance capital in a structure of neo-colonial power; and its military apparatus is not an alien invading force, as in the case of China when the Japanese presence afforded Mao the opportunity to make his movement one of national liberation, but is thoroughly Peruvian in personnel, although it, like other Latin American military organizations, is increasingly trained, equipped and funded by its North American ally in a process of military transnationalization.

Sendero's ideology combines Maoist interpretation with Andean messianism, representing a mixed urban and rural point of view. It suffers all the defects of a movement composed of uprooted urban and rural elements, most of whose leaders are steeped in a poverty-stricken provincial university background. The University of Huamanga, in Ayacucho, according to Gutiérrez Aparicio (1984:234), since its opening in 1959 has graduated only 22% of its students. Millones (1983b:11) characterizes this academic atmosphere as one with "neglected and delayed financing, a multitude of students with deficient nutrition and education, and professors worn out by multiple and unending tasks." Only the test of history, as it is made in the short-term future, will show whether or not Sendero's popular support is sufficient to make up for its narrow-mindedness, dogmatism and provincial vision of Peruvian realities.

Peru has just elected Alán García to be its next president. This election represents not only legitimacy but the victory, at long last after over half a century of struggle, of a *petit bourgeois* party whose slogan has been anti-imperialism. If the new president can, as promised in his campaign, restore peace in southern Peru by demilitarizing it, he will have taken a major step to counter Sendero's influence, which has fed on repression, but he will also have to counter Peru's appalling poverty by applying a break to Peru's galloping inflation, providing full employment, redistributing national income, holding off transnational creditors and halting the creeping transnationalization of his country. Such heroism could easily be viewed as a threat by foreign creditors who might use the country's already transnationalized military to liquidate that threat. In that case, the genocide will continue.

NOTES

1. For the purpose of this essay, "ideology" refers to the viewpoint of a social sector differentiated by the conditions of its existence from other sectors.
2. This focus on the rural sector consists of several different trends of thought, together referred to as *indigenismo,* nativism or Indianism. See Stein (1984c).
3. The word "Indian" is an epithet in Peru, applied mainly to rural dwellers and persons in small towns. Originally, it referred to native Andean people, but both urban and rural Peruvians are so mixed genetically at the present time, and so culturally distinct from the prehispanic societies of the area, that it makes little sense to use it, especially with regard to people who would be insulted by it. The term *"runa,"* Quechua for countrypeople, although slightly exotic, would be appropriate; but I have chosen to use the terms "peasant," "countrypeople" and "rural sector." For discussions of this theme, see the collection by Fuenzalida (1970) and Mayer's (1979) recent article. By "peasant," I do not mean an exotic social condition but simply rural small producer whose priority, but not exclusively so, is self-subsistence, in accord with Wolf's (1966) formulation. Also see Stein (1985b).
4. The tendency in Andeanist anthropology is to focus on relating communities to their social contexts, rather than on viewing them as isolates as in the past. There has been debate recently, however, on whether communities or households should be the units of study (see Stein 1984a).
5. Wolf (1965:93) defines cultural "brokers" as persons "who are able to operate both in terms of community-oriented and nation-oriented expectations." For a discussion of colonial Andean brokers, see Spalding (1984:209). Flores Galindo (1981:259–260) brings out the broker character of Túpac Amaru II, describing him as "speaking in Quechua and Spanish, knowing the *Royal Commentaries* and Latin, understanding the Andean messianic hope, and revering Christian religiosity, . . . not an exceptional person in the eighteenth century."
6. The term *"mestizo"* originally referred to the offspring of mixed Spanish and Andean parentage, as distinguished from *"criollo" (creole),* the offspring of

Spanish parents and born in the New World. With time, physical characteristics ceased to distinguish the several population categories. At present, the word is better interpreted as "intermediary" in a social system which links peasants to the urban world (see Mayer 1979:94). Macera (1981:36) says of *mestizos* that "they do not know well what they are, but, still, they know what they do not want to be: they do not want to be Indians."

7. I am indebted, for the summary of Andean myth presented here, to the following works: Ortiz Rescaniere 1973, Urbano 1981 and 1982, Silverblatt 1982, Szemiński 1983, and the collections in Ossio 1973 and Urbano 1977.
8. I have elsewhere acknowledged my appreciation of several persons and institutions who have assisted my work on the Atusparia movement. I hope they will all forgive me for omitting mention of them here. Interested readers may consult several of my published works cited in the text.
9. To cite only works more likely to be available to North Americans, see Reyna 1932, Valladares and Piel 1977, Klaiber 1977a, and Stein 1980, 1981, 1982a, 1982b, 1984b, and n.d.
10. Changing conditions in Peru's rural sector are discussed and references are cited in Stein (1983, 1985a).
11. Let readers not misunderstand my intention: the term "professional revolutionaries" is not an epithet; it refers as much to a profession of faith as it does to a professional occupation and identity.
12. Millones (1983a:99) notes that in 1975 ten cattle rustlers were lynched by the members of one of the Iquicha communities. Information on community patrols in southern Peru is difficult to obtain at present. For a description of how such patrols are formed, and how they function, in another region of the country, see Gitlitz and Rojas (1983).
13. Ortiz Rescaniere (1973:3–4) says, fittingly: "Peruvian peasants understand with difficulty the content of the concepts Revolution or Dialectic. Neither does the person from our capital city understand the meaning of terms like "the world is going to turn over . . . when the Inca's son is grown and moving about."
14. An impressive parallel may be drawn between the left's treatment of peasants and its treatment of women. MacKinnon (1983:230) says: "Feminists have often found that working-class movements and the left undervalue women's work and concerns, neglect the role of feelings and attitudes in a focus on institutional and material change, denigrate women in procedure, practice, and everyday life, and in general fail to distinguish themselves from any other ideology or group dominated by male interests." The point is well made: a proletarian utopia with sexism is an absurdity. It is tragic that rural people have not had as articulate an advocate!

References

Amnesty International, 1983, Peru: Torture and Extrajudicial Executions, Letter of Amnesty International to President Fernando Belaunde Terry. London: International Secretariat, Amnesty International.

———. 1985, Peru Briefing. London: Amnesty International Publications.

Bak, János M., and Gerhard Benecke, 1984, Religion *and* revolt? *In* Religion and Rural Revolt, János M. Bak and Gerhard Benecke, eds. Manchester, England: Manchester University Press.

Barton, Carol, 1983, Peru—"dirty war" in Ayacucho. NACLA Report on the Americas 17(3):36–39.

Bartra, Roger, 1978, El Poder Despótico Burgués. México: Ediciones Era.

Brown, Cynthia, ed., 1985, With Friends Like These, the Americas Watch Report on Human Rights and U.S. Policy in Latin America. New York: Pantheon Books.

Burga, Manuel, and Alberto Flores Galindo, 1980, Feudalismo andino y movimientos sociales (1866–1965). *In* Historia del Perú, V. 12, Fernando Silva Santisteban, ed. Lima: Editorial Juan Mejía Baca.

———. 1982, La utopía andina. Allpanchis Phuturinqa (Cuzco) 20:85–101.

Castelli, Amalia, 1978, Tunupa: divinidad del altiplano. *In* Etnohistoria y Antropología Andina, Primera Jornada del Museo Nacional de Historia, Marcia Koth de Paredes and Amalia Castelli, eds. Lima: Museo Nacional de Historia.

Cavero, Ranulfo, 1983, La Otra Cara de la Medalla que Algunos No Quieren Ver: A Propósito de la Semifeudalidad y la Problemática Agraria en el Perú. Ayacucho, Peru: Universidad Nacional de San Cristóbal de Huamanga, Dirección Universitaria de Investigación.

Choy, Emilio, 1976, Contradicciones y trascendencia de la revolución. *In* Flores Galindo (1976a).

Cornblit, Oscar, 1976, Levantamientos de masas en Perú y Bolivia durante el siglo XVII. *In* Flores Galindo (1976a).

Custred, H. Glynn, Jr., 1973, Symbols and Control in a High Altitude Andean Community. Ph.D. Dissertation, Indiana University. Ann Arbor, Michigan: University Microfilms International.

———. 1980, The place of ritual in Andean rural society. *In* Land and Power in Latin America, Agrarian Economies and Social Processes in the Andes, Benjamin S. Orlove and Glynn Custred, eds. New York and London: Holmes and Meier Publishers.

Davies, Thomas M., Jr., 1984, The Shining Path to Nowhere: Guerrilla Warfare in the Andes. Paper presented to the Midwest Association of Latin American Studies, November, 1984. Electrostatic copy. San Diego: Center for Latin American Studies, San Diego State University.

De Trazegnies Granda, Fernando, 1983, Informe. Appendix *in* Guzmán Figueroa, et al. (1983).

Deane, Hugh, 1985, Mao's rural strategies: what went wrong? Science and Society 49:101–107.

Deustua, José, 1983, Sobre movimientos campesinos e historia regional en el Perú moderno: un comentario Bibliográfico. Revista Andina 1(1):219–240.

Engels, Frederick, MECW, See Marx and Engels (MECW).

Espinoza Soriano, Waldemar, 1981, 1780: movimientos antifiscales en la sierra norte de la audiencia de Lima y repercusiones tupamaristas en la misma zona, nuevas perspectivas. Allpanchis Phuturinqa (Cuzco) 17/18:169–201.

Fernández Salvatteci, José A., Mayor E. P., n.d., Guerrillas y Contraguerrillas en el Perú (Sendero Luminoso y el Gobierno del Arq. F. Belaúnde T.). Mimeographed pre-edition. [Lima, 1984].

Fisher, Lillian Estelle, 1966, The Last Inca Revolt, 1780–1783. Norman: University of Oklahoma Press.

Flores Galindo, Alberto, 1976a, Sociedad Colonial y Sublevaciones Populares: Túpac Amaru II—1780. Lima: Retablo de Papel Ediciones.

———. 1976b, Túpac Amaru y la sublevación de 1780. *In* Flores Galindo (1976a).

———. 1981, La revolución tupamarista y los pueblos andinos (una crítica y un proyecto). Allpanchis Phuturinqa (Cuzco) 17/18:253–265.

Fuenzalida V., Fernando, ed., 1970, El Indio y el Poder en el Perú. Lima: Instituto de Estudios Peruanos.

García Sayán, Diego, 1982, Tomas de Tierras en el Perú. Lima: DESCO, Centro de Estudios y Promoción del Desarrollo.

Gitlitz, John S., and Telmo Rojas, 1983, Peasant vigilante committees in northern Peru. Journal of Latin American Studies 15:163–197.

Golte, Jürgen, 1980, Repartos y Rebeliones, Túpac Amaru y las Contradicciones de la Economía Colonial. Lima: Instituto de Estudios Peruanos.

González Carré, Enrique, and Fermín Rivera Pineda, 1983, Antiguos Dioses y Nuevos Conflictos Andinos. Ayacucho, Peru: Universidad Nacional de San Cristóbal de Huamanga.

González Vigil, Fernando, 1984, More on human rights in Peru. Latin American Studies Association Forum 14(4):24–26.

Gott, Richard, 1971, Guerrilla Movements in Latin America. Garden City, New York: Doubleday and Company.

Gutiérrez Aparicio, Luis, 1984, Realidad Económica Peruana, Problemas Actuales y Alternativas. Lima: Instituto de Investigaciones Económicas de la Universidad Nacional Mayor de San Marcos.

Guzmán, Virginia, and Virginia Vargas, 1981, El Campesinado en la Historia, Cronología de los Movimientos Campesinos, 1956–1964: Lima: IDEAS.

Guzmán Figueroa, Abraham, Mario Vargas Llosa, and Mario Castro Arenas, 1983, Informe de la Comisión Investigadora de los Sucesos de Uchuraccay. Lima: Editora Perú.

Handelman, Howard, 1975, Struggle in the Andes, Peasant Political Mobilization in Peru. Austin and London: University of Texas Press.

Hobsbawm, Eric J., 1974, Peasant Land Occupations. Past and Present 62:120–152.

Hocquenghem, Anne Marie, 1984, Moche: mito, rito y actualidad. Allpanchis Phuturinqa 23:145–160.

Hünefeldt, Christine, 1980, Conciencia étnica y conciencia de clase: el levantamiento campesino de 1780–1783. *In* El Hombre y la Cultura Andina, III Congreso Peruano, Segunda Serie, T. 3, Ramiro Matos Mendieta, ed. Lima: Editora Lasontay.

Kapsoli, Wilfredo, 1983, Ensayos de Nueva Historia. Lima: Francisco Gonzales A. Editores.

———. 1984, Ayllus del Sol, Anarquismo y Utopía Andina. Lima: TAREA, Asociación de Publicaciones Educativas.

Klaiber, Jeffrey L., S. J., 1977a, Religion and Revolution in Peru, 1824–1976. Notre Dame, Indiana: University of Notre Dame Press.

———. 1977b, Religión y revolución en los Andes en el siglo XIX. Histórica 1:93–111.

———. 1982, Religión y justicia en Túpac Amaru. Allpanchis Phuturinqa (Cuzco) 19:173–186.

Landa, Francisco, ed., 1984, Uchuraccay, el crimen impune, homenaje y protesta. Cuadernos Peruanos 4:1–64.

Lauer, Mirko, ed., 1977, Frente al Perú Oligárquico (1928–68), Debate Socialista 1. Lima: Mosca Azul Editores.

Lazo García, Carlos, and Javier Tord M., 1978, Grupos de poder y movimiento social en el Perú colonial: algunas evidencias. *In* Etnohistoria y Antropología Andina, Primera Jornada del Museo Nacional de Historia, Marcia Koth de Paredes and Amalia Castelli, eds. Lima: Museo Nacional de Historia.

Lenin, V. I., CW, Collected Works. 45 volumes. Moscow: Progress Publishers.

Lewin, Boleslao, 1957, La Rebelión de Túpac Amaru y los Orígenes de la Emancipación Americana. Buenos Aires: Librería Hachette.

Loveman, Brian, and Thomas M. Davies, Jr., 1985, Case histories of guerrilla movements and political change. *In* Guerrilla Warfare, Che Guevara. Lincoln, Nebraska, and London: University of Nebraska Press.

Macera, Pablo, 1981, Arte y lucha social: los murales de Ambaná (Bolivia). Allpanchis Phuturinqa (Cuzco) 17/18:23–40.

———. 1983, Las Furias y las Penas. Lima: Mosca Azul Editores.

MacKinnon, Catharine A., 1983, Feminism, Marxism, method, and the state: an agenda for theory. *In* The *Signs* Reader, Women, Gender and Scholarship, Elizabeth Abel and Emily K. Abel. Chicago and London: University of Chicago Press.

Mao Tse-Tung, 1967, Selected Works, Volume 1. Peking: Foreign Languages Press.

Marx, Karl, MECW, See Marx and Engels (MECW).

Marx, Karl, and Frederick Engels, MECW, Karl Marx, Frederick Engels, Collected Works. New York: International Publishers.

Mayer, Enrique, 1979, Consideraciones sobre lo indígena. *In* Perú: Identidad Nacional, César Arróspide de la Flor, et al. Lima: Ediciones CEDEP.

Marzal, Manuel M., S. J., 1971, El Mundo Religioso de Urcos. Cuzco, Peru: Instituto de Pastoral Andina.

———. 1977, Estudios sobre Religión Campesina. Lima: Ponticifia Universidad Católica del Perú, Fondo Editorial.

———. 1983, La Transformación Religiosa Peruana. Lima: Pontificia Universidad Católica del Perú, Fondo Editorial.

McClintock, Cynthia, 1983a, Sendero Luminoso: Peru's Maoist guerrillas. Problems of Communism, October, pp. 19–34.

———. 1983b, Democracies and guerrillas: the Peruvian experience. International Policy Report (Center for International Policy, Washington, D. C.), September, pp. 1–9.

Mercado, Rogger, 1983, Algo Mas sobre Sendero. Lima: Ediciones de Cultura Popular.

———. 1985, El Partido Comunista del Perú: Sendero Luminoso. Third edition. Lima: Ediciones de Cultura Popular.

Millones, Luis, 1979, Sociedad indígena e identidad nacional. *In* Peru: Identidad Nacional, César Arróspide de la Flor, et al. Lima: Ediciones CDEP.

———. 1983a, La tragedia de Uchuraccay: informe sobre Sendero. Appendix *in* Guzmán Figueroa, et al. (1983).

———. 1983b, Prólogo. *In* Antiguos Dioses y Nuevos Conflictos Andinos, Enrique González Carré and Fermín Rivera Pineda. Ayacucho, Peru: Universidad Nacional de San Cristóbal de Huamanga.
O'Phelan Godoy, Scarlett, 1976, El Carácter de las Revueltas Campesinas del Siglo XVIII en el Norte del Virreinato Peruano. Cuadernos del Taller de Investigación Rural No. 19. Lima: Pontificia Universidad Católica del Perú.
———. 1977a, Cuzco 1777: el movimiento de Maras, Urubamba. Histórica 1:113–128.
———. 1977b, El norte y los movimientos antifiscales del siglo XVIII. Histórica 1:199–222.
———. 1979, La rebelión de Túpac Amaru: organización interna, dirigencia y alianzas. Histórica 3(2):89–121.
———. 1983, Tierras comunales y revuelta social: Bolivia en el siglo SVIII. Allpanchis Phuturinqa (Cuzco) 22:75–91.
Ortiz Rescaniere, Alejandro, 1973, De Adaneva a Inkarrí, una Visión Indígena del Perú. Lima: Retablo de Papel Ediciones.
Ossio, Juan M., 1978, Las cinco edades del mundo según Felipe Guamán Poma de Ayala. *In* Etnohistoria y Antropología Andina, Primera Jornada del Museo Nacional de Historia, Marcia Koth de Paredes and Amalia Castelli, eds. Lima: Museo Nacional de Historia.
Ossio A., Juan M., ed., 1973, Ideología Mesiánica del Mundo Andino. Lima: Edición de Ignacio Prado Pastor.
Pease G. Y., Franklin, 1973, El Dios Creador Andino. Lima: Mosca Azul Editores.
Ponte Gonzáles, Alfonso, 1945, Por la Senda, Breve Ensayo Histórico Biográfico. Lima: Imprenta Gráfica "Stylo."
Quijano, Aníbal, 1983, Notes on human rights in Peru. Latin American Studies Association Forum 14(2):5–8.
———. 1979, Problema Agrario y Movimientos Campesino. Lima: Mosca Azul Editores.
Reyna, Ernesto, 1932, El Amauta Atusparia. Lima: Ediciones de Frente.
Rowe, John, 1976, El movimiento nacional Inca del siglo XVIII. *In* Flores Galindo (1976a).
Salcedo, José María, 1984, Las Tumbas de Uchuraccay. Lima: Cóndor Editores/Editora Humboldt.
Sánchez Enríquez, Rodrigo, 1981, Toma de Tierras y Conciencia Política Campesina. Lima: Instituto de Estudios Peruanos.
Silverblatt, Irene, 1982, Dioses y diablos: idolatrías y evangelización. Allpanchis Phuturinqa (Cuzco) 19:31–47.
Sivirichi Tapia, Atilio, 1979, La Revolución Social de los Túpac Amaru. Lima: Editorial Universo.
Spalding, Karen, 1980, Class structures in the southern Peruvian highlands, 1750–1920. In Land and Power in Latin America, Agrarian Economies and Social Processes in the Andes, Benjamin S. Orlove and Glynn Custred, eds. New York and London: Holmes and Meier Publishers.
———. 1984, Huarochirí, an Andean Society Unver Inca and Spanish Rule. Stanford, California: Stanford University Press.
Stein, William W., ———. 1980, Rebellion in Huaraz: the newspaper account of an "obscure" revolt in Peru. Dialectical Anthropology 5:127–154.
———. 1981, The Role of Non-Peasants in a Peasant Revolt: Mestizos and Indians

in Nineteenth Century Peru. Paper presented in a panel on Third World Agrarian Labor History, Annual Meeting of the American Anthropological Association, Los Angeles. Mimeographed. Amherst, New York: Department of Anthropology, State University of New York at Buffalo.

———. 1982a, Myth and ideology in a nineteenth century Peruvian peasant uprising. Ethnohistory 29:237–264.

———. 1982b, The Limits of Peasant Movement: Leaders, Followers, and Allies in the Atusparia Uprising of 1885, Peru. Special Studies No. 147. Amherst, New York: Council on International Studies, State University of New York at Buffalo.

———. 1983, The Condition of the Rural Working Class in Peru. Paper presented in a panel on Peru in Transition, Annual Meeting of the American Anthropological Association, Chicago. Mimeographed. Amherst, New York: Department of Anthropology, State University of New York at Buffalo.

———. 1984a, The Practice of Economic Anthropology in the Peruvian Andes: Community, Household, and Relations of Production. Paper presented in a symposium on Units of Analysis in Economic Anthropology, Annual Meeting of the American Anthropological Association, Denver. Mimeographed. Amherst, New York: Department of Anthropology, State University of New York at Buffalo.

———. 1984b, Religion and clergy in the Atusparia uprising, Peru, 1885. *In* Religion and Rural Revolt, János M. Bak and Gerhard Benecke, eds. Manchester, England: Manchester University Press.

———. 1984c, Images of the Peruvian Indian peasant in the work of José Carlos Mariátegui. Historical Reflections/Réflexions Historiques 11:1–35.

———. 1985a, Introduction: metropolis and hinterland in Peru. *In* Peruvian Contexts of Change, William W. Stein, ed. New Brunswick, New Jersey: Transaction Books.

———. 1985b, Townspeople and countrypeople in the Callejón de Huaylas. *In* Peruvian Contexts of Change, William W. Stein, ed. New Brunswick, New Jersey: Transaction Books.

———. n.d., La Sublevación de Atusparia. Lima: Punto y Trama Editores, *in press.*

Stern, Steve J., 1982, Peru's Indian Peoples and the Challenge of Spanish Conquest, Huamanga to 1640. Madison, Wisconsin: University of Wisconsin Press.

Szemiński, Jan, 1976, La insurrección de Túpac Amaru II: ¿guerra de independencia o revolución? *In* Flores Galindo (1976a).

———. 1983, La Utopía Tupamarista. Lima: Fondo Editorial, Pontificia Universidad Católica del Perú.

Szemiński, Jan, and Juan Anisón, 1982, Dioses y hombres de Huamanga. Allpanchis Phuturinqa (Cuzco) 19:187–233.

Taber, Robert, 1970, War of the Flea, a Study of Guerrilla Warfare, Theory and Practice. New York: Citadel Press.

Urbano, Henrique-Osvaldo, 1981, Del sexo, incesto y los ancestros de Inkarrí, mito, utopía e historia en las sociedades andinas. Allpanchis Phuturinqa (Cuzco) 17/18:77–103.

———. 1982, Representaciones colectivas y arqueología mental en los Andes. Allpanchis Phuturinqa (Cuzco) 20:33–83.

Urbano, Henrique-Osvaldo, ed., 1977, Mito y utopía en los Andes. Allpanchis Phuturinqa (Cuzco) 10:1–174.

Valcárcel, Daniel, 1947, La Rebelión de Túpac Amaru. México: Fondo de Cultura Económica.

Valladares, Manuel, and Jean Piel, 1977, Sublevación de Atusparia. *In* Los Movimientos Campesinos en el Perú: 1879–1965, Wilfredo Kapsoli, ed. Lima: Delva Editores.

Vargas Llosa, Mario, 1983, Inquest in the Andes. The New York Times Magazine, July 31.

Wolf, Eric R., 1965, Aspects of group relations in a complex society: Mexico. *In* Contemporary Cultures and Societies of Latin America, Dwight B. Heath and Richard N. Adams, eds. New York: Random House.

———. 1966, Peasants. Englewood Cliffs, New Jersey: Prentice-Hall.

5

Revolution in the Tradition of Jan Hus: The Confluence of Christian Religion and Marxist Ideology in Czechoslovakia

MARTIN RUMSCHEIDT

Introduction

The interaction of Christian religion and Marxism ideology in Czechoslovakia (ČSSR) is producing remarkable results as each is finding new sources of hope and energy in dialogue with one another. But these results are less surprising when viewed against the long history of revolution that dates back to a great fifteenth century reformer named Jan Hus. Like so much of Europe in the later Middle Ages, the region now known as Czechoslovakia was under the governance of the clergy and aristocracy, an arrangement that provided these two estates with privileged status. That period of history was also a time when orders of monks and nuns traveled far and wide preaching voluntary poverty and a new piety, which included a renewed preoccupation with the study of the Bible. Their preaching sounded a distinctive anti-hierarchical note which was especially welcome in commercial, intellectual and administrative centers such as Prague. Due to popular interest in this new piety, the eloquent preacher Jan Hus was called to Prague in 1402. But jealousy and anger among academics led to his downfall in 1412 and, after a broken promise of protection by the Emperor, to his execution.

Of course, his death made Hus a martyr to his numerous followers and a symbol of protest against throne and altar. Under his inspiration, their populist piety took a revolutionary turn and fostered a populist uprising bent on fashioning a new kind of church and civil community. For fifteen years, these parish-based peasant commandos fought back whole armies while spreading their religious protest against existing ecclesiastical and social hierarchies throughout central and western Europe. Massive destabilizing efforts by Church and Court succeeded in dividing the movement into a pacifist and a militant group, thus robbing it of its unity and power. But the seeds of revolution had been planted by Jan Hus and were embedded in a Hussite tradition that continued through the centuries to the present day.

Not surprisingly, these old Hussite visions were rekindled by the various European revolutions of 1848 as theological motivations were clearly married to revolutionary aspirations. Thus, when the state of Czechoslovakia was established as a result of the Allied victory of 1918, the old dreams of political and religious freedom seemed realized at last. The throne of Habsburg had been replaced by a new republic which had the power to keep aristocrisy and clergy under control. Unfortunately, the young republic quickly fell victim to the Nazi invasion, but the victory of the Allies in 1945 again restored the prospect of Czechoslovakian self-determination. In 1948, a political party with determined orientation set out to establish new structures of civic and church life, which removed the clergy and the aristocracy from their places as privileged institutions with assured existence. That social revolution which is yet incomplete was Communist directed and organized. But it was no less a Christian revolution for all of that, since the Czechoslovakian dream of populist rule had been nourished by a Hussite heritage of five and a half centuries.

In the continuing interaction of Christianity and Marxism in Czechoslovakia, the long tradition of Hussite faith is proving itself capable of resisting the demodernizing tendency of Soviet ideology and Christian theology as well as renewing both Christianity and Marxism in their revolutionary quest toward a more noble humanity. Attention will be given in this paper, after some general comments about Marxism and Christianity, to the Czechoslovakian Christian-Marxist dialogue in the early 1960s and after the fall of Dubcek in late 1968. The position of two Marxist and two Christian participants in the dialogue will be explored, with special attention to the way the category of revolution has been appropriated in Christian theology. A concluding section will argue the case for a genuinely "public" approach in the political processes of shaping human life in community.

I

Some definitions are required. Even though there is no unanimity in defining religion, revolution and ideology, one owes the reader an indication of how these terms are being used. This obligation is all the more pressing because these terms are themselves subjected to propagandistic use in the mass media.

"Revolution." People generally believe nowadays that current revolutions are little able to establish primary human-social relations of freedom, equality and brother/sisterliness. The revolutionary struggle for justice so quickly lapses into obsession with domestic and national security, as can be seen in the multiplication of military regimes, in the accelerating arms-race and in the disappointed hopes that lead either into unbridled terrorism or egocentered passivity. This raises a question about what a revolution is and when a revolution has occurred.

To her lasting credit, Hannah Arendt has brought some firm guidelines into this confused situation. Establishing a line of thinking about "revolution" that runs from 1776 and 1789 to 1848 and 1917, Arendt summarizes the characteristic elements of a "genuine" revolution in the popular phrase "government of the people, by the people, for the people." Thus, notions of hierarchies or elites of a so-called "new class" are by definition excluded from genuine revolutions. If elites exist in the revolutionary process, they are there merely as functionaries of the process. Their destiny is to self-destruct as various phases of the revolution are attained. The presence of an "expertocracy" is always a signal that something is "rotten in the state of Denmark." Not surprisingly, by this reckoning, Arendt regards the American Revolution of 1776 as the only successful revolution in modern times.

Still the world has lived in a revolutionary situation for two centuries and something must be said about those revolutions that have failed or have yet to succeed. More accurately, revolution must be seen as something other than a strictly American achievement or monopoly. This need is especially urgent for Christian theologians who see history as the theater of God's revolutionary activity and faith as the summons to humankind's revolutionary destiny. Their's is not a theology of revolution but a theology for revolution. Their reflections on human nature and social change do not take rise in law and order, in that which is static, but in justice and liberation, in that which is dynamic. Drawing on biblical images and visions, their theologies draw attention to the fact that within the society of the "old Adam" a new society is being created by the "new Adam."

Thus, for purposes of this study, we must define the way the word "revolution" is used in the framework of both the Christian religion and Marxist ideology. Within the Christian framework, "revolution" is defined as a long term process of radical humanization which, given that it is beset by opposition, necessarily becomes a deep incision in the processes of historical development. These incisions seek, in the first instance, to create freedom, dignity, peaceful living and cultural values but also to assure bread in sufficient quantity. At the same time, a true revolution will also guard the great values created by earlier generations. When spoken of in the Marxist frame of reference, "revolution" means the overthrow of the *basis* of all that is in existence, to be precise, the complete overthrow of the existing production forces by the masses of people which revolt not only against individual conditions of hitherto existing society but against the very "life-production" hitherto existing, the whole of the activity on which that society and its sustenance rest.

As shall be shown later, even the differences in these two conceptions, namely that the former views reality in light of the conditions of the "new Adam" who is said to have already lived in our midst, whereas the latter views reality in a utopian vision for which we humans struggle without the aid of the transcendent present among us, have a confluence in the perception of the human as the Promethean.

"Ideology." Defined in a neutral way, an "ideology" is a system of norms and principles in which two things have happened, in this order: reasons are given to justify something which was done in the past and thereby becomes a part of the rational and moral foundation of actions which are undertaken in the future. Defined in this way, ideologies are ways of viewing reality and methods of justifying behavior that have a collective character, since they are subscribed to by entire groups. "Ideology", in current usage also has a decided negative flavour. Marx called an ideology any system of thought which is based on false consciousness and which confers privileged status on a group or a class. In his view, ideological thinkers may or may not be aware of these underlying motives.

It is this negative dimension that I need to expand: for even though embodying a false consciousness, one in which what *truly* motivates a collective is concealed, ideologies are conscious of what I earlier called the "demodernizing tendency." Ideologies seek to shape a wholistic outlook on life and eliminate choice for subjects: ideology is the fabric of de-differentiation.[1] Demodernizing or dedifferentiating is a community's coercing assent in the offering of single, total solutions. "One's club finds people either in or out. The book of spiritual directions has precise engineering solutions, with none of the doubleness that humans have to live with. A generation is untrained to look for something different in spirituality than in engineering, where things in the end always work, or in advertising, where promises always look true."[2] What primarily characterizes the "spirit" of modernity is precisely the ability and the *right* to choose freely and, as a consequence, the existence of community in plurality, in the openness of the "public" dimension. As Hannah Arendt puts it, the space where women and men can speak openly and be heard. A genuine "public" approach "critically appreciates modernity because it stresses free choice, but presents the vision of wholeness that keeps it from simple fragmentation. Brokenness and wholeness, complexity and simplicity, pure hunger and total fulness, each pair can tyrannize with their false alternatives."[3] Ideology shapes wholistic outlooks around false alternatives and then seeks to present that outlook as a goal already arrived at; that goal achieved then becomes the foundation from which all else yet to be done follows consistently. Ideology—the precise opposite to revolutionary consciousness—seeks to defend the status quo; revolution calls for entry into a journey toward promises yet to be fulfilled, toward existence in hope. The deep danger of ideology is that, because of its totalitarian claims, truth dies, the *logos* departs from life. Even if the truth were *One,* it cannot exist apart from diversity and, therefore, has to find its living space in the open, democratically functioning existence of free people. And that imperative may, indeed, be the author and sustainer of revolution.

"Religion". It is my guess that there are in the literature even more definitions of religion than of revolution. Because religion has so much to do with the depth dimension of people's individual existence and public life and praxis, no attempt will be made to provide a "generic" definition, such as "ultimate concern" or "the feeling of absolute dependence." What such definitions do indicate well, however, is that religion cannot be grasped in terms of specific assertions or dogmas to be held by adherents but has to be seen as a specific activity of people.

In this paper "religion" refers to the manifestations—personal, institutional, communal—of a particular tradition. The Christian "religion" is that activity which centers in a perception of reality in which Jesus of Nazareth, a historical figure, the Christ is seen as embodying the revelation of what is believed in as "God" and claiming an allegiance overriding all others. That such a "definition" is restrictive and, possibly, argumentative, is conceded; it does express, however, how the term figures in this paper.

II

The dialogues between Christians of various Reformation and Roman Catholic traditions and Marxists in Europe—from both sides of the so-called East-West divide—have made it quite plain that neither Christians nor Marxists today can maintain an either-or dichotomy about each other, except for reasons of ideology, of false consciousness. The clear embrace of and reflection upon revolution as a praxis of private and public human existence by Marxists has given Christians access to dynamic anthropological dimensions of religion that had hitherto been swamped by different ontological and highly static theories. It has also opened doors to reflection on revolution far more in line with the post-aristocratic and populist-democratic political realities that shape modern life. The powerful iconoclastic tradition of biblical religion has provided for Marxists access to critical evaluation of two specific areas of their philosophy and praxis. 1) Even without destabilization, Marxist revolution "devours its children" insofar as it tends to lack the ability to prevent the emergence of a "new class". (Milovan Djilas of Yugoslavia argued this matter clearly in his book of that title.) 2) The balance between the "individual" and "collective" dimension of a human being is generally resolved in Marxist politics in favor of the latter and then detrimental to basic human rights. Christianity's iconoclasm of hierarchies and elites and its insistence that all persons, through belonging by their very nature to community, are creatures of God and, therefore, irreplaceable, provide for Marxist consciousness new foci for human praxis.

Marx and Engels, but also Luxemburg and Gramsci, were not only very sharply critical of religion but also very appreciative of the ethics, the life and death of Jesus. With the almost singular exception of Lenin, there is no significant Marxist who has not perceived and acknowledged the significance and uniqueness of the man from Nazareth. It requires no faithful apperception of Jesus as "truly God and truly Human" to see that following in his ways does not justify, in a quietive manner, passive acceptance of given conditions and injustices. It took the public, theological activity of politically responsible Christians to cause Marxists to question their view of religion as "the opiate of the people." It took the Christians' *practical* denial of the opiate-like function of religion in their lives that introduced them to the idea that for Christians the substantiation of their faith lies precisely in the will to change the world. Faith here does not spend itself in stating perceptions of God nor in explaining the world; faith is rather an activity, to be precise, a way of living that gets along without the supranatural, otherworldly conception of a heavenly being and without the consolation that such a conception offers. Faith is a manner of being without a metaphysical advantage over against the people without religion in which, however, Jesus' opposition to and transformation of given conditions and injustices is firmly grasped.

Such a Christianity does not lead necessarily to Marxism. But the disappearance of the opposition between world-renouncing contemplativeness and other-worldly metaphysics on one side and immanentist, world transforming social activity on the other caused the dialogue to start "between Marx and Christ"[4] and made apparent that they could well complement one another. The pathos of Marxist rhetoric is the rage against passive acceptance of inhuman conditions, against that "Christian resignation" that seems to perpetuate the suppressed existence of people. The pathos of much recent, "modern" theology is the denial that religion is to be seen as an objectifiable, a "reified" deposit of faith which, like other kinds of deposits, needs to be guarded with what turns out to be an ideology. When the intended humanism of Marx' program was thwarted, as it was under Stalin's bureaucratic Marxism (which reduced socialism to the establishment of optimal possibilities for the development of production energy and then restricted these energies to the production only of material goods, giving the well-being and dignity of human beings a secondary position to that of the "planned goal of production") a corrective became necessary. The Christian "religion" was seen as such a corrective, albeit not the only one conceivable. Many revolutionary Marxists were sure enough of their foundations to feel confident in the ability of Marxism to adopt into itself the dimensions of Christian personalism.

After these general comments, we turn to the specific example of the dialogue in the ČSSR. The thinking of four participants is to be touched upon. The Marxists are Vitezslav Gardavský and Milan Machovec, the Christians Josef Hromádka and Milan Opočenský.

III

Gardavský and Machovec wanted to give atheists access to Jesus. The latter published a book entitled *Jesus for Atheists,*[5] the former one called *God is not Yet Dead.*[6] Note a curious coincidence: Gardavský's book appeared at the same time when theologians in the United States published works declaring that God was, indeed, dead!

Viteslav Gardavský, born in 1923 at Ostrava, taught philosophy at the military academy at Brno until late 1968 when, in protest of the August invasion of his country by five Warsaw-Pact-member-armies on the orders of President Brezhnev, he retired. He worked for a time as a stoker, but died a few years later—a man silenced. He had studied German Catholicism, Freud, Fromm, Bultmann and D. Sölle; he was fascinated by the differences between Greek and Hebrew mythology. The story of Icarus demonstrates that the gods have set limits to what humans can achieve; the story of Jacob shows that the god of the Hebrews sets no unalterable limits to the development of human reality. The relation of Hebraic-Christian mythology to Marxist atheism is what interests him. It is significant that, in relating the person of Jesus to that atheism, Gardavský should insist on stating that "Jesus is a Jew." Jacob's humanity—more general: Hebrew anthropology—perceives humanity as being revolutionary, as being Promethean in the sense Marx had depicted it. Jesus' form of revolutionary humanity is told in the gospels in the category of love: "Jesus is convinced that before we can come to a radical decision. . . , we must be filled with love: we must be aware . . . that we only exist when we surpass ourselves. . . , and when we know that this act of transcendence challenges our minds, our strength of purpose, our passion . . . and demands that we should bring all our senses into play"[7] . . . "And if we look at it this way, love turns out to be the radically subjective element of history."[8]

It is precisely revolution where this lever of love must be put into action; "the world must really be changed, but the problem has now shifted. The world has gone through a head over heels transformation and must be interpreted anew if it is not to sink into ashes altogether."[9] How is the world to be interpreted so that appropriate changes can be made which prevent the loss of the world into ashes?

For Marxist thought it is programmatic that the symbols we live by have no transcendent, that is, otherworldly functions. Gardavský is convinced, however, that in the search for existence that can be called *truly* human, it is not necessary to regard religion as an opiate under all circumstances. The Marxian insight that "*religious* distress is at the same time an *expression* of real distress and a *protest* against real distress. Religion is the sigh of the oppressed creature, the sentiment of a heartless world, and the soul of soulless conditions. It is the opium of the people,"[10] remains unaltered in force. But when Marx described religion as suffering and protest, he made the connection between the individual's religious and social worlds; he drew attention to the social function of religious symbols. Gardavský's inference is that once the illusory and ideological facets of religion have been uncovered by the activity of rigorous logical and scientific analysis, then the whole range of religious, particularly Hebraic, mythology will assist tremendously in that search for genuine humanness. "Christians do not have to think of God as a prism in which the world is refracted [leaving the world to us for mere interpretation, presumably], for God can also represent a direct call for a socially and humanly responsible decision to act [that is, to act with a view to change the world]. In that case, the concept of God loses its dreamlike quality and challenges us to action in human terms."[11] Here, the concept of God functions as the spring of protest against the real suffering of people, which that concept had, indeed, helped to expose. The question of God can, therefore, be brought together with that of the human without dissapating it into illusion or ideology. It may be argued that Gardavský is concerned with the essence of religion in the interogative.

Radical Marxism means for Gardavský the search for all that has made up the human value of history. As atheism this Marxism seeks to bring that value to bear on the new, all-embracing, all-*human* future that is to be created by revolution. Here interpreting and changing the world converge. But here radical Marxism and radical Christianity also converge, for the symbols of Gardavský's atheistic metaphysics overlap with those of biblical mythology.

He cites three symbols which he derives from the Bible and applies to his metaphysics: the subjectivity and transcendence of the human, love which conquers death, and playful creativity which renounces the use of force. Through these symbols Marxism can do its best for the vision and praxis of true humanness; they express an obviously not yet present human era of communism.

It would lead too far afield now to describe these symbols and their substance; that is done in the article referred to above in note 6. What is useful to indicate is that a secular or "non-transcendent" reading of the biblical material can unearth a depth of meaning which a concern with orthodox exactitude or with apologetic polemics tends to ignore. Such reading certainly stimulates dialogue with Christians.

God is Not Yet Dead begins with the words *credo quia absurdum,* I believe because it is absurd; it ends with these: "we do not believe in God, although it is absurd."[12] Both protest the notion that it is simple to believe or not to believe. There is a huge distance between the view that we humans may live because God lives, the classic Christian affirmation, and the view that God is not quite dead, therefore, we humans are not fully alive yet, the classic atheistic affirmation. The atheist accuses the Christian of holding to an "absurd" religion in which the life humans long for rests on the death and resurrection of us all and that means that we are never really ever quite alive. Gardavský submits that religion to criticism and offers a vision of life with faith, hope and love; of transcendence, a vision without belief in God. But, he says it is absurd not to believe in God. The critique of religion as a symbol system with references to a realm beyond the human shows why there cannot be belief in God: it prevents humanity from ever attaining full humanness. To believe, therefore, is absurd. Atheism is a precondition for true humanness. But atheism is now also called an absurdity. Why so? The search for existence that can be called by the worthy name 'human', as Gardavský puts it, made him speak of the hope which in Marxist terminology is called communism—the community of women and men truly alive. His atheistic metaphysics expressed the vision of that community and the means of attaining it in terms of biblical symbols. But biblical symbolism is firmly rooted and has its life in Israel's faith in God, God the focal point of all our human potential and possibilities. A *theistic* faith in God is an absurdity, an *atheistic rejection* of faith in God is an absurdity because it robs the quest for truly human existence of its focus on and means towards real humanity. Therefore, the critique of religion as the opiate of the people becomes, in its search to find a way to interpret the world anew and to change it, the protest against the real distress of a world experiencing deep oppression and bondage. According to Marx, that protest was the sigh of the alienated creature, was religion.

J. Bentley summed up his discussion of Gardavský as follows: "Gardavský remained an atheist . . . an atheist *de profundis*. His atheism had nothing in common with the self-confident propagandistic atheism of the Enlightenment . . . He asked what were the functions that belief in God apparently still fulfilled (however inadequately) and Marxism, properly understood, ought better to fulfill. The question could be answered, he said, only when Marxism had soaked up Christianity. 'The Marxist', he wrote, 'is convinced that Christianity as a religious movement can be altered to fit in with socialism.' And he considered it 'patently obvious that until we are capable of making a fair assessment of the epoch-making phenomenon that is Christianity, we shall not be able to establish how far it has failed to live up to its own potential.' "[13]

The approach to the phenomenon of Christianity taken by Machoveč is relatively similar. Bentley speaks of him as "gentle and persuasive, unaggressive in his Marxism and in his leanings toward Christianity, [he] was nonetheless prepared to accept disgrace in his own country instead of finding, as he readily could, academic reward in exile."[14]

Milan Machoveč was born in 1925. From 1953 until 1970 he taught philosophy at the Karl's University in Prague. Since then, having been suspended from his teaching position, he is active as a "private scholar". His work *Jesus for Atheists* was not published in the ČSSR but in Germany and not in the author's native language but in German. A companion with Machoveč in the dialogue between Marx and Christ, Helmut Gollwitzer, wrote a brief introduction to it; he begins with a citation from Bonhoeffer, which sets the tone for the reader. "What does it mean when proletarians say, in their world of distrust, 'Jesus was a good man?' It means that nobody needs to mistrust him. The proletarians do not say, 'Jesus is God.' But when they say, 'Jesus is a good man,' they are saying more than the bourgeois say when they repeat, 'Jesus is God.' God is for them something belonging to the Church. But, Jesus can be present on the factory floor as the socialist; at a political meeting as an idealist; in the worker's world, as a good man. He fights in their ranks against the enemy, Capitalism."[15] Machoveč's new reading of the Bible—as a book which had claimed so deeply the life and work of his admired co-citizen Hromadka—led him to see it as a book which can bring people together or pull them apart. In reading it, people—now to use a biblical image—who were far away may come near, the first may become the last and vice versa. Machoveč makes it plain that he is an atheist. What constitutes his Marxist atheism? First of all, the modern perception of immanence: no divine interference in the course of the world, no revelation, no resurrection, no eschatological future of God. Secondly, the conviction that humans are the shapers of their history and that it is time that they shape that history responsibly for the greatest possible good of all people. The first of these views is not specifically Marxist; the second is specifically Marxist but not un-Christian. That Jesus' Word drives toward human deeds Machoveč himself demonstrates in the book; he and all Marxists greet—with total justification—those Christians, who are not put to sleep by the gospel but marshalled into activity as comrades in the struggle for a human shaping of the world. Jesus stands no longer between us as a dividing wall, says Machoveč; in Jesus' call for new action we can find one another.

His critique begins with the declaration that every Marxist knows something of Christian mercy, goodness, love of neighbour and universalism, none of which is denigrated. The problem is that, by and large, Christianity knows really only the dispensing of charity, that is merely individualistic initiative, incidental acts of well-intentioned betterment for thousands that cannot alter the fact that the existing antagonistic structures of classism continue to throw hundreds of thousands into deeper distress. Despite the noble drives of holy dreamers, there are more miserable people in this world than people on whom fortune has smiled due to Christian charity, including those who suffer unnecessarily and who could have been helped with the means proposed by Marxism. Instead of calls for mercy and love of neighbor there is to be the planned construction of hospitals and schools; instead of enthusiastic talk of non-violence there is to be gradual progress toward the classless society which—yes, only then!—will also be non-violent; no more speeches about the omnipotence of love but the establishment of the kinds of social institutions in which no longer the market-place and profit, money and power relate individuals one to another, but loving hearts and other natural human gifts.[16]

But is this not too beautiful to be true? Are the results of over half a century of Marxist practice so demonstrably clear? Are those who criticize what that practice has achieved only motivated by the base, egotistical interests of private capitalism?

Machoveč wants to know whether in the many contemporary appeals to Marx and the declarations of adherence to his thought there remain, apart from the faded name of the founder, any clear constants which, *mutatis mutandis* in Christianity, have remained untouched by the great, observable difference in the ethical stances of Marxists? When one examines the main concepts of the theoretical structure of Marxism, namely the classless society as the goal to be achieved, internationalism, political struggle against reactionaries and the commitment to scientific methods, one sees that they, too, are subject to values of peoples' current lifestyle, which value-hierarchy they subscribe to. The existence of powerful structures of state, of Marxist bureaucracies has created large numbers of *petit-bourgeois* and servile people who represent in their daily lives and their fundamental suspicion of those who probe more deeply a praxis in which the most sublime in internationalism meant blind obedience to the strongest centers of power. This only renders the moral-political dimension monotonous and impoverishes it.[17] People who are utter cynics and egoists may be called "good" here; others who seek and declare new values are called "dangerous" and every attempt to give Marxism new drives and powers may be called "revisionism". What Marx took to be the most crucial element of the commitment to scientific methods, radical critique, open critique of the key problems of social development, is prohibited by the "good" people in power. "To silence those who think different thoughts by forceful means has always been the highest wisdom for the *petit-bourgeois* soul when it felt its advantages threatened."[18]

Machoveč concluded that a genuinely Marxist, scientific view of reality requires that it be personally active in every individual and tied to quite specific values, namely those which have aided the advance of the scientific outlook on life, values such as searching energy, a Faustian unrest, a spiritual freedom that cannot be limited by a government's censure. The absence of such values will cause Marxism to be betrayed and cause its bearers to become the learned experts of the gradual, and peaceful, self-destruction of humankind. "Even though we may know only little of the substance of Jesus' cause, e.g. his call to help even those who think differently or his warning against pharisees who, while preaching correct and quite laudable ideas, still compromised them by their life-style: is it surprising or perfidious when in recent times hundreds of renowned Marxists, given the inner experiences of what has happened to Marxism, have shown growing interest in the cause of Jesus?"[19]

Like Gardavský, Machoveč questions the thesis of the primacy of the economic-material dimension; spiritual-moral values do not, like Athena from the head of Zeus, arise automatically from the economic basis. How can people who truly love the movement they participate in still believe in the sole healing power of the new economic basis? Is such belief faithfulness? Why does Marxism have to follow the path of another institution of not too long ago in which, it being so rigorously self-contained, one would have to become pope before one was allowed to show the full range of one's Christian conviction?[20] Machoveč sees real hope in the influence of certain "primordial-humanistic" feelings of people, certain relationships and archtypes which are not open to manipulation, which cannot be alienated: a mother's love, a father's protectiveness, erotic enchantment, the longing for a friend's openness. It is in relation with these archetypes (he actually calls them "stereotypes"[21]) that he praises the open and self-critical dialogue of Christians and Marxists: such dialogue uncovers those "primordial-humanistic" feelings that are not easily influenced by ideology. "In dialogue one finds that people differ from and are alike one to another in ways quite other than *Weltanschauungen*, isms, political diversities and ideologies. This insight helps demythologize systems and ideologies and to put them into the place where they really belong. One looses that panic-stricken fear of the seemingly all-powerful systems."[22]

"When I, as a modern human being, have taken cognizance of the full extent of Marx' work . . . and identified myself with its historical and liberating goals, when I am unable to 'believe' in a dualistic nature of the world, then I do not know why I should be not permitted to be deeply touched by the life and death of Jesus, why I should not regard it as 'my inheritance,' and understand it as a claim on myself, a claim that calls me into freedom and into deeper responsibility in the modern movement to which I belong and which I love. Nor do I know which goals and methods, which political and scientific parts of Marxist theory I would have to 'betray' as a consequence. For in both there stand at the center basically different but not opposed teachings."[23]

It is the Christianity of traditional fideism, of miracles and otherworldliness that appears as ideology to Machoveč. "The result of (such a view of religion) could neither be profound nor imaginative but merely a relapse into customary dogmatics and ethics which, in terms of substance, are clearly conservative and meagre in theory. For that reason, there is nothing interesting, remarkable or instructive in it for us: we can find this kind of servant of God and the intellectual level that goes with it easily within the generally known ABC of Marxist teaching on religion."[24]

Machovec was, clearly, influenced in his positive assessment of the cause of Jesus and its contemporary promise and possibilities by his reading of the theologians like Karl Barth, Dietrich Bonhoeffer and, particularly, his compatriot Josef Hromádka. In relation to the latter he wrote: "The sources of his thought are to be found in his earlier spiritual formation . . . especially in the Czech past, in the tradition of the Bohemian Brethren . . ."[25] Machovec refers to an immediately noticeable component of Hromádka's thought: the emphasis of a joyful and fulfilled human life. (It is *apropos* here to recall the remark of the ancient church's bishop, St. Irenaeus of Lyons, who commented that God's greatest glory is men and women fully alive. A slightly emendated version would be that God is not fully alive until human beings are, which then could be juxtaposed to Gardavský's reversion of Marx's comment that as long as God is alive human beings will not be fully alive.)

The gospel is "the way to humans," says Hromádka, toward people, without making ideological or political differentiations, to call people into further growth in humanization. This Christian humanism is to be traced to "the old tradition of the Czech Reformation, of Hussite visions and those of the Bohemian Brethren. . . , or of Chelčicky . . . In many of his thoughts, which in their theoretical sense are less radical than those of Barth, Hromádka can proceed quite far beyond the Swiss professor, simply because he is not Swiss, but Czechoslovakian."[26] He is a minister in a socialist country and he does not only see and observe Socialism, but experiences it as a lived reality in which he participates and is a part of, says Machovec. "Yet already in 1911 he set out to attack the professionalism, the comfortableness and the spiritual laziness of Christians. After the changes of 1918 he became nauseated by the [ever-present] cowardice. In his letters one perceives the abhorrence with which he characterizes Christians of his country. They are afraid of everything: Germans, Hungarians, Bolsheviks. Where was their faith? He wrote full of anguish even then that the tragedy of Christians consisted in the fact that they meant nothing anymore to society. 'What an amusing religion when one discovers that the constantly satisfied members of our churches rejoice over the fact that *in the past* we had Communists at Tabor [a reference to the old Taborites] and Bohemian Brethren who fought against sin and the world', he wrote in 1920. The provincially patriotic and humanitarian products of 'churchmen' evoked only loathing in him. He was aware that piety became a mantle for comfortableness and fear of social transformation, and knew that reactionaries, rural aristocrats, crafts people and cowardly middle-class folk fled en masse to the churches, only to praise the egotistical fear for their property, their opportunism and the reactionary stance as 'Christian'."[27]

Machoveč describes Hromádka's relation to Communism as follows: "He did not agree with Communists in every aspect. He was, however, sure that neither the petit-bourgeois in their fear nor the selfish land-owners have a moral right to criticize Communists but only they who made politically and morally more radical, challenging and lofty demands."[28]

Machoveč, finally, calls attention to the new dimensions Hromádka contributed to the inner-Marxist discussion, in addition to a truly challenging theology. "Hromádka asked whether the pathos of Marxist atheism that was allegedly so great and wonderful under capitalism and during the revolution, inspired as it was by the misery and suffering of millions and the heroic struggle of others to do away with all that, can remain at that level in subsequent periods. Will atheism sooner or later not leave an emptiness of heart in the lives of relatively satisfied people without distress and hunger, something like a vacuum which would give Christianity a new opportunity and hope?" And Machoveč comments: "The fact is that one cannot deny that the morale of communists, their activity and verve of life cannot rest in the epoch of Socialism in opposition to capitalism but need to find new resources in life . . . It is clear that science alone cannot give us a sense of life that provides sufficient value to us, for that requires other factors, especially that we have strong interpersonal relations and a solid foundation for the struggles of life . . . It is not surprising that especially this theologian should believe that precisely in the coming society a great and lofty mission awaits the true church. We Marxists do not share that view, but a state directed by Marxists must give believing people full opportunity to work for that mission."[29] And he ends with the unusual assertion: "Christians must have faith, must be strong in that faith, strong . . . Right now we ask: where is such faith, such strength? *Vox clamantis in deserto* . . ." (a voice crying in the desert).[30]

IV

In this section the discussion will focus on the Czechoslovakian theologians, Hromádka and Opočensky, and attempt to indicate their positions.

In a recent conversation with me, Josef Smolík, Professor of practical theology at the Comenius Faculty in Prague, said that a number of Christians in the ČSSR were sure right from the beginning that what had happened in 1948 was a new orientation, that the socialist change was not something to be regarded as provisional or as a mere historical episode. Rather, they argued, this change was taking them out of their traditional, optimistic confidence in the thinking of Europe and North America; it was leading them out of the culture of European traditions. He also drew my attention to a declaration, published in July 1962 by a number of people, both ordained and lay, about this "new orientation".[31] Of specific reference to this paper is the statement that in Czechoslovakian philosophy, as represented by T. G. Masaryk and E. Rádl, truth is seen to be personal commitment and concrete command in the actually existing situation. And that is seen to be a strain as well of the tradition of the Hussite Reformation and of the Czech National rebirth during the middle of the 19th century: truth requires personal engagement to be discerned, to be precise, truth requires engaged intervention in the events of the world.[32] But this view is held to be that of the Christian gospel also: "This gospel is an urgent challenge for us to strive for the radical renewal of all things human."[33] The declaration climaxes in an article, which expresses well what that great theologian and pastor Josef L. Hromádka had endeavoured throughout his life to teach his students and co-citizens. "With deep understanding we shall observe and follow the way of secularized, modern men and women. We shall listen seriously to their profound questions and affirmations including their atheistic arguments against Christianity and Church. We seek a living and truthful answer to those questions, which are also ours. To seek a concrete way and appropriate answers is the endeavour of a worldly interpretation of biblical themes and concepts. This undertaking presupposes that we consider constantly what is going on in technology and science, philosophy, sociology, politics and the arts. It presupposes that we observe the always changing mentality of urban and rural populations; it presupposes that we have constant contact with real life, with people of all generations and all spheres."[34]

But how is such an endeavour to avoid, as Smolik puts it, the *Scylla* of triumphalist religiousness, so characteristic of the Christian theological tradition, and the *Charybdis* of the opiate which such a gospel has often become in face of adversity? He believes that it requires a concentrated theological effort towards a Christian humanism. The specifics of that effort are for him "the engagement for men and women in suffering and hunger, deprived of dignity and subjected to economic pressure and exploitation. [But] this struggle for a foundation for humanity is associated for us Christians with extraordinary difficulty, because our ecclesial institutions are so closely allied with the rich nations. A new humanity, changed by the gospel and freed from the church's position of power and the temptation of wealth, can alone build bridges between rich and hungering peoples."[35]

Often, latterly all too often, such an affirmation is called into question by being called a politically one-sided theology. In truth, however, such affirmations reside *theologically* in a perception of the biblical God which Latin American theology describes in the concept of "preferential option for the poor", *ecclesiologically* in the perception of Christendom as universal, in the sense of embracing *all* Christians irrespective of their political stances, and *politically* in the basic visions of socialism.

The work, life and thought of Josef Hromádka can be well summed up in those three categories. He was born in 1889 in Hodslavice in Moravia, the same town from which Frantisek Palacky, the leader of Czechoslovakia's national rebirth in the 19th century had come. The radical piety and the radically practical orientation of the Czech Brethren, the twofold heritage of theirs, namely the critique of church and of society founded in the view of *ecclesia semper reformanda* and of *societas semper reformanda* (the church and the human community are continually to be reformed), combined in him with the ecumenically radical tradition of the Scottish Presbyterians. He died soon after his eightieth birthday, on December 26, 1969.

We have to deal with this central figure of recent Czech history at some length, and I begin the discussion with an autobiographical comment from 1968.

"I, too, am preoccupied today with the question why church institutions all over the world, in spite of their external historical and cultural differences, manifest a *bourgeois* mentality with all its limits and inertia that varies from one to the other only in degree. Why are they all so convinced that they have to be composed of serious and decent folk who should not soil their hands on account of having something to do with this restless, corrupt world? Why does one see so little of that gift of discernment in them that would make them able to overcome the boundaries of normal national, political and ecclesial life? Is it that way because we are not sufficiently rooted in the Bible? Or because we have not advanced far enough toward the heart of the gospel's revolutionary secret? Why have the churches of the Reformation retreated in theology and praxis into a few old Reformation themes, such as justification by faith alone or *soli deo gloria* [to God alone be glory]? Why have we not taken seriously the fact that Jesus of Nazareth was tossed out of synagogues and the temple and condemned to death by priests and theologians? Why do we refuse to follow Jesus' example, who went among the lepers and the marginalized, declaring that he would lead those to his kingdom who had been pushed outside the gate, living now as the marginalized for whom no one cared? Why so little understanding for the reverberations of the social revolution? And why even now so halfhearted an attempt in the broad majority of the churches, including those in socialist countries, to come to terms with the events of 1917? These were and remain the theological questions which I have been preoccupied with since the end of World War I."[36]

Hromádka raises the same concern in a non-theological form: who is going to assume the responsibility for a backwards looking orientation at a time when the peoples of the so-called Third World are making radical demands for a just participation in the means to sustain and advance life, when liberal-bourgeois democracies could not perceive the question for world-wide social justice and when the promises of the French and Russian revolutions have by no means all been kept?[37]

The fruit of his questionning was the "socialist humanism" he developed over the years; it interlocked with the Christian humanism of which Smolík speaks. For both, such humanism, if advocated by Christians, resides in an anxiety-free option for men and women, whom Christians and churches owe nothing other than peace and justice, love and freedom in the shape of personal and political forms of life.[38] But bearing responsibility for peace and justice in society, when that is being shouldered in a situation of both minority-existence and numerous sacrifices, requires a tradition and practice of resistance. A church without privilege, living a *diaspora,* a dispersed existence, experiences the challenges of a society which resolutely secularizes itself in a way much more alertly and critically than a church that is still associated with the centers of political power. Such a church has also a clearer eye for the substitutionary religions which often undermine resolute secularization and revolution. The tradition of Hussite Christianity provided precisely the requirements for resistance, critique and iconoclasm that Hromádka has marshalled in his work of nourishing the responsibility for the renewal of church and society and which caught the attention of Czech Marxists.

Hromádka was not interested in a theology of revolution but in a theology for revolution. I believe that one must not interpret that to mean that he rejected revolution as an option for Christians, rather that he rejected theological transfigurations of revolutions. It was plain to him that the road back to a bourgeois society was closed off to Christians in the ČSSR because that would, in the first instance, require a counter-revolution there and, in the second, demand specifically of Christians that their own revolutionary consciousness, shaped in the crucible of their tradition and concrete reality, was a false one.

All the crucial questions concerning the reality and meaning of God's self-revelation in the people of Israel, through the prophets and in the incarnation of the Word in Jesus of Nazareth are *the* focal point of our theological work. Tied to that is the struggle about the being and mission of the church of Jesus Christ. We find ourselves in a total transformation of our Central and Eastern European society. At issue is not simply a political change in the international situation, not only a political reform of our nations, but a deep historical change of our civilization, our life-style and the secular aspirations for the future. The highest ideals and standards of Western democracy have, in our judgment, ceased to be the norm, standard and arbiter of human future and civilization.

I am personally convinced that Western democracy, having failed in the critical years between 1918 and 1938, would not be in a position to master the problems of those areas with its institutions, standards and spiritual power . . . I want to ask those in the West who do not understand us whether they are so sure of their faith, whether the spiritual situation in the countries in the West is so obviously better than it is with us and whether it is indeed possible to work successfully for the gospel in a *bourgeois* capitalistic country . . . The manner in which socialist countries or Communism are opposed 'in the name of Christianity,' is basically wrong, ill-placed and perverse. That process is rapidly becoming the undertaker of the church in many countries—and not only of the East.[39]

This Christian insistence on "doing repentance" is what leads Hromádka to accept that the birthright of primogeniture has been lost by the so-called Christian nations of Europe and North America, that the era of the predominance of Christian civilization is over. Gone is the certainty that only a form of society, erected on the patterns of Western cultural traditions, can guarantee the future of the Christian church. It is still highly perplexing for many that a large part of the world, including some European nations, have broken loose from those traditions and have begun a new experiment of social, economic, political and ideological transformation.

[And yet] the atheism of Marxist ideology is nothing new. It is only a radical expression of modern European revolutionary consciousness. From the days of the Renaissance and the Enlightenment there moves, somewhere deep in the heart of every European and American citizen, the vision of humanity without God . . . But that atheism has become the uncompromising, official ideology of Communist and radical socialist parties and has rocked the traditional churches everywhere. This shock has also facilitated the victory of conservatism, anti-socialism and anti-communism of post World War times in the hearts of the great majority of Christians . . . Christian Churches have been prevented [by this ideological split] from moving forward to the most essential problems of the postwar years, from understanding men and women in their anxiety and restlessness, their guilt and aspirations, in that which mortally endangers them and brings them greatest hope.[40]

Before addressing specifically the perception of revolution in recent Czech Protestant theology, a brief summary description is required of what Communism means to Hromádka. He sees Communism to be a revolutionary, a dynamic movement which in November 1917 (according to the Russian calender in late October) opened a new historical epoch to which people everywhere have to relate in one way or another. Communism is so gigantic a factor, that we have not finished with it by any means. From the end of World War I to this day the Russian Revolution marks history in a way that some view with suspicion and, yes, fear, others with anticipation and joy. Hromádka warns against abstract discussion of Communism as much as of Christianity. How easy it is to reduce them to religious and political doctrines, to abstract scholasticism. Yet the failure of such discussions to comprehend and deal appropriately with historical changes are apparent to astute observers of history.

Communism is not only a doctrine, a theory or a political conception. As we speak of it today Communism is an historical phenomenon that turns things around, a complicated stream of communal life. Communism—it is the Soviet revolution and Soviet Russia. Communism—it is the workers movement based on the program of Marx. Communism—it is a specific philosophy, Marxism, scientific socialism and dialectical materialism. It is also the Communist parties in Russia, China, here and in many other countries. But Communism is also the dynamic of current history that is so hard to define, something which hangs in the air and that acts, to speak in human terms, as an unstoppable striving so that our shattered world of today be built up again not on personal advantages, interests, profits and privileges but on social equality, security, collective cooperation of the peoples' masses. Communism—it is that, in part obscure, in part definite, consciousness that the nations and countries [that] until 1938 bore the responsibility for leading and organizing the order of the world are no longer able morally or politically to master the tremendous tasks of the world after the [Second World] War.[41]

However much the fact of living in a socialist-communist country shapes a view of revolution, it would be false to say that Czech theologians, at least those discussed here, perceive revolution simply in terms of Soviet ideology.

Hromádka's approach is that of an historical analyst. For him revolutions inevitably are deep incisions into the process of historical development. Revolutions are steeped in dreams and longings on the one hand and in errors, sins and failures on the other. The single concept of "suffering" brings these two sides together. Born in suffering, revolutions also bring suffering; but this suffering is worth bearing. The old Hussites sang in one of their chorals "Christ is worth bearing all this suffering for." There, in the Hussite struggles the old Bohemians and Moravians discovered that the gospel of Christ was indeed a mighty driving force of revolution: of the search to have here new, better mutual relations in society, a search, fraught with hardship, but made bearable by that gospel. Hromádka cites the dimensions of the gospel in the revolutions of Wyclif and Cromwell, in the Scottish revolution of Knox, or, without citing the names of Christian leaders, the influence of theocratic convictions in the American revolution.

Yet not every storm or coup is a revolution; revolution is not born from capricious protest against old orders or from fanatic haste. A real revolution is founded in indisputable facts. It is a matter of human existence, it seeks to make human orders more just, to fit them better to current historical reality and to give people the opportunity to replace old, unfruitful orders with something else. "A true revolution is guided by responsible, patient people who are determined to shoulder the burdens of decision-making and leadership. Yes, the danger of senseless destruction lies in every revolution; from time to time unworthy people have pushed themselves forward in revolutionary struggles . . . True revolutionaries must be circumspect and defend the revolution against meanness, unnecessary harshness and arbitrary actions . . . Revolution creates the conditions in which what has been achieved in the human struggle for real humanness, may be cleansed and safeguarded and not only for today but also for tomorrow . . . Counterrevolutions renew that which was outlived, that which, attempted to be revived by artificial means, leads to the decline of society with all the concomitant moral and political repercussions. A true revolution is costly . . . It demands so much from people . . . That is why every revolutionary time forces people to examine their inner moral and spiritual abilities and to determine whether these abilities are strong enough to deal with these tremendous and taxing tasks."[42] Hromádka wrote this not during the "Czechoslovakian Spring", 1968, but in the "darker" days of 1957.

Milan Opočenský was Hromádka's assistant as a student—that onerous and exhilerating existence of intellectual and, at times, even physical symbiosis with one's teacher. For several years he served as secretary to the World Christian Student Federation; in 1966 the then 35 year old carried major responsibility for the absolutely pivotal WSCF conference on "Church and Society" in Geneva, which turned out to be the event that reoriented most of the significant Continental and American Protestant theologians. He is now professor of Christian social ethics at the Comenius Faculty in Prague. In reading his much more "scholarly" treatment of revolution, one senses unmistakably the influence of his great teacher.

Christianity helped formulate, propagate and put into practice the revolutionary ideals of a class-less society, of freedom, equality and justice. Even Communism cannot be understood without the spiritual and ethical heritage of Christianity. If Christianity has helped decisively in the development of these ideas then it is impossible to deny its participation in the victory of a socialist revolution. If that is so "then one can claim that the most valuable aspects of the Communist revolution and its achievements cannot be maintained without Christianity."[43]

One must distinguish between short-term goals of revolution, such as assuming power and establishing a new situation for the oppressed, and long-term ones, such as the ideal of a class-less society and an integrated multi-racial world. In order to avoid stagnation or even counterrevolution, the original motives of a revolution must be kept constantly alive. "It is perhaps a Christian duty to be concerned with permanent revolution."[44] The aims of a revolution, Opočenský asserts, are relative. No revolution can completely solve problems. That is why a revolution should be viewed as a long-term process of radical humanization, a process that has immediate significance for matters of peace and justice. For him it is also clear that for a Christian to look upon revolution with hope is not a leap away from the gospel: "When Christians work for the revolution they derive their right to do so not from an idea of revolution but from the gospel. And so the revolutionary aims of justice and humanization, as propagated by the revolution, are not relativized."[45]

For the Christian and the Marxist the question is: what in the position of the other need I reconsider, respect and, possibly, accept into my own? What in mine need I think about in the light of the other without, at the same time, distorting it? Outsiders might observe that such questions, arising from dialogue, are at best indications of relaxed phases in the encounters of Marxism and Christianity, of times when "socialism puts on a human face," as it did under Dubcek. At worst they are the symptoms of two antiquated systems moving towards each other that, having lost their powers of attraction, seek through mutual interaction to call attention to themselves.

Whatever one may say about the Christian-Marxist dialogue in other countries, such as the USSR, Poland, the Germanies, France, Italy, Hungary, the mutuality of the Czechoslovakian partners in the tradition of Jan Hus provides for a confluence that needs careful attention. Hromádka's and Machoveč's references to Hus and the Czech Brethren are clear in the discussion thus far. But Gardavský, too, refers explicitly to the heroic struggle against feudalism, adding that the "Reformation has a special significance for us Czechs and Slovaks, for our ancestors were among the first to herald its arrival."[46] Opočenský discusses the ethos of Jan Hus' work and that of his successors under the insightful title of "resistance against the spirit of the Constantinian era", the age of too close an identification of the church with the powers of the throne.[47] There is a common revolutionary tradition, a humanism steeped in hope and passion, which, while not leading to a commonly held view of reality, alerts both sides to commonly held, albeit differently assessed, ideals and goals. In these revolutionary goals and programs Jesus figures significantly "for both partners in the dialogue." The Marxists have a christology that is about a Christ without God; the christology of the Christians is, of course, about a Christ with God. For both, however, clearly it is a Christ who is with and for human beings, a man of the people, for the people.

The Czechoslovakian theologian, Jan Milic Lochman, who now teaches in Switzerland, puts the overlap and divergence of these views of Christ into the insightful question: if Prometheus is the quintessence of the Marxian anthropological symbolism and Jesus that of the Christian, is there room for both Prometheus and Jesus in *both* symbolisms? Must Prometheus be the antipode of Jesus and the "gentle Jesus" the one of Prometheus? For many centuries Prometheus was seen in Christian theology as representing symbolically all that Jesus was not: rebellious, defiant of the gods' will, self-reliant. And when Karl Marx spoke of Prometheus as the best embodiment of the revolutionary spirit of Communism, since he, damned by the gods, is representative of the proletariat, the abhorrence in Christianity grew even worse. Yet, Lochman's study concludes that the Christian-Marxist dialogue in the ČSSR shows that in no other calendar of saints Prometheus has a better place than in the Christian one![48]

The biblical God does not bind rebellious Adam-Eve in chains, turning them into creatures to be pitied; this God "is no jealous cosmos police-officer, who guards the boundaries of an untouchable principality. The God of the Bible creates humans in the image of divinity. . . , (they) are born partners of the covenant. This God does not hoard the 'fire' of creation but shares it with humans. And not only the fire: the very self of this God is communicated to humans; in Jesus Christ God so walks the way of humans that they may walk their way by themselves."[49] In the biblical view, humans are free and creative beings who in nature and imagination are oriented toward self-transcendence; they are beings who question what and where they are because they desire what, precisely because of God's creation of them in their image, is already burning in them. These God-created beings are Promethean. And that is their glory and danger. Gardavský's Jacob takes on the role-model of Prometheus; he is the first true human since he wrestled with the deity and won, with wounds, the right to shape his ways. For Jacob there could exist no more metaphysical division between humans and the divine; they no longer stood on separate steps of the ontocratic ladder of being. Gardavský repudiates a long-held religious class-structure of gods and humans by pointing to Jacob. And Christian theologians saw in that Marxist mirror how the great weight of Christian tradition has pushed aside over and over again the dynamic aspects of that radical biblical heritage in favor of otherworldliness or inwardness, the aspects Marxists call the opiate.

Hromádka's anthropology, founded on his christology, held up a Christian mirror in which Marxists saw how their critique of religion reckoned with a God that had all the features of Zeus but not the one the prophets, whom they called upon in the name of YHWH. Zeus has the features of a religious-repressive class-structure; atheism is, of course, the only way of emancipation from such repression.

Machovec's study of Bonhoeffer had alerted him to the fantastic critique of 'cheap grace' found in *The Cost of Discipleship:* cheap grace is grace that has no echo, no responding works; cheap grace is consolation without repentance. It is an opiate. And the whole Hussite tradition was a sharp repudiation of cheap grace. Of course, the Hussites could have survived had they chosen the road of quietism, had they made grace an opiate instead of seeing it as the very hope in their lives and deaths for freedom, justice and peace.

But what if the Promethean "salvation by revolution alone" indeed turns out to make humans like the gods, what then? What will it be like to exist after "salvation" and without revolution? How will that "salvation" be prevented from devouring its children? The *problematique* of Marxist ideology concerning revolution resides precisely in the fact that revolution is far more than a political event: the ultimate possibilities of human life are made manifest in it. "The triumph over unjust economic structures releases a universal process of salvation. The self-realization of the working men and women brings fulfillment to nature and history. Revolution, too, has salvation dimensions."[50] Here Christians say: No! The hope for the world's redemption that is focussed in the God of Jacob and of Jesus indeed beholds history but that redemption which takes place in history is not the achievement of history.

But must the Promethean rebellion be interpreted always as a successful, though back-firing, drive to be like the gods, the attempt to have what they have even without being one of them? Must it always be the desire, yes, the lust, to be like God (Genesis 3:5)? What if Promethean rebellion means to suppress the self-transcendent spirit, to quench the fire of God in us, and through sloth deny participation in the liberating action of that God in history? Then sin against God would not be to engage in revolution, to refuse abhorrence of Prometheanism, but would be to conserve what exists now at any cost.

Precisely because the goal of this struggle for a more human existence is *not* to make gods of people but to establish political structures that further men and women to become and then remain human in freedom, equality and sister/brotherliness it is a revolutionary struggle. After all, the "divinization" of humans may well stay in the individualistic, private sphere, may be a "religious" process of inwardness and otherworldliness. Not so the "hominization" of people; it is a political, public and Promethean process which, as will be shown later, is anti-ideological and open to atheistic as well as religious input.

V

Dialogue is a modern concept inasmuch as conversation among persons that meet beyond boundaries of otherness or enmity so as to clear up misperceptions and to learn from one another is essential to pluralistic, democratic life. It is thoroughly modern that Christianity and Marxism, two 'closed systems', should have opened themselves one to the other for such conversation. To disrupt or destroy such dialogue is anti-modern, whether that happens in socialist or non-socialist countries is irrelevant to that assertion.

Dialogue implies openness to legitimate critique and the readiness to accept better judgment, to become an 'open system'. Whenever all values are questioned and examined, genuine encounter of people becomes truly possible. That was one of the irreducible insights which the Enlightenment in Western Europe in its various French, English, Scottish, American and German forms defended. In the terminology of Christian theology that insight is expressed like this: only they who are ready to enter into the depths of human existence, in full cognition of their own fragility and guilt, are capable of encountering others. Dialogue and modernity require going deeper in encounter than to the levels of *Weltanschauung* and ideology. Dialogue does not have to aim at consensus or the disappearance of boundaries; at the same time opposition in views of reality need not exclude dialogue.

While uncovering the foundational positions of its participants, dialogue also allows development of available options. When encounter makes plain that implementing the "moral" options proscribed by one's foundational position is not possible—it may be exclusivist—the search for "real" options is dependent on the mutual exchange of ideas which characterizes democratic politics. When Aristotle was asked: who is human? he answered: the one who has a voice in the *polis* in the public life of community. For him that meant in fact the aristocracy. Large segments of the population had no part in any *polis* and were, consequently, not 'humans'. Under the conditions of modernity full participation in the political order is enshrined as a basic human right. When asked: what is it to become and remain human? Christianity and Marxism need to show what they legitimate or sanction in respect to that aspect.

Both have demonstrated in their histories that they can legitimate almost everything from the loftiest to the basest in the realm of public policy. It was their advocates' assumption that providing a religious or, in the case of Marxism, a 'scientific' legitimation meant also supplying a sufficient moral foundation for specific programs; but that assumption is fallacious in a democratic community. For the issue of "who" provides the legitimation is not irrelevant to the morality put forth. Predominant values of a community reflect always who predominates in that community. Legitimation, therefore, becomes a question also of power; in modern, democratic states power is, at least constitutionally, shared by the citizens. It is the aim of populist revolutions to assure that a nation's political power be open to the participation of all citizens; in that feature revolutions differ markedly from revolts, in which one group wrests power from another only to possess it in equal exclusiveness.

This paper maintains that a truly "public" approach to politics requires an anti-ideological view of reality, a view that stresses the open space between people in which they may freely speak, critique and dialogue and has a perception of wholeness that is not dominated by one view alone. If that view were then to gain access to a community's center of power, seeking to supplant other views, it would become an ideology—it demodernizes, de-differentiates plurality and becomes a solid mass, inasmuch as the open space of dialogue is gone.

Ideology operates in terms of simple fragmentation; in a political constellation people are either in or out. Ideology, therefore, creates a moral universe in which adherence to party politics is virtue. Soviet ideology in Czechoslovakia made it plain to those Hussite Christians who, through their own rootage in revolution, experienced that the course of the Russian revolution, ever more excluding internal critique and dialogue with others, was increasingly devouring its children. The attempt of those Christians to turn their church into a "public" church, one critically appreciating modernity and the factual existence of the course of their own history, opened the possibility for dialogue with similarly sensitive Marxists. Just as a de-ideologized Christian religion can assist in democratizing politics and become Promethean, so a de-ideologized Marxism can appreciate the cause of Jesus and appropriate its human resources for truly open political life.

It appears to me that if not only the consciousness of a people is shaped by the stuff that makes for revolution but also its most 'sacred' public institutions of law and order, then the people, in their defense of that consciousness and those institutions cannot afford to depend on bureaucracies beyond critique, such as those Stalinist governments built up, or on religions that assign faith to the private and inward sphere, as it is argued by the churches of the "new right." For these are demodernizing forces. Permanent revolution promises the best chances for de-ideologizing religion and politics if the vision of an open and public life of community remains at the centre of the view of reality, of who is truly human. So much that is human is being sacrificed to Christian "standards" these days, to Marxist "doctrines" and in the name of the opposition that each drums into its adherents against the other. The dialogue of those modern Hussites raises hopes—for both sides, since both sides, exhausted or past the bloom of their own revolutionary struggles, discovered in that openness the sources of hope and energy that lay in them from the start.

NOTES

1. Martin E. Marty, *The Public Church:* New York: Crossroad, (1981), p. 37. (Cited as Marty)
2. Ibid., p. 37
3. Ibid., p. 43
4. J. Bentley, *Between Marx and Christ;* London: Verso Editions, (1982). (Cited as Between)
5. *Jesus für Atheisten;* Stuttgart: Kreuz Verlag, (1972). It is typical of British publishers to turn evocative titles, such as the one of this book, into lifeless ones, such as *A Marxist Looks at Jesus,* London: Darton, Longman and Todd, 1975?
6. Harmondsworth: Penguin Books, (1973). An extended, albeit introductory study of this book and Gardavský's *Hoffnung aus der Skepsis* is found in Martin Rumscheidt: "Religion as Critique; The Atheism of Gardavský" in *Studies in Religion/Sciences Religieuses,* vol. vi., no. 2, pp. 149–157.
7. *God is Not Yet Dead,* p. 48–9. (Cited as God)
8. Ibid., p. 33
9. *Hoffnung aus der Skepsis;* Munich: Chr. Kaiser Verlag, (1970), p. 15.
10. Karl Marx: "Toward the Critique of Hegel's Philosophy of Right" in *Marx and Engels: Basic Writings on Politics and Philosophy,* Lewis S. Feuer, ed; Garden City: Anchor Books, (1959), p. 263.
11. *God,* p. 200
12. Ibid., pp. 7 and 218
13. *Between,* p. 144
14. Ibid., p. 159
15. *Jesus für Atheisten,* p. vii
16. Milan Machoveč, "Die Sache Jesu und marxistische Selbstreflexionen" in Fetscher, Machoveč, eds., *Marxisten und die Sache Jesu;* Munich-Mainz: Kaiser-Grunewald, (1974), p. 85–6. (Cited as Marxisten)
17. Ibid., p. 89
18. Ibid., p. 90
19. Ibid., p. 92

20. Ibid., p. 95
21. Ibid., p. 98
22. Ibid., p. 99
23. Ibid., p. 101
24. Milan Machoveč, *Marxismus und die dialektische Theologie: Barth, Bonhoeffer und Hromádka in atheistisch-kommunistischer Sicht;* © of the German translation, Zurich: Theologischer Verlag, (1965), p. 126. (Cited as Theologie)
25. Ibid., p. 129
26. Ibid., p. 131
27. Ibid., p. 131–2
28. Ibid., p. 135
29. Ibid., p. 140–2
30. Ibid., p. 143
31. Bé Ruys, Josef Smolík, eds., *Stimmen aus der Kirche der ČSSR;* Munich: Chr. Kaiser Verlag, 1968, pp. 99–103. (Cited as Stimmen)
32. Ibid., p. 9
33. Ibid., p. 101
34. Ibid., p. 103
35. Ibid., p. 123–4
36. In Martin Stöhr, ed., *Der Geschichte ins Gesicht sehen;* Munich: Chr. Kaiser Verlag, (1977), p. 347. (Cited as Geschichte)
37. Ibid., p. 348
38. Ibid., p. 349
39. Ibid., p. 282–5
40. Ibid., p. 275–6
41. Ibid., p. 157
42. Ibid., p. 254–5
43. Milan Opočensky, *Widerstand und Revolution;* Munich: Chr. Kaiser Verlag, (1982), p. 87. (Cited as Widerstand)
44. Ibid., p. 115
45. Ibid., p. 133
46. *God,* p. 13
47. *Widerstand,* p. 42–6
48. Jan Milic Lochman, "Platz für Prometheus" in *Evangelische Kommentare,* vol. 5 (1972), pp. 136–41. (Cited as Prometheus)
49. Ibid., p. 137
50. Ibid., p. 140

6

Religion, Ideology and Economic Justice

RICHARD L. RUBENSTEIN

On November 10, 1984, immediately after President Reagan's stunning electoral victory on an unabashedly pro-capitalist platform, the U.S. Bishops' Ad Hoc Committee on Catholic Social Teaching and the U.S. Economy made public the first draft of a proposed pastoral letter on the economy. On October 7, 1985 the Bishops issued a second, modified draft. The first draft letter was presented at the annual national meeting of all U.S. Catholic bishops. Although the draft was, of necessity, a tentative statement, it did indicate that in the final letter, the majority of the bishops were likely to express profoundly ambivalent opinions about the capitalist system. The same ambivalence is evident in the second draft.

The proposed letter had its origins in the U.S. bishops' 1980 pastoral letter on Marxist communism. At the time some bishops suggested that a critique of capitalism also be undertaken. This was in keeping with the admonition expressed in the 1980 letter against identifying Christian social principles "with our own social-economic structure" and the observation that consumerism and America's failure to deal seriously with the sources of global injustice "weaken our credibility" and heighten the attraction of communism to the less developed countries of the world.[1] In both drafts the Bishops were especially critical of the extreme economic inequality in contemporary America and the world at large which they judged "morally unacceptable." To remedy the situation, the bishops proposed the following:

1. A national commitment to reduce the unemployment rate to 3 to 4 per cent, partly implemented by federally-sponsored job-creation programs targeted on the structurally unemployed. The bishops also urged the funding of public and private job-training programs.

2. Proposals for a drastic overhaul of the welfare system including: (a) uniform national eligibility standards; (b) a uniform minimum benefit level; (c) welfare programs restructured to encourage rather than discourage gainful employment; (d) annual cost of living adjustments; (e) participation by welfare recipients in the design of public assistance programs; (f) programs designed to strengthen rather than weaken the family.
3. Curtailment of the arms race which diverts energy and resources away from the economic problems besetting the nation and the world.
4. New labor laws designed to help workers organize unions, to prevent worker intimidation, and expeditiously to defend workers against unfair labor practices.
5. A changed U.S. foreign policy that would re-emphasize human needs rather than military programs. The bishops were especially critical about the militarization of the U.S. economy and American arms sales and arms grants to developing nations.[2]

The bishops' draft letter has been the object of considerable comment from both Catholic and non-Catholic supporters and critics. Coming so soon after the president's reelection, the bishops' critical posture towards free-enterprise capitalism undoubtedly surprised many Americans. Among those who have criticized the bishops on economic issues is Edward L. Hennesy Jr., a Roman Catholic layman and Chairman of the Board of the Allied Corporation. Hennesey comments:

> As a Catholic, I listen carefully and sympathetically when the bishops describe the plight of the poor as a special concern of the church. As a businessman responsible for managing an enterprise with 117,000 employees, I worry that the bishops' remedies, while giving a larger handout to the poor, might injure the economy on which all of us depend.[3]

Hennesy notes that approximately $72,000,000,000 is currently (1984) spent by the Federal Government on anti-poverty programs, with state and local governments spending a further $26,000,000,000. In addition, 36,000,000 Americans receive $190,000,000,000 in Social Security benefits. Without these benefits the Census Bureau has estimated that the number of retirees below the poverty line would quadruple. In the face of monumental budget deficits, Hennesy argues that the bishops ignore the fact that, as a country, we are living beyond our means. Thus, while the bishops go into considerable detail to propose measures that would increase Government assistance to the poor, according to Hennesy, they offer no serious counsel concerning how to attain the kind of economic growth that would materially diminish poverty. While the Christian Right has stressed the importance of wealth production, the Catholic bishops appear to have been been primarily concerned with its redistribution.

Father Andrew M. Greeley was another well known Catholic critic of the bishops' first draft. Although Greeley is best known as a popular novelist, he is in fact an important sociologist. Greeley commented:

> The bishops . . . have produced a document that is little more than a rehash of the party-line conventional wisdom of five to 15 years ago, with a touch of class conflict ideology (the poor against the powerful) that hints vaguely at pop-Marxism. They have, in other words, provided religious underpinning for the latter day New Deal of the 1980 Democratic party platform.[4]

The bishops' second draft was less subject to the kind of criticism leveled by Greeley. There was less emphasis on redistribution and more on macro-economic policies that could create the basis of a full-employment economy. In both drafts, however, the bishops emphatically rejected the idea that an "unfettered free market economy . . . provides the greatest possible liberty, material welfare, and equity."[5] The bishops' views were consistent with the traditional Catholic attitudes toward capitalism. Joseph Califano, Secretary of the Department of Health, Education and Welfare from 1977 to 1979, tells of a private audience he had with Pope John Paul II on November 11, 1978 in which the Pontiff declared that *both* capitalism and communism had serious moral flaws—in the case of capitalism, its maldistribution of material wealth, in the case of communism its repression of the human spirit.[6] The Church has traditionally been suspicious of ethically unregulated market economies. There is little in Catholic ethical doctrine that could concur in Adam Smith's faith in an economic system in which the sum-total of self-regarding economic actors yields the greatest good for society as a whole. Historically, the Church has tended to view society in organic terms and to reject the economic individualism of free-enterprise capitalism.

Long before Pope John Paul II expressed his dissatisfaction with contemporary capitalism, the German sociologist Max Weber outlined some of the reasons why the Church and many other religious traditions have had a tradition of deep distrust for capitalism. Writing of the antipathy between religious institutions and capitalism, Weber observed:

> The reasons for this mutual antipathy must be sought in the fact that the domination of capital is the only one that cannot be ethically regulated, because of its impersonal character. Most of the time this domination appears in such an indirect form that one cannot identify any concrete master and hence cannot make any ethical demands upon him. . . . Decisive are the need for competitive survival and the conditions of labor, money and commodity markets; hence matter-of-fact considerations that are simply non-ethical determine individual behavior and interpose impersonal forces between the persons involved. The penalty for non-compliance is extinction, and this would not be helpful in any way. More important is the fact that such economic behavior has the quality of a *service* toward an *impersonal* purpose.[7]

The extreme anonymity, moral neutrality and depersonalization characteristic of the contemporary economic order is a consequence of a market economy. Again Weber can instruct us:

> The market community as such is the most impersonal relationship of practical life into which human beings can enter with one another. . . . The reason for the impersonality of the market is its matter-of-factness, its orientation to the market and only to that. When the market is allowed to follow its own autonomous tendencies, its participants do not look toward the persons of each other . . . there are no obligations of brotherliness or reverence, and none of spontaneous human relations that are sustained by personal unions. They all would just obstruct the free development of the bare market relationship . . . Market behavior is influenced by rational, purposeful pursuit of interests.[8]

Having described the market system, Weber offers the following comment:

> Such absolute depersonalization is contrary to all the elementary forms of human relationship. . . . The "free" market, that is, the market which is not bound by ethical norms . . . is an abomination to every system of fraternal ethics. In contrast to all other groups which always presuppose some measure of fraternal relationship or even blood kinship, the market is fundamentally alien to any type of fraternal relationship.[9]

It is therefore not surprising that a highly influential group of Roman Catholic bishops found themselves in fundamental opposition to the Reagan economic philosophy in spite of agreement on such issues as abortion, school prayer and economic relief for parents of children attending non-public schools. No administration in recent history has been as committed, at least in theory, to free enterprise capitalism as President Reagan's. In spite of the President's assurances, undoubtedly made in good faith, that a "safety net" will be maintained for the poor, the logic of free enterprise capitalism is likely to lead to a progressive lessening of such support by the state. The poor have failed the ultimate test of the system, namely, the ability to prosper in the market place. When their failure is given a religious interpretation as a sign of divine rejection, there is even less incentive to be concerned with their fate. This does not mean that there will be no "safety net." Historically, a principal motive for state support of programs of poor relief has been the control and bureaucratic policing of potentially disruptive elements within society.[10] Such motives are, however, very far removed from Christian charity and compassion as understood by the bishops.

While capitalism has yielded an extraordinary advance in the material wealth, no system is as inherently destabilizing of fixed economic relationships. A major consequence of this tendency has been the misery experienced by the millions of human beings who have been unable to adjust to the technological and social revolution engendered by so dynamic a system. Those religious leaders, whose traditions are rooted in an era of relatively greater stability, are likely to find much that is wanting in American capitalism, especially if they focus their attention, as did the bishops, on the millions who have been unable to adjust to the system. Moreover, in addition to the ethical and doctrinal sources of the bishops' criticism, there is a demographic and socio-economic reason for the bishops' emphasis on the poor: The native-born, non-Hispanic whites of the South and the West, the regions that had prospered most in the 1970s and 1980s until the recent drop in oil prices, are predominantly Protestant. By contrast, large Roman Catholic working class populations are to be found in those Northeast and Midwestern states which have been most seriously injured by the decline of America's "smokestack" industries.

The Catholic bishops are not the only leaders who have evaluated contemporary America in the light of their religious commitments. Of all the developments in recent American politics, none has been as significant as the rise of the New Right to a position of influence and power in American politics. Until the end of the 1960s, those intellectuals and social scientists whose opinions influenced public-policy decision-makers included few conservatives and fewer right-wing intellectuals. Since then, conservative and right-wing academics and intellectuals have become increasingly influential in the shaping of the national political agenda. Similarly, conservative Protestant evangelical and fundamentalist leaders have moved from a posture of relative political quiescence to one of extreme political activism. Indeed, it is impossible to imagine that the political New Right would have achieved its spectacular gains absent the political activities of the New Christian Right.[11]

It would appear that the political program of both the political and religious Right is characterized by three distinct concerns. As we shall see, the three are somewhat contradictory. Yet, it is their very contradictory character that gives the Right's platform much of its strength. These concerns are *economic libertarianism, social traditionalism* and *militant anti-communism*.[12]

We have already noted the underlying assumption of the New Right's economic libertarianism, namely faith in the power of the self-regulating market place to transmute individual economic egoism into the common good. A corollary of this view has been a tendency of the Right to blame economic crises either on direct government interference in the market place or on indirect intervention through programs which transfer resources from the economically productive classes to the dependent and unproductive. Yet another source of economic distortion, according to the Right, is needless government regulation. The New Right would, if it could, dismantle almost all of the liberal New Deal and Fair Deal programs of the last half century. As President Reagan has reiterated, the least government is the best government.

Implicit in the New Right's economic libertarianism is a commitment to individualism and personal freedom. As noted, this position is profoundly at odds with the traditional views of the Roman Catholic Church. In contrast to the Roman Catholic view, the pursuit of individual self-interest is not regarded by the Right as disruptive but as the basis of the social bond. Although most New Right thinkers would accept Weber's description of the market community as essentially accurate, they would vehemently reject his social and cultural pessimism.

The New Right's optimism concerning economic libertarianism is dependent upon its commitment to social traditionalism. Fundamental to the Right's program is a reversal of what they regard as the breakdown of the family, religion and traditional morality. We need not dwell on the forms this program has taken on such issues as abortion, school prayer, womens' rights, school busing, pornography and the general secularization of culture. The Right's social traditionalism stresses the themes of community and behavioral restraint in which society is regarded as a network of shared values and integrating institutions. The Christian Right holds that it is society's function to bind individuals together, placing limits on their egoism, destructiveness, and self-indulgence. It is hardly surprising that the morals revolution of the 1960s and 1970s brought in its train a negative response on the part of conservative Americans. From the perspective of the Christian Right, religious people have at least as much right to restore moral and religious values to American society as secular relativists, often identified as secular humanists, have had in vitiating them. One astute observer has commented that what is at stake is the "struggle to define America."[13]

The third New Right concern is militant anti-communism. Communism is the political and cultural antithesis of the New Right's economic libertarianism. To the extent that right-wing thinkers regard the free-enterprise system as divinely ordained, as many do, its polar opposite must be viewed as satanic or, at the very least, an "evil empire." A practical consequence of anti-communism has been strong support for increased military expenditures and an active, anti-communist foreign policy. This in turn has helped to create the unprecedented budget deficits of the Reagan Administration. Although conservatives have traditionally sought a balanced federal budget, the current deficits go a long way to assure that, no matter which party comes to power in the decade after Reagan, the Federal government will be compelled to continue to reduce its support of social and welfare programs. The future has been so effectively mortgaged to military expenditures that, absent large and unpalatable tax increases, the Federal government has come close to reaching the limits of its capacity in non-military expenditures. Moreover, there exists the suspicion that this strategy was clearly understood by the Reagan administration and one for which Democrats were wholly unprepared.

The Christian Right has set about to transform America. It regards liberalism, which it sees as a bi-partisan phenomenon, as responsible for the monumental failures in the American system.

These became evident in the 1960s and 1970s, namely, the rise of a class of unemployed individuals wholly dependent upon a bloated welfare system, the collapse of personal morality and acceptance of religiously-taboo life-styles, decline of religious faith especially among established elites, the turning away from continuity with historic American cultural and social traditions (which are perceived to have had their origins in Evangelical Protestantism), rampant inflation, a punitive and dishonest tax system, the defeat in Vietnam and the contempt heaped upon America by the seizure of American hostages in Iran and by Third-World beneficiaries of American largesse in the United Nations.

Above all, it would be unwise to underestimate the importance of the Vietnamese defeat and the Khomeini hostage seizure in the formation of the new pro-military posture of the American Right or of the long-term bitterness caused by liberal opposition to the war. The Right is convinced that the war was lost at home, a defeat for which they hold liberal academics and media professionals largely responsible.

On the surface there would appear to be a very strong contradiction between the economic libertarianism and the social traditionalism of the New Right. By itself, untrammeled economic individualism has little interest in the constraints of social traditionalism. It knows no value more important than the "cash nexus." Recently, American society has witnessed all too many examples of unprincipled behavior in the service of the "cash nexus": illegal overcharges and deliberate cost overruns by defense contractors; the conviction of a former Asistant Secretary of Defense on charges of perjury in connection with his admitted misuse of insider knowledge to gain stock market profits for his mistress; the failure of a number of banks and dealers in federal securities as a consequence of the misconduct of their senior corporate executives. Indeed, the very decline in morals and religion that the New Right has decried may have been a direct consequence of a society whose commitment to unadulterated economic freedom knows few restraints. Such freedom can easily end in the very materialism, self-indulgence and selfishness which the New Right has opposed so vigorously.

Moreover, social traditionalism normally entails a pessimistic view of life which tends to encourage conservative constraints not only on individual behavior and morals but on economic growth and development as well. Such pessimism has not been a predominant element in American cultural mainstream. It goes counter to the optimism concerning the power of human inventiveness which is so much a part of the New Right's values and which has very deep roots in American experience. By themselves, neither economic libertarianism nor social traditionalism would be capable of generating the kind of political and social dynamism the Christian Right has exhibited in the last decade. However, when the two concerns are linked, they do not conflict. On the contrary, they generate an enormous motivating force which is rooted in the Protestant ethic and which, according to Max Weber, facilitated the growth of modern western capitalism in the first place.[14]

Traditionally, the most potent legitimations for material success in America have been those which endowed this striving with religious meaning. The Protestant tradition of serving God through one's calling gave to a career in business a status and a dignity it had never attained in pre-capitalist society. The conviction that one's business or profession was a means of serving God transformed what could have been unvarnished economic individualism into the basis of a world of stable social relationships.

The religious Right has flourished *because* of its combination of social traditionalism and economic libertarianism. Each component overcomes the weaknesses of the other. American conservatism captures the libertarian emphasis on material progress and individual success but transforms it into a calling, thereby placing it within the context of divine providence. At the same time, it adopts a traditional concern for social stability and spiritual values but without otherworldliness or pessimism about progress and human nature. The New Right is thus able to affirm *both* God and capitalism, social stability and economic and technological dynamism, thereby encouraging the individual to maximize his economic and professional potential without appearing to destabilize the traditional order.

One of the criticisms most frequently leveled at the New Christian Right is that its injection of religious issues into the national political agenda is inherently divisive and distracts attention from pressing national problems, such as the declining ability of America's older industries to compete in the world market, mass structural unemployment, and the long-term dangers inherent in the massive federal deficit. Those who criticize the New Christian Right are convinced that in a multi-religious, multi-ethnic community like the United States, government must be neutral in religious matters and that no religious group has the right to impose its views on others.[15]

Regretably, the Right's critics seldom appear to understand that the Right's insistence on the political significance of religious issues involves far more than blind dogmatism. Given the Right's non-negotiable commitment to free-enterprise capitalism, its insistence upon the political significance of religious values becomes an absolute necessity. By diminishing government's capacity to constrain the moral abuses and the human desolation a free market economy can visit upon the losers in the battle for economic survival, the only remaining constraint is religion. At the outset of this study, we noted Max Weber's pessimistic observations concerning the destruction of all "obligations of brotherliness or reverence" entailed in a depersonalized, self-regulating market economy. Weber was opposed to socialism and saw capitalism as by far the better system. Nevertheless, he spoke of the future under capitalism as an "iron cage," for he could foresee no force capable of restraining the amoral and dehumanizing characteristics of the system. At some level, the New Christian Right seems to have had a comparable insight and would create a godly, if not a Christian, commonwealth to counter the worst excesses of a purely market economy. Moreover, its vision of a godly commonwealth can hardly be said to be without indigenous roots in the American history.

Nevertheless, a godly commonwealth requires a common moral universe with its shared sense of obligation. One must ask whether such a community exists in America even among conservative white Protestants. Given the extraordinary diversity of origin, belief and values of the American people, is the kind of value consensus required by the New Christian Right realizable? Moreover, the problem of achieving an American value consensus is exacerbated by the recent tendency of some extreme Fundamentalist Churches to pray for the death of those who have been prominent in opposing their stand on issues such as abortion. Supreme Court Justice William Brennan has been the target of a number of such prayers. In spite of the best of intentions, it may not be possible for the New Christian Right to extricate itself or the nation from Weber's "iron cage."

Whether or not its public objectives can be achieved, the Christian Right can be expected to remain a permanent and highly influential aspect of the American political landscape. In part, its rise reflects the fact that a decisively important group has ceased to be politically quiescent and has gained an effective political voice. Its rise also reflects something of an Evangelical-Catholic and an Evangelical-Mainline Protestant power shift; in both cases favoring the Evangelicals and Fundamentalists. While American financial and corporate elites have remained predominantly Republican, Protestant and Anglo-Saxon, Catholic influence has traditionally been far stronger in the Democratic than in the Republican party, save for the South where the inclusion of conservative, white Southern Protestants in the Democratic party was largely a legacy of the Civil War and the Reconstruction period.[16] Although many conservative Southern Democrats identify with the Christian Right, the Republican party, especially under President Reagan, has been the Christian Right's party of choice. Moreover, in spite of attempts to win a permanent national majority, the party remains more fundamentally white Protestant in its leadership and ethos than the Democrats.

A number of social theorists have used the hypothesis of "status politics" to comprehend right-wing American religious and political movements.[17] According to this hypothesis, these movements cannot be explained solely in terms of economic or class conflict but as responses to challenges to their values, life styles and traditions. Thus, the 1919 ratification of the Eighteenth Amendment to the Constitution, which resulted in Prohibition, has been interpreted as the high point of middle-class Protestantism's ability to enforce its definition of social reality on the entire country. Prohibition was thus a "status triumph" for conservative Protestantism and a "status degradation" for Catholics and Jews who (a) did not share Fundamentalism's ethic of abstinence, (b) were more likely to be urbanized and concentrated in the Northeast and the Midwest than Evangelical and Fundamentalist Protestants, and (c) were far more likely to be immigrants or the offspring of immigrants, and hence less "American," than the Protestants. It is not irrelevant to this hypothesis that the era of Prohibition coincided with the enactment of the Johnson Immigration Act of 1924 which drastically curtailed immigration from Eastern and Southern Europe while favoring immigration from the Protestant nations of Northern Europe. At the time, conservative Protestants tended to be far more hostile to Catholics and Jews than are their contemporary counterparts. In 1924 the Ku Klux Klan's membership reached an all-time high and numbered in the millions.

Fundamentalism's "status triumph" proved to be short-lived. The 1933 Repeal of the Eighteenth Amendment represented a repudiation of the values of indigenous conservative Protestantism. However, this "status degradation" could never have been achieved solely by a Catholic-Jewish coalition. The active participation of the Eastern Protestant establishment and the mainline Protestant denominations was indispensable. These denominations were modernist and tended to regard the Fundamentalists in a patronizing manner as provincial, culturally backward, poorly educated and "fanatic." On issues regarded by the Fundamentalists as non-negotiable, such as the literal truth of Scripture and a triumphalist religious self-interpretation, the modernist position can best be described as compromising and relativizing. The patronizing attitude of the Protestant mainstream was reinforced by the fact that all of America's most prestigious academic and theological institutions were affiliated in fact if no longer in name with the mainstream, modernizing denominations.

The situation of the Fundamentalists began to change in the 1960s. According to John H. Simpson:

> Increasingly, Fundamentalist, Evangelical and Conservative Christians realized that the real enemy was not the Roman Catholic or Jew but the smiling, flexible, civil Protestant modernist who wrote them off as "religious fanatics" unwilling to take the rough edges off their beliefs and practices and glide along smoothly with others in the prosperity of post-war America.[18]

According to Simpson, it was not the challenge of modernity but "the failures of modernity in its guise as establishment America that provided the Protestant religious Right with the opportunity to go public once more." The Fundamentalists had always been convinced that their conception of a Christian life-style is divinely-sanctioned. By contrast, the modernists had difficulty identifying any behavioral norm as either literally sanctioned or prohibited by God. On one issue after another, such as birth control, pre-marital sex, abortion, homosexuality and even extra-marital sex, the modernists tended to take relativizing and compromising positions. Without a belief in the inerrancy of Scripture or an alternative source of moral and religious authority, it was impossible for them to do otherwise. Faced with the multiple crises besetting America in the 1960s and 1970s, mainstream denominations have had little that was indubitably Christian to contribute. As noted above, without a sense of divinely-sanctioned constraints, modern capitalism can easily become little more than economic egoism. After Vietnam, Watergate, the morals revolution and the Iranian hostage crisis, the Christian Right no longer appeared to be, or felt themselves to be, outmoded fanatics.

If the Protestant Right has experienced great status enhancement in recent years, the same cannot be said for the liberal wing of America's Roman Catholic Church. The bishops' letter is clearly a product of that sector of Church leadership which is politically and economically (if not theologically), liberal. Catholic liberalism can be seen as having experienced a considerable status decline recently. Within the Church, the appointment of conservatives such as John Cardinal O'Connor of New York and Bernard Cardinal Law of Boston to positions of preeminent leadership have been widely taken as signifying a trend away from liberalism. Indeed, it is difficult to imagine a committee led by either Cardinal as producing the bishops' first draft letter. Moreover, the growing strength of the conservative wing must be seen as a parallel to the rise of the new Christian Right and the relative decline of the mainline Protestant denominations.

The liberal origins of the drafts are all too obvious. As such, they reveal the letter's principal weakness. The bishops assign the "highest priority" to the fulfillment of "the basic needs of the poor." The document calls for the "evaluation of decisions, policies and institutions in the light of their impact on the poor." In the first draft the bishops took their stand with those who favor income redistribution rather than income incentives although this position was somewhat moderated in the second draft. By contrast, the Reagan administration and the Christian Right have a very different set of priorities. Neither the administration nor the Christian Right would accord "highest priority" to the problems of the poor, as do the bishops in the first draft.

As noted, even Catholic conservatives take issue with the bishop's call to base public policy on a "preferential option for the poor." To do so, they argue, would seriously injure America's prospects of achieving genuine economic growth and, hence, an enhanced capacity to alleviate poverty. It is this writer's opinion that the bishops have performed an important service by calling upon the nation to confront the moral dimensions of economic policy, both private and public, but they would have strengthened their case had they spelled out the economic as well as the theological rationale for their own position more fully.

This writer is also convinced that a crucial ommission in the bishops' drafts was the failure to deal with the multi-dimensional consequences of the rise of Japan to the position of the world's leading creditor nation, as well as the consequences of the rise of the so-called "little tigers," (South Korea, Taiwan, Hong Kong and Singapore). At no point do the bishops deal with the fact that Japan rather than the United States is in the process of becoming the world's dominant economic power, a development of enormous consequence for America's future. On the contrary, the bishops appear to take America's wealth and prosperity as a given. There is little recognition of the fact that this nation's wealth and prosperity can easily be lost, an issue discussed in greater detail below. Much of the bishops' concern in international trade is focussed on what they regard as America's obligation to assist underdeveloped countries and to assure those nations that they receive a fair price for their goods and services. Nowhere do the bishops deal with the fact that throughout the underdeveloped world, Japan and the "little tigers" are rapidly displacing the United States as the predominant trading partners. The bishops have little to say about the unpleasant, large-scale domestic consequences that will follow from our failure to enhance our trading and financial position in the international economy. Even America's ability to support the poor will depend on how well America meets the Asian challenge.

Nor have the bishops asked whether there is anything we can learn from Japan's "economic miracle." Obviously, Japan is a very different kind of society than the United States and what worked for that nation will not necessarily work for us. Nevertheless, there is one overridingly important lesson the Japanese "miracle" can teach us: *Japan's rise to economic preeminence was not the consequence of redistribution but of national policies aimed at the creation of new wealth.* Largely guided by MITI, Japan's Ministry of International Trade and Industry, postwar Japan utilized the most sophisticated, long-range economic planning to achieve her current worldwide preeminence.[19] While we cannot emulate Japanese managerial style, we had better take seriously the political and economic strategies employed by the Japanese to achieve what they have. The bishops have focussed their attention on some of the most urgent problems confronting American capitalism. They have, however, had little to say concerning how America can grow as a productive society, and it is only as a productive society that we will have the resources to meet the needs of the weaker members of our society who are the objects of the bishops' special concern.

The Christian Right has addressed, perhaps intuitively, a question which is absolutely fundamental to the American future, namely, "What is required to give capitalism an ethical valence?" Their answer is, as noted above, religious. Its obvious difficulty is that what Fundamentalism means by religion cannot easily be reconciled with American pluralism. A less obvious but perhaps equally important problem is the triumphalism of the Christian Right *vis-a-vis* mainline Protestant denominations, Catholics, Jews and America's increasingly numerous adherents of other traditions. Given that triumphalism, the Christian Right's insistence on the place of religion in the public realm cannot be divorced from its status politics. As such, it is not a unifying insight but an element in a struggle for power. In that struggle, it must be noted that the vast majority of the poor are not middle-class, white Protestants. Because the Christian Right is more closely identified with America's original religious and cultural tradition, it undoubtedly has the capacity to fare exceedingly well in any long-term status struggle. While the Right would not be likely to win a total victory—few victories are total—it may be able to create a cultural and political climate which is increasingly conservative in religious matters for all traditions.

A victory of the Christian Right could, however, prove to be pyrrhic. In their justifiable concentration on the challenge of the Soviet military strength and communist ideology to American interests, the Christian Right has all but ignored an equally serious challenge. As with the bishops, the Christian Right gives no evidence of having taken seriously the long-range challenge of Japan to America's economy and society. Regarding least government as best government, the Christian Right has had little, if anything, to say concerning the challenge to American interests of a competing society like Japan in which government and industry cooperate intimately in long-range planning which has as its objective the economic debilitation, if not destruction, of one American industry after another.

The Christian Right would relegate the problems of unemployment and poverty to the workings of the market place and private charity. The bishops propose to alleviate the problems by greater government expenditures on welfare and public works. By contrast, Japan has largely solved the problem of unemployment by an extraordinarily successful combination of planned industrial development and trade. In industry after industry the Japanese have "destroyed" their foreign competitors and made them dependent upon Japanese products. The process is relatively simple but requires the kind of cooperation between government and business which American conservatives reject: In the first stage Japan imports a technology, such as automobiles, television, computers and telecommunications equipment, from the West. While the new industry develops, its home market is protected against foreign competition. Since the Japanese market is one of the world's largest, the new industry is able to acquire the experience and achieve the economies of scale that will later permit it to win a dominant position overseas. In the next stage, the new industry enters the world market and offers its products at lower prices than its foreign competitors. This process has taken place in such fields as transistor radios, color television, cameras and automobiles. It is currently taking place in such crucial fields as microprocessors and advanced computers. In field after field, as Japanese industry translates cost advantage into ever larger market shares, it is able to improve quality to such an extent that foreign competitors can compete neither in price nor quality.

In the final phase of what is in reality a major battle in a long-term trade war, the Japanse company invests in manufacturing capacity in foreign markets, as has been done in the United States by Sony, Matsushita (Panasonic), Honda, Toyota and Mazda, thereby assuring a continuing market share for their product abroad. By contrast, foreign industries find it difficult, if not impossible, to invest on the same scale in Japan in spite of constantly repeated assurances by Japanese leaders to foreign governments that Japan is "about to take steps" to liberalize entry by foreigners into the Japanese domestic market. The same "assurances" have been offered for over two decades with the same predictable outcome.

Once the trade battle has been won, a successful Japanese industry can safely dispense with protectionism and Japan can honestly claim that it does not bar most foreign imports. For example, there is no longer any need to protect Japanese producers of videocassette recorders against foreign competitors. Japan's protectionism is currently concentrated on such industries as biotechnology, telecommunications, advanced computers and aircraft. After Japan achieves dominance in these fields, it will no longer be necessary to protect them.[20]

There is real danger to the United States in this trade war. Japan's trade strategy has proven far more effective in "destroying" American factories than could the bombs of an adversary. As one American industry after another atrophies or collapses altogether, increased mass unemployment becomes an obvious danger. Recently, the editors of *Business Week* published a lengthy "Special Report" entitled "The Hollow Corporation." The editors began by observing:

> A new kind of company is evolving in the U.S.—manufacturing companies that do little manufacturing. Instead, they import components or products from low-wage countries, slap their own names on them and sell them in America. Unchecked, this trend will ultimately hurt the economy-retarding productivity, innovation and the standard of living. And even the rise of a strong service economy is not likely to offset the decline of manufacturing.[21]

Obviously, there are many factors which have contributed to the decline of America's older industries which cannot be attributed to Japan's trade war with the United States. For our purposes, it is important to note that Japan has utilized the combined resources of government and business to devise a practical long-range program for keeping unemployment and poverty at a minimum in a period of revolutionary economic and technological change. Unfortunately, neither the bishops nor the Christian Right have addressed themselves seriously to these problems.

Undoubtedly, the small-town and rural roots of the predominantly middle-class Christian Right have played a part in its inability to consider seriously the Japanese challenge. Nor has the Christian Right's religious triumphalism served that movement well with regard to the Japanese challenge. Its contacts with the Orient have been largely mediated by its own missionaries who have tended to emphasize what the Christian world can teach non-Christians more than what can be learned from them. Nevertheless, if Evangelical and Fundamentalist Protestantism are responsibly to take the leading role in American life to which they aspire, they will be unable to ignore the long-term challenge posed by Japan, especially the intimate connection between Japanese industrial and trade policy and the problem of unemployment, poverty and economic justice in both Japan and the United States.

In conclusion, there is yet another reason why both the Christian Right and the bishops would do well to consider the utter seriousness of the Japanese challenge. On May 29, 1985 Mr. Kenichi Yamamoto, President of the Mazda Motor Corporation, participated in groundbreaking ceremonies for the new Mazda plant in Flint Rock, Michigan. The Governor of Michigan was present and took part in the ceremonies which included a two-hour dedicatory service conducted by a Shinto priest. When groundbreaking ceremonies were held for the automobile factory jointly owned by Chrysler and Mitsubishi in Bloomington, Illinois, there was a similar Shinto service. Unlike the United States, the sacred and the public realms are intertwined in Japan. One can never speak of any significant Japanese activity as being purely secular. On the contrary, as the Shinto ceremonies in Michigan and Illinois demonstrate, there is no such thing as a purely economic activity for the Japanese. The union of business and religion in Japan has been acknowledged by no less an authority than Soichiro Honda, founder and President of the Honda Motor Company. Honda has observed:

> . . . the people who shoulder the responsibility for the Japanese economy are also genuinely Japanese in the sense of being worshippers of the Japanese deities. These people are guided in their economic rationality, and they pray to the *kami* for the safety and prosperity of the enterprises over which they preside.
>
> Such Shinto belief is hidden at an unconscious level in the minds of the Japanese people and is the spiritual ground of belief tacitly controlling this industrial society.[23]

The Japanese challenge is thus as spiritual as it is economic. At stake is the question of which spiritual universe, the Shinto or the Christian, can produce the better society for all of its people. As yet, neither the bishops nor the Christian Right has seriously dealt with what may prove to be one of the most serious long-term challenges ever to confront the Republic.

NOTES

1. See *Origins: NC Documentary Service,* November 15, 1984, p. 338.
2. The text of the bishops' first draft letter is to be found in *Origins: NC Documentary Service,* November 15, 1984. See also Kenneth Briggs, "Catholic Bishops Ask Vast Changes in Economy of U.S." in *New York Times,* November 12, 1984, pp. 1, 15. The text of the second draft is to be found in *Second Draft: Pastoral Letter on Catholic Social Teaching and the U.S. Economy,* Washington: National Council of Catholic Bishops, 1985.
3. Edward L. Hennesy Jr., "A Pastoral for the Poor, Not for the Economy," *America,* January 5–12, 1985.
4. Andrew M. Greeley, "The Bishops and the Economy: A Radical Dissent," *America,* January 5–12, 1985.
5. Second Draft, p. 37.
6. Joseph A. Califano, "The Prophets and the Profiteers" in *America,* January 5–12, 1985, pp. 5–7.
7. Max Weber, *Economy and Society: An Outline of Interpretive Sociology,* eds. Guenther Roth and Claus Wittich, New York: Bedminster Press, 1968, Vol. III, pp. 1186–7.
8. Weber, *loc. cit.*
9. Weber, *op. cit.,* Vol. II, pp. 636–7.
10. See Richard L. Rubenstein, *The Age of Triage,* Boston: Beacon Press, 1983, pp. 60 ff.
11. For an overview of this development, see Thomas Byrne Edsall, *The New Politics of Inequality,* New York: W. W. Norton, 1984.
12. This author is indebted to Jerome L. Himmelstein, "The New Christian Right," in Robert C. Liebman and Robert Wuthnow, *The New Christian Right,* New York: Aldine, 1983, pp. 15–27, for the analysis of these concerns.
13. See Donald Heinz, "The Struggle to Define America" in Liebman and Wuthnow, *op. cit.,* pp. 133–49.
14. The classic source of Weber's ideas on Protestantism and capitalism is Max Weber, *The Protestant Ethic and the Spirit of Capitalism,* trans. Talcott Parsons, New York: Charles Scribner's Sons, 1958.
15. See Kenneth Connors, "Public Issues and Private Morality," *The Christian Century,* October 22, 1980.
16. See Edsall, *The New Politics of Inequality,* pp. 26–28, 68–70.
17. See Joseph R. Gusfield, *Symbolic Crusade: Status Politics and the American Temperance Movement,* Urbana Ill.: 1963; Richard G. Hofstadter, *Anti-Intellectualism in American Life,* New York: 1962.
18. John H. Simpson, "Moral Issues and Status Politics," in Liebman and Wuthnow, *The New Christian Right,* p. 201.
19. The story of MITI's extraordinary achievements, as well as its darker origins in the wartime Ministry of Munitions, is told by Chalmers Johnson, *MITI*

and the Japanese Miracle: The Growth of Industrial Policy, 1925–1975, Stanford: Stanford University Press, 1975.

20. See William L. Givens, "The U.S. Can No Longer Afford Free Trade," *Business Week,* November 22, 1982.
21. Cover, *Business Week,* March 3, 1986.
22. Soichiro Honda, "Shinto in Japanese Culture," *Nanzan Bulletin,* No. 8/1984, p. 30. This article originally appeared as "Bunka no naka no Shinto," *Shukyo Shinbun,* February 1 and March 1, 1984.

7

The Religious Legitimation of Counterviolence; Insights from Latin American Liberation Theology

WILLIAM R. JONES

Liberation Theology: Saint or Satan?

Unquestionably both the content of liberation theology and the approach it proposes . . . [namely] its insistence on a total economic and political structuring through violence (if necessary) . . . create a difficult if not dangerous atmosphere . . . [and] complicate the ability of the United States to conduct business in the Western Hemisphere. . . .[1]

This citation from a recent participant in the Strategic Studies Program at the National War College summarizies what the current administration and its apologists calculate to be the intrinsic morality and geopolitical impact of liberation theology. The core of this calculation is a condemnation of liberation theology in general and Latin American liberation theology (LALT)[2] in particular on the grounds that they provide "the license and possibly the inspiration for violence in the underclass' struggle for economic social and political equality."[3] Critics of liberation theology also seize upon its alleged commitment to revolutionary violence to link it with Marxism and further excommunicate it from the circle of legitimacy. It goes without saying that crucial geopolitical decisions have and will continue to flow from this understanding of liberation theology.

Proponents of liberation theology have endorsed what for many is a dubious even nihilistic right: the right to violence. Detractors of LALT find it particularly ironic that liberation theologians legitimate this right on moral and religious grounds. Some twenty years later, the image of the Colombian priest Camilo Torres—calling his people to rise up and revolt, taking up arms himself and being killed by government troops—is still vivid. This and similar images continue to fuel a caricature of liberation theology as a "bible and bazooka" Christianity where ultimate homage is rendered to the cannon instead of the crucifix.

The purpose of this essay is to challenge this portrait of liberation theology. I want to show that its perspective on violence is grossly misinterpreted and misunderstood. In what follows, I want to provide a more accurate and adequate picture of how LALT views the role, value and morality of violence in social change, a view which, if accurate, dictates a radically different rationale for opposition to liberation theology.

It should be clear to all that if policy makers are responding to an inaccurate picture of liberation theology's theory of violence, their game plan can not be trusted. What is at stake here extends beyond a faulty strategy based on background information that is inaccurate or incomplete. I want to suggest that the enormity of the logical and moral inadequacy of this criticism of liberation theology forces one to search for a hidden agenda and ask what appears to be a loaded question: is this criticism part of a calculated strategy to demolish liberation theology's moral legitimacy and thereby defuse a major threat to the economic, social and political status quo that the current administration wants to maintain in the Southern hemisphere? However, this question is entirely appropriate if one illuminates the maintenance needs of oppression, in particular the concepts and values it needs to perpetuate itself. It will become clear that the attack on LALT's theology of social change incorporates the basic operation of oppression itself.

The importance of isolating the inner logic of LALT and its theology of social change should be clear for public policy makers. The geopolitical implications of LALT's ultimate resolution of this issue are especially acute for the United States because of the obvious proximity of our borders. There is also the factor of numbers. Latin America is part of the so called Third World where it is estimated that the majority of Christians will be located by the year 2000.[4] Liberation theology's popularity must also be taken into account. Richard C. Brown, himself, concludes that an estimated "20 to 30 percent of the bishops (including archbishops and cardinals) are probably dedicated proponents" and "40 to 50 percent among the rank-and-file clergy could be classified as enthusiastic advocates." In addition, he allows that "possibly over 60 percent of the hierarchy" is also sympathetic, eschewing, however, its advocacy of "revolutionary violence."[5]

The impact of liberation theology's theology of social change also looms in importance once we consider what its popularity reveals: large numbers of the underclass, with life long commitments to the Church and Christianity, no longer swallow this food of non-violence as the only or even the best fare. And it must not be forgotten that these are individuals claimed to be the church's most loyal and dedicated followers. A similar movement beyond non-violence is clearly documented in the civil rights struggle in North America. Nor can we be blind to a similar demystification in South Africa at this very hour. What I draw from these connected events is this fact: policy makers can no longer praise non-violent models as the ideal and condemn revolutionary violence as a strategy for keeping the underclass in their place at the bottom of the economic, social and political ladder. This strategy is exposed daily as a hypocritical policy with an inner design that maintains the status quo with its massive inequalities. This, in essence, is the case that I will make in this essay.

Method, Scope and Semantic Clarifications

Because of a possible misunderstanding, it is important to identity more precisely my approach. To the extent that I challenge certain criticisms directed against liberation theology and seek to establish the presence of ideological taint in the critics' argument, my general approach can be regarded as *apologetic*. Technically, however, I am advancing an *interim assessment* of selected criticisms of liberation theology. An interim assessment is, in essence, a corrective enterprise, a criticism of criticism. Like Janus, it looks both backward and forward. It peers backward towards an earlier criticism—here the attack on liberation theology's theory of revolutionary change—that is seen as deficient and invalid. Given its forward bearing, an interim assessment becomes a proposal for a new method and a more adequate critical apparatus that seeks to avoid the errors of the earlier analyses. In this sense, my concern is not to establish the validity of LALT's theology of social change. Rather, it is to show that specific attacks upon LALT have been neither accurate nor successful, thus leaving the door open for LALT's critics to reestablish their charges on other grounds.

Let me outline the basic strategy of liberation theology's apologetic that we will explore in this essay—a strategy that boldly removes the moral onus from itself and places it on the shoulders of its critics! For our purposes, the heart of liberation theology's apology is the refocusing of the issue as the moral and religious legitimacy of *counter*-violence—rather than violence. This means apologetically that the violence of the oppressed, the group for which liberation theology speaks, is a response to a prior, "original" violence that created and maintains the oppression that liberation theology attacks. Hence the moral rationale of *counter*-violence, of *self*-defense, and of the *just* war. Any criticism of liberation theology that fails to engage this moral position as the fundamental issue is attacking a straw man.

Liberation theology's moral rationale for counterviolence, we will argue, is also misinterpreted if we fail to see it as the outcome of a specific understanding of the nature and operation of economic, social and political oppression. This understanding must be also regarded as foundational to avoid the unsound policy that accompanies a faulty decoding. For instance, to establish the legitimacy of counter-violence, liberation theology is obliged to show that the group for which it speaks is "oppressed." Obviously, this makes the category of oppression normative for the debate. The category of oppression is preeminent as well at another level; it serves to back LALT's critics into a corner, forcing them to respond to the charge that their criticism, almost without exception, is hypocritical, self serving and part of the ongoing operation of oppression itself. In this way liberation theology reduces the "legitimate" critics of counter-violence to that of the strict, absolute and consistent pacifist—a creature as rare as the statistical nonentities in the Kinsey Report who don't masturbate.

Two comments should be made about the scope of the materials in this essay. My purpose here is not to give a general survey of the literature on these issues, but to anticipate the religious justification for revolutionary violence that public policy makers in the future are almost certain to encounter in Latin America and the Third World. This means that our purpose here is not simply to focus on the general argument that LALT has already advanced but also to anticipate the further evolution of its defense of counter-violence. To facilitate this, LALT will not be my exclusive focus. Illustrative materials will be drawn as well from other representatives of liberation theology, in particular the black theology movement in the United States. Materials from the latter are valuable for several reasons. Drawn from our own recent national history, they provide an earlier, but parallel, evolution of this issue that is more familiar to us. In addition, the response of the establishment class in America to these contrasting models of social change, associated with Malcolm X and Martin Luther King are part of the history that informs liberation theology's own theology of social change.

Finally by way of introduction, let me outline the major sections of this essay and discuss some semantic stipulations. "LALT and Violence: The Critics' Case" summarizes the basic argument that we want to critique. "Towards a Phenomenology of Oppression," articulates the particular understanding of oppression that informs liberation theology's moral rationale for counterviolence. "Violence and Moral Legitimacy: The Not So Odd Couple," establishes and documents liberation theology's rationale for counter-violence. "Quietism, Anti-Powerism and Violence: The Mechanism of Oppression," illustrates the ideological manipulation of values to maintain oppression.

It is also important to unpack the meaning of ideology for this essay, since a specific negative connotation of ideology controls an essential part of the liberation theology argument. Ideology, on the one hand, can be used in a neutral sense "as a person's basic systems of goals and values, plus the means to achieve them—"[6] in sum, one's belief or faith system. On the other hand, we can speak of ideology in a pejorative sense "as a mental mechanism that serves certain class, race or other interests by concealing or sacralizing a given situation. . . ."[7] The latter definition's stress on conceptual manipulation and deception is usually coupled with a call for critical demystification and exposure. Certain methodological consequences follow from this second understanding of ideology, one of which is crucial for our argument. The presence of ideological taint can only be established by identifying a basic inconsistency between what one preaches and what one practices.

The term, violence, also presents critical problems that demand special attention. I will argue below that the very definition of violence includes a subjective component that is characteristically question-begging. Moreover, the counterviolence advocated in the liberation theology apologetic is not simply a negative mirror image of violence. For that reason, I will speak initially of liberation theology's "theology of social change" rather than "revolutionary violence."

LALT and Violence: The Critics' Case

Richard C. Brown's article noted above is representative of the typical strategy and argumentation of the critics of liberation theology. Their argumentative strategy, which can best be described as a "Saint and Satan" approach, is intended to destroy the theological basis for LALT's theory and practice of counter-violence. The logical scenario proceeds as follows: first, the "Saint" of the Christian, biblical or Catholic tradition embodies the definitive norm for Christian moral theory and public policy; second, liberation theology's theory and practice of social change contradicts this saintly prerequisite for economic, social and political holiness; therefore, liberation theology's moral imperatives and revolutionary policies must come from some "Satanic" source that is unwholesome and unprincipled. Most often, this satanic influence is identified with Marxism.

It is important to show how the specific category of violence links up with the "Saint and Satan" strategy. The argument begins by establishing that violence is antithetical to the Christian's moral strategy. Here, papal citations, some of which were directed specifically to LALT and others from an earlier context, are cited. The following are representative:

> We are obliged to state and reaffirm that violence is neither Christian nor evangelical, and that brusque, violent structural changes will be false, ineffective in themselves, and certainly inconsistent with the dignity of the people.[8]
>
> The sort of liberation we are talking about knows how to use evangelical means, which have their own distinctive efficacy. It does not resort to violence of any sort, or to the dialectics of class struggle. Instead it relies on the vigorous energy and activity of Christians, who are moved by the Spirit to respond to the cries of countless millions of their brothers and sisters.[9]

Next, the Marxist insistence on the necessity and legitimacy of violent revolution is stressed and compared to liberation theology's alleged commitment to revolutionary violence. Thus, LALT's moral imperative for radical social change is undercut in two ways. Its Christian legitimation is denied and its alleged Marxist inspiration is exposed.

Further consideration of Brown's refinement of the "Saint-Satan" strategy provides additional background for understanding liberation theology's apologetic position. The "bottom line" of this strategy is the charge that liberation theology's vital concerns are basically political and sociological, not spiritual or theological. Moreover, Brown insists that liberation theology's theological warrants for radical social change are only "secondarily" biblical. They are actually derived from the Roman Catholic social doctrines of the 1960s, particularly, the papal encyclicals—*Mater et Magistra, Pacem in Terris, Popuiorum Progressio*—the conclusions of Vatican II and the Conference of Latin American Bishops held in Medellin, Colombia, 1968.

These papal encyclicals contained a number of revolutionary economic and political ideals. They affirmed that "the absolute right to private property and the virtues of individualism over collective action" must be challenged, that "wealthier nations [have] a responsibility to provide aid to underdeveloped nations in such a way as to avoid creating a new form of colonialism," that the "fulfilling of people's social as well as their spiritual needs is central to the definition of the Church's mission," that "the Church must take a more verbal stand on social, political and economic issues," that "the rigid anti-communism of Pius XII is deemed no longer adequate. [Accordingly], capitalism, imperialism and underdevelopment [are] all subject to review and criticism."[10]

Catholic leaders in Latin America, Brown concludes, translated these papal pronouncements into the agenda and norms of liberation theology. This translation is especially evident in the controlling affirmations of the Medellin conference. The Bishops declared that Latin America was living in "dependency" on foreign powers and suffering from "economic colonialism." Within this interpretive framework, the causal nexus of poverty is redefined. "The poor are poor because the rich are rich, and the rich are rich because they exploit the poor, and the rich want to stay rich badly enough to keep on exploiting the poor."[11] In sum, poverty did not come about because of the poor's failures and shortcomings, but it was the result of a defect in the structure of the prevailing economic and political systems. From the recognition that Latin America was the victim of systemic oppression, followed in lock step the recognition that it was also the victim of institutional violence.

Brown's analysis of LALT's explicit ties to Roman Catholic teaching would seem to provide a "saintly" foundation for its theory of social change. But, even this foundation is judged "satanic." The Church's social teachings that emerged during the 1960s are tainted, Brown claims, because "they were tailored to meet several underlying realities confronting the Church in Latin America," particularly the "conviction that if the Church did not radically change its policies, it would simply not survive as a relevant institution."[12] Thus we see the critics "satanize" and contaminate the liberation motifs that LALT stresses by tying them to a particular pope at a specific historical juncture, motivated by self-interest and controlled by self-preservation, with all the desperation that this involves.

In all of this we see several things that are significant for our analysis: The first matter of import follows from the fact that, though Brown correctly traces the foundational elements of LALT to movements internal to the Roman Catholic tradition itself, he invalidates these elements by virtue of his normative conclusions about the essence of the faith and practice of Roman Catholicism. Brown's acknowledgement is, however, grist for liberation theology's mill, for it shows us that the saint and satan criticism revolves around a specific interpretation of the Church's tradition. Accordingly, for this strategy to be valid and, particularly, to avoid a questioning-begging foundation, its advocates must substantiate that their particular reading is the only acceptable reading of the tradition.

What this shows us apologetically is that Marxism need not be the source for the tenets of liberation theology and that LALT and its critics are endorsing rival interpretations of Roman Catholic faith. Thus the crucial, and yet unanswered question here is: "What is the essence of Roman Catholicism, and by extension, Christian and biblical faith?" This leads to the question of questions: "Who is to define this?" or as Humpty Dumpty, in *Alice in Wonderland,*" poses the issue: "Who is to be the master?"[13]

Finally, in the next section, we will call attention to the central role that economic, social and political oppression plays in the LALT apologetic. It should be now obvious why LALT must document such oppression in a manner that moves beyond idiosyncratic and arbitrary judgments. By demonstrating that it is responding to an established oppression, it documents part of the moral base that an *apologia* for counter-violence requires.

Towards a Phenomenology of Economic, Social and Political Oppression: LALT's Apologetic Norm

Liberation theology is "a theological reflection born . . . of shared efforts to abolish the current unjust situation and to build a different society, freer and more humane."[14]

Liberation theology claims that counter-violence is a permissible Christian means for radical social change in the context of historic economic, social and political oppression. This crucial qualification establishes a normative grid that critics of liberation theology tend to overlook, namely its understanding of oppression. Fleshing out this category is the purpose of this section.

Deciphering liberation theology's rationale for counter-violence begins with its claim that economic social and political liberation is a necessary dimension of Christian and biblical faith. It is on this principle and its corollary—the definition of oppression as sin and its eradication as fundamental for any understanding of salvation—that liberation theology constructs its methodology, rank orders its moral imperatives, establishes its policy norms, and assesses its moral and theological rivals. Speaking politically then, the first purpose of liberation theology is to eradicate economic, social and political oppression. Speaking religiously, its purpose is to establish the orthodoxy and orthopraxy of this mission as a Christian, biblical, moral and spiritual imperative.

Liberation theology links its program of economic, social and political liberation to biblical and Christian faith. This account, however, falls outside the scope of this essay. For the validity of our argument here it is sufficient to note that, drawing upon a wide range of theological and biblical resources, including mainstream elements of the church tradition, liberation theology affirms and impressively documents this connection as its explicit point of departure. Given this documentation, critics can no longer blithely point to Marx as liberation theology's unquestioned parent; Mark is an equally probable womb.[15] This documentation also relocates the nature of the debate as one between different Christian factions, thus forcing the question of whether liberation theology or its critics presents the more accurate interpretation of biblical and Christian faith.

A further preliminary observation: liberation theology's description of oppression should be interpreted as a phenomenological analysis that aims to move beyond idiosyncratic and arbitrary judgments—indeed, a picture that can be drawn with biblical as well as Marxist strokes. For this reason the accuracy of its description should be approached as an unsettled empirical question that can and must be negotiated independently of its rationale for counterviolence. The apologetic importance of this approach should not be overlooked. It means that to establish a sound criticism, the critics must first show that liberation theology's description of oppression is an inaccurate and inadequate account of its existential and historical situation.

One final observation is needed to introduce liberation theology's concept of oppression. Liberation theology approaches its task from the context and the vantage point of those labeled variously as the oppressed, the wretched of the earth. These are the people who view the parade of history from that place where the "trickle down," theoretically, but not actually, reaches its final destination. This is the population whose economic, social and political situation constricts it to a "worm's eye view" of reality.

With these preliminary observations as background, we can obtain an overview of liberation theology's understanding of oppression if we do two things: reflect on why the *worm* has often been chosen to symbolize the oppressed and unpack some of the important nuances in the contrasting images of a worm's eye and bird's eye view.

There is a singular reason why the worm is the preferred symbol for the oppressed, rather than the snake or some other creature that has to see things from the ground up instead of from the sky down. The worm expresses the essence of defenselessness against a more powerful, wide-ranging and far-seeing predator. Translating the issue into economic, social and political categories, the enormous armaments of the bird—its superior size and speed, its menacing beak—represent the immense surplus of death-dealing power and spacious access to life-enhancing resources of the elite in the society that equip them for their role as exploiters of the oppressed. From the vantage point of the worm and its gross deficit of power and resources, it appears that not only the early bird gets the worm, but the late bird as well. Only in death, when the body returns to the earth from whence it came, does the worm have its day in the sun. The oppressed are also aware of the time-honored justification for the gross inequalities of power and privileges that mark the respective roles of the elites and the masses; these inequalities are legitimated by appealing to the heavens, the abode of the creator and ruler of the universe, and, not accidently, as the worm sees it, the playground of the bird.

The Binary Logic of Oppression

With this understanding before us, let us now take a "creature from Mars" perspective and indicate how we would explain oppression to our visitor.

1. Speaking in the most general terms, oppression can be seen as a form of economic, social and political exploitation; as a pervasive institutional system that is designed to maintain an alleged superior group at the top of the ladder, with the superior accoutrements of power, privileges and access to society's resources.
2. If we move from a general to a more detailed description of oppression, the following should be accented. Oppression can be analyzed from two different perspectives: objective and subjective. The objective elements can be reduced to pervasive economic, social and political inequalities. But inequalities, *per se,* are neutral. There is nothing that forces one automatically or as a matter of course, to appraise any inequality as negative or instinctively to seek its eradication. Both the negative and positive features lie outside the mere identification and description of the inequality. The most exhaustive, detailed and factual description of the inequality will not uncover its unjust or negative quality; the same applies for the positive label. Both the negative and positive tags are generated by a particular world view, a specific value system, a discrete theology or identifiable picture of ultimate reality—in short, something that is not part of the facts in question. This, for our purposes, comprises its subjective component, the *belief and value system* that anchors oppression.

This feature of oppression—and this is the crucial point for our analysis—tells us that the oppressed are oppressed, in fundamental part, because of the beliefs, values and theology they adopt or, more accurately, are socialized to accept. Benjamin Mays' criticism of "compensatory ideas" in Afro-American Christianity is a classic statement of this insight.

> The Negro's social philosophy and his idea of God go hand in hand. . . . Certain theological ideas enable Negroes to endure hardship, suffer pain and withstand maladjustment, but . . . do not necessarily motivate them to strive to eliminate the source of the ills they suffer. . . . The idea has also persisted that 'the harder the cross, the brighter the crown.' Believing this about God, the Negro . . . has stood back and suffered much without bitterness, without striking back, and without trying aggressively to realize to the full his needs in the world.[16]

This leads, in the vocabulary of liberation theology, to *quietism,* the stifling of any desire to attack or eradicate the economic, social and political inequalities that characterize oppression. Whether the wretched of the earth embrace nonviolence or take any means necessary to eradicate their maldistributed suffering depends upon the kind of God in which their faith resides and what one thinks that God demands. The implications of this for valuing or disvaluing violence are obvious.

Since liberation theology's apologetic connects violence and quietism, it is helpful to look briefly at the inner logic of the latter and its close relation to oppression. Quietism, in the lexicon of liberation theology, is a refusal to reform the status quo, especially where traditional institutions and values are involved. Conformity, accommodation and acquiescence are its distinguishing marks.

Quietism becomes our operating principle if we believe that economic, social and political correction is unnecessary, impossible or inappropriate. Corrective action is unnecessary, for instance, if we believe that some agent, other than ourselves, will handle it. Another quietist tendency is found in the familiar adage, "If it ain't broke, don't fix it." This bespeaks the attitude that correction is gratuitous if the good, the ideal, is already present or in the process of being realized. We are also pushed to quietism if remedial action is thought to be impossible. We apparently reach this conclusion when we encounter an invincible force or when the item to be corrected is a structure of ultimate reality. Finally, change is rejected if changing things will make things worse or involve us in actions deemed inappropriate, e.g., violence. (This will be discussed in more detail below.)

3. The inner logic of oppression affirms a two-category system. It divides the human family into at least two distinct groups, hierarchically arranged into alleged superior and inferior classes: in-group, out-group; male, female; rich, poor; Greek, barbarian; Aryan, non-Aryan; and master, slave are familiar examples.
4. This hierarchical arrangement is correlated with a gross imbalance of life-extending and life-enhancing power, resources and privileges. The alleged superior group will possess a grossly conspicuous surplus and the alleged inferior group, a grossly disproportionate deficit. To make the same point in different terms: the alleged superior group will have the most of whatever the society defines as the best, and the least of the worst. In stark contrast, the alleged inferior group will have the least of the best and the most of the worst.
5. This hierarchical division and the economic, social and po-

litical inequalities it expresses are *institutionalized*. The primary institutions are constructed to maintain an unequal distribution of power, resources and privileges. This is their inner design and the actual product of their operation.

Religious Legitimation and the Mechanism of Oppression

6. The next component of oppression demands special attention, for it brings us to the heart of the topic: the religious legitimation of economic, social and political oppression which introduces the possibility of ideological taint. The hierarchical division, with the accompanying inequalities of power, resources and privileges institutionally installed, is alleged to be grounded in ultimate reality—God or nature—or blame is shifted to the oppressed themselves for their status at the bottom of the ladder.

This maneuver is in line with the maintenance of oppression. To perpetuate inequalities, the oppressor must persuade the oppressed to accept their lot at the bottom of the economic, social and political totem pole and to embrace these inequalities as good, deserved and inevitable. In all of this, responsibility is conveniently lifted from the shoulders of the oppressor. To accomplish this, the inner logic of oppression claims that basic inequalities are the product of and in conformity with reality itself. By invoking the supernatural/divine order—one could just as well appeal to nature as its foundation—oppressors accomplish several things that the maintenance of oppression requires. On the one hand, they establish a superhuman foundation that by virtue of its superior power compels conformity and obedience. On the other, they guarantee the goodness and moral superiority of the existing social order. Rearranging social inequalities is unthinkable if the economic, social and political order expresses the will of God. Even if we had the power to reform things, such remodeling would still be inappropriate and blasphemous. Whatever status we have is just; it is the station that God intends for us; what is, is what ought to be. A similar conclusion would also follow if we interpret economic, social and political suffering and inequality as divine punishment.

We have identified the central role that religion plays to legitimate both the objective and subjective elements of oppression. At this juncture it is important to identify the implications that liberation theology draws from this use of religion, recognizing, of course, the checkered history of religion as both goad to the oppressed and guardian of the oppressor.

For liberation theology, this means that moral and theological authenticity can no longer be determined solely or primarily by certifying that it is part of the tradition of the church. Religion's checkered history—where the church usually has sided with the powerful and the wealthy—tells us that the tradition itself is suspect; even the core tenets of the faith can be part of the scaffolding of oppression. Accordingly, a new test is necessary. For liberation theology, that test comes down to whether or not religion supports or subverts oppression.

Liberation theology also concludes that a total and comprehensive audit of the faith must be executed. Like the discovery of the single med-fly, nothing at the outset can be regarded as uncontaminated. Rather, each theological and moral imperative must be provisionally regarded as suspect and, accordingly, must be quarantined until it has been certified to be free of contamination.

To illustrate this method, it is helpful to recall the critical challenge of black theologians in North America to theological formulations, like those of Martin Luther King, which reduce Christian and biblical faith to agape, self-sacrificing love for the other. These reductions were attacked as ideological tools to maintain oppression.

> By emphasizing the complete self-giving of God in Christ . . . the oppressor can then request the oppressed to do the same for the oppressors. If God gives himself without obligation, then in order to be Christian, men must give themselves to the neighbor in like manner. Since God has loved us in spite of our revolt against him, to be like God we too must love those who . . . enslave us. . . . In fact, they are permitted to do whatever they will against black people assured that God loves them as well as the people they oppress.[17]

7. Historically speaking, oppression is initiated through the violence of the oppressor. The pattern that history reveals is this: there is an original violence that initiates and establishes the economic, social and political inequalities that comprise oppression. "With the establishment of a relation of oppression, violence has *already* begun."[18] However, the oppressor invariably suffers historical amnesia regarding this original violence, or that violence is transmuted into a more "benign" action through the oppressors' power to legitimate. Stressing

original violence as part of the very definition of the problem is central to liberation theology's apologetic, as is implied in its accent on counter-violence.

Allied with this understanding is a particular conclusion about how power is transferred in human history, namely that force is required to effect a more equitable distribution of economic, social and political power, resources and privileges. No upper class, Gunnar Myrdal concludes, has ever stepped down voluntarily to equality with the lower class or as a simple consequence of moral conviction, given up their privileges and broken up their monopolies. To be induced to do so, the rich and privileged must sense that demands are raised and forcefully pressed by a powerful group assembled behind them.[19]

Powerism and Anti-Powerism

8. To explain the final dimension of oppression to be treated here, it is necessary, first, to differentiate between two antithetical philosophies: *anti-powerism* and *powerism*. Anti-powerism regards power as essentially negative or evil. The essence of this position is best expressed by Jacob Burkhardt: "Now power, in its very nature, is evil, no matter who wields it. It is not stability but lust and, *ipso facto,* insatiable. Therefore, it is unhappy in itself and doomed to make others unhappy."[20]

Powerism expresses a quite different understanding about the role, status and value of power in human affairs. Power, from this perspective, is neutral—neither evil nor good; rather its quality depends upon who wields it and for what purpose. Advocates of this position advance power as a preeminent interpretive category for all aspects of human affairs as well as the natural and supernatural world. Disciples of powerism would consider the following an appropriate description. "In any encounter of man with man, power is active, every encounter, whether friendly or hostile, whether benevolent or indifferent, is in some way, a struggle of power with power."[21]

Part of the mechanism of oppression is to socialize the oppressed to adopt a philosophy of anti-powerism, though the oppressor lives by the opposite philosophy of powerism, not only regarding the origin of oppression but its maintenance as well. Below, we will show how the advocacy of anti-powerism and non-violence meets one of the maintenance needs of oppression.

William R. Jones

Violence and Moral Legitimacy: The Not So Odd Couple

It is not difficult to understand liberation theology's rationale for counterviolence if we begin with this assumption: individuals and groups regard their actions—no matter how heinous they may appear to others—as moral and right. In the case where actions are defined as morally reprehensible, what we find is exactly what we discover for morally approved actions; both are advanced as a legitimate and moral means to an end that is also regarded as morally correct. If this is the case—and slavery, the holocaust, and terrorism warrant this conclusion, as well as the checkered history of religion as moral exemplar—we will always misinterpret those actions we deem immoral if we fail to ferret out the "moral" rationale that underlies these alleged "reprehensible" acts.

This methodological axiom is peculiarly crucial when we are analyzing a category like violence which is used in a highly partisan fashion. However, most of liberation theology's critics ignore this approach. They apparently start with the questionable assumption that certain actions, such as violence, cannot be legitimated morally or religiously. But any action can be wrapped in a moral or religious justification, depending upon what a given moral or religious perspective allows. There is hardly any action—I have yet to uncover one—that has not been morally and religiously sanctioned.

If this is an accurate view of what is at stake, it is important to consider liberation theology's moral base for counterviolence. Other features of liberation theology's social ethics must also be treated here: (a) the actual status and value of the violence that it affirms; (b) the distinction it makes between types of violence; (c) the critical qualifications that hedge the sanction of counterviolence and show that there is no absolute endorsement even of counterviolence; (d) its identification of an inevitable subjective component in the very definition and classification of violence; (e) a contextual approach that excludes the *a priori* classification of any act as violence; (f) a logical grid that convicts its critics of hypocrisy and inconsistency; and (g) establishing counterviolence as a form of self-defense. Obviously the soundness of this argument depends upon liberation theology's success in showing that its clients are the oppressed and this, in turn is contingent upon the accuracy and adequacy of its account of economic, social and political oppression. Nothing more needs to be said about this point except to alert future critics of liberation theology that attention should be riveted on this issue.

At the outset, let us note that critics of liberation theology label it a theology of violence. As part of the Saint and Satan strategy, liberation theology's critics reduce its theology of social change to one that glorifies violence. But liberation theology's actual position says something quite different.

Liberation theology does not glorify violence or counterviolence; nor does it make counterviolence the preferred or even the necessary response to oppression. Nor should we reach the erroneous conclusion that all liberation theologians endorse counterviolence. As the debate among black theologians in North America reveals, this issue splits liberationists into opposing camps though I sense that the larger group in the future will be the advocates of counterviolence.

An Anatomy of Violence

A fuller sense of liberation theology's theory of social change requires us to identify some of the different types of violence that inform its analysis. A helpful starting point is Dom Helder Camara's phenomenology of violence, now more than a decade old.

Camara labels the first appearance of violence as *violence number 1*[22] or what might be termed "original" violence or what has been categorized as "structural" or "institutionalized" violence.[23] This is the violence that lays the initial foundation for the oppression and maintains it. Violence number 1, in Camara's analysis, calls forth the response of violence number 2, i.e., counterviolence. And violence number 2 triggers violence number 3, "repressive violence." To maintain their surplus of power and privilege, the established authorities invoke repressive actions to put down the usurpers, the practitioners of violence number 2. This, in turn, triggers further counterviolence, and the spiral continues—unless we move, as Camara recommends, to the level of active non-violence.

Several features of Camara's analysis require further clarification. First, given this typology, one can say that liberation theology legitimates only violence number 2 and even this, as we will see below, is not endorsed absolutely but only in highly selective and rigidly defined contexts. Next, the meaning of violence in violence number 1 has been enlarged beyond the conventional definitions which reduce violence to an overt physical act of injury or destruction. "Violence is physical force resulting in injury or destruction of property or persons in violation of general moral belief or civil law."[24] We will critique this definition below as question-begging. Camara and liberation theology extend the meaning of violence to include institutionalized covert actions or injustices of the type described as: "The violence of hunger, helplessness, and underdevelopment, . . . of persecution, oppression and neglect, . . . of organized prostitution, of illegal but flourishing slavery, and of social, economic, and intellectual discrimination."[25]

Understanding the rationale for counterviolence also requires that we recall the composite character of violence—its objective and subjective elements. Reducing violence to its essentials, we find objective force or power. But we also find that this power/force is labeled or classified. There is always a labeling, generated from the subjective side, that is added to the objective power and force, a labeling that the most minute description of the force itself will not reveal. Thus the same force or power in the hands of different persons yields different labels. Deadly force for the soldier or policeman would escape the label of violence; the same force used by the mugger would not. The difference is not in the amount of force but in the context; who uses it and for what purpose.

This feature of violence, liberation theology contends, entails the conclusion that violence is a political category which can only be defined contextually. Whether the destruction associated with violence goes "too far" can only be determined with reference to a concrete situation. Any *a priori* labeling is problematic.

Given this understanding, liberation theology challenges all definitions of violence in terms of "the violation of civil law," as question-begging. Is not the final logic of this stipulation that the state can never be convicted of violence until it is overthrown? Does it not give the government the right and power to legitimate its use of force, no matter what its character, as "legal" and therefore not violent? Moreover, this political and contextual nature of violence means that the definition of violence itself is always an exercise in power. This means in turn, that any discussion of the legitimacy of violence, counterviolence (or the new pariah, terrorism), ultimately rests on the logically prior question, "Who will define?"

At this juncture, the imbalance of power that defines oppression comes to the fore in liberation theology's apologetic. The oppressed's deficit of economic, social and political power means that they do not participate in the labeling that determines whether a given instance of force is violence. Their lack of co-equal power to define and authorize violence is seen by liberation theology as simply another mode of oppression. Given this sense, any definition of violence by the establishment is provisionally suspect and question-begging.

A Moral Defense of Counterviolence

Liberation theology's rationale for counter-violence, as Alfredo Fierro correctly indicates, is ethical. "Its talk centers around the conditions that make violence licit. What is more, and also somewhat surprising, this discussion tends to remain within the context formulated by classic moral theology."[26] In the final analysis, the case for counterviolence rests on the legitimacy of self-protection or self-defense.

"To be specific, it tends to adopt as its basic criterion the age-old moral principle of legitimate defense and its proper proportions. Thus the new current theology of violence tends to be no more than a new application of an old principle; it takes the classic principle of the individual's right to defend himself by violence against an unjust aggressor and then applies it to revolutionary violence perpetrated by a group. Almost everything that has been written by Christians on this topic . . . remains within this relatively traditional framework."[27] Gustavo Gutierrez makes the same point:

> [Liberation] theology's position on violence is the same as the Church's traditional teaching on 'just wars' that date to Thomas Aquinas that violence is possible as a lesser evil and last resort against a greater violence. One of the crucial decisions in that choice is whether counterviolence is effective. If it is not, it should not be chosen.[28]

LALT remains within the mainstream of traditional moral theology when it interprets unjust laws as a form of violence. "Laws not derived from eternal law," according to Aquinas, "lack the true nature of law [and are] rather a kind of violence."[29]

Two things stand out in liberation theology's rationale for counterviolence: its preeminent use of traditional arguments from moral theology and, on the other side, the failure of its critics to engage and accommodate this point in their condemnation. The critics construct a false picture of liberation theology's rationale which they then conveniently demolish. Their error is two-fold:

they omit liberation theology's essential and traditional moral defense for counterviolence, seeing instead a borrowing from Marxist ideology which is interpreted as basically nihilistic or amoral. In addition, they refuse to debate a major plank in liberation theology's rationale: that the group or class which is advancing counterviolence is oppressed. As shown above, the validity of liberation theology's case for counterviolence as self-defense depends upon the accuracy and adequacy of its analysis of economic, social and political oppression, in particular the assertion of the latter's substantial presence. Accordingly, to rebut liberation theology's case requires the critics to demonstrate that the situations which have spawned liberation theology do not constitute oppression.

Note the consequences if critics are allowed to skirt this part of liberation theology's argument. Violence number 1 becomes invisible, thus providing an illegitimate escape exit from the other part of liberation theology's argument: the charge of a hypocritical endorsement of non-violence only when it serves to protect the status quo. Richard Brown's inaccurate criticism[30] of Gutierrez's analysis of the just war theory points to precisely such a consequence. Brown contends that Gutierrez "strays outside the [just war] theory confines," and moves the question of whether to commit violence beyond the matter of its "justnesss" to the "application of the amoral criterion of 'effectiveness'. . . . This new standard admits to a high degree of pragmatism and neatly coincides with Marxist-Leninist dogma."[31]

Quietism, Anti-powerism and Violence: Ideological Perpetuation of Oppression

It is evident that recommending nonviolence to blacks is an effort to retain the Christian vocabulary which has kept them imprisoned in passivity for so long. Asking blacks to be non-violent means that whites are demanding a Christian virtue which they themselves do not possess. That means that whites are once again trying to dupe the blacks.[32]

A conceptual and value system has been built up to destroy the ability of the oppressed to see the exploitation to which they are subjected and to understand its causes. The system we now want to consider involves the ideological manipulation of the maintenance concepts of oppression—in particular the establishment of anti-powerism and non-violence as ultimate moral imperatives.

We also will examine liberation theology's response to this ploy: the charge that its critics are guilty of an unrighteous hypocrisy.

One aspect of the ideological use of religion to maintain oppression is the establishment of anti-powerism and its correlate nonviolence as preeminent moral ideals. To decipher this feature of oppression we should recall the gross imbalance of power that characterizes the unequal status of oppressor and oppressed. To the degree that the oppressed accept the logic of anti-powerism (that power is evil), they will regard their deficit of power as good and as necessary for their highest good. In this way their pursuit of co-equal economic, social and political power, a necessary condition for their liberation, is aborted at the outset. In short, one of the maintenance formulae for oppression is "anti-powerism equals quietism." The formula, "violence equals evil," produces the same result.

This strategy of the oppressor, however, can be undercut in several ways, the most effective of which is the charge of hypocrisy against those who attack the violence of the oppressed against the system, but not the violence ingrained in the system itself. The charge is easy to document and difficult to escape, as this rhetorical question suggests: "Why, in a world of violence, should only the proletariat not have the right to use violence?"[33]

It also appears to be the case that any effort to invalidate LALT's use of the just war theory or self-defense has a boomerang effect. If the use of force by the oppressed against an unjust *internal* order is ruled invalid, is not the traditional justification of war against an *external* threat likewise invalidated?

Consider also that if one is not a rigid and consistent pacifist or practitioner of non-violent resistance, the logical and moral barriers for the legitimation of counterviolence have already been scuttled. Any movement away from pacifism (e.g., just war, self-defense, counteracting a greater evil, the American invasion of Grenada), means that violence has been sanctioned or legalized at some point. Add to this the actual historical situation where force was used to establish oppression, violence number 1, or to continue oppression, as in violence number 3. The norms used to justify these instances of force provide all the maneuverability that the moral rationale of counterviolence requires and more. Moreover, if violence number 2 is not granted to the oppressed, their critics are required to defend a superior-inferior arrangement where they assign to themselves rights and privileges that are denied to others. In short, the critics must show that their rejection of counterviolence is not the operation of oppression in a new guise.

Another strategy relocates and broadens the parameters of the moral issue in several significant ways. If violence is already part and parcel of the situation of oppression—and this is implied in the category, violence number 1—the moral issue is not simply the question of non-violence as the only permissible action. Nor can the issue of moral obligation be collapsed, as do the critics of liberation theology, to the oppressed's obligation not to negate the life and person of the oppressor. A context of oppression spawns other moral dilemmas. The fact of violence number 1 raises the question of one's moral responsibility to the oppressed, the object of violence number 1 as well as 3. The oppressor is not the only neighbor whose humanity must be considered; the oppressed, the object of the oppressor's violence are equally one's neighbor. Thus, one has to decide not simply between non-violence or violence towards the oppressor but between violence towards the oppressor or violence towards the oppressed. "I do not opt for violence, it is forced upon me. I have no other choice. If I opt for non-violence, I am the accomplice of oppression. I take sides on behalf of the violence of the state. . . ."[34]

If this is the case, then responding to the oppressor in a manner that leaves violence number 1 essentially intact means that one is perpetuating violence against one's other neighbor, the oppressed. Given this dilemma, that one can choose only violence, liberation theology argues that one must simply take sides or, as Robert M. Brown has aptly put it, change sides.

Non-violence and Its Ideological Manipulation

Some examples from our own recent history, the establishment response to Martin Luther King, Jr. and Malcolm X, also help to illustrate the ideological manipulation of non-violence to further oppression. King's philosophy of non-violence was incessantly pressed upon blacks—when faced with the alternative of a Malcolm X—as the sole instrument for economic, social and political change. Yet when King advanced the same policy for Americans in Viet Nam, he was dropped like a hot potato. This refusal to acknowledge that what is good for the goose (the oppressed) is good for the gander (the oppressor) unwittingly documented for blacks the establishment's ideological manipulation of non-violence.

A similar manipulation is also apparent in the gross caricature of Malcolm X's philosophy of social change, particularly the attribution of a theory of violence that was in fact alien to his actual position. Malcolm X never rejected the validity of non-violence. He only challenged its absolute validity, which is to say, its validity for all contexts. Malcolm X opposed Mao's contention that the gun is necessary and violence inevitable,[35] arguing instead for the "ballot or the bullet." Violence is not advanced as the superior or the oppressed's *first* response to their plight. The ballot is to be the first strategy, and only if the oppressor rejects the ballot is the bullet permitted. Rather the oppressed's method of social change is dictated by the context, specifically by the severity of the oppression and the character of the oppressor's response to demands for social justice. Indeed, Malcolm X even allowed that America could spawn a revolution "without violence and bloodshed" if "the black man is given full use of the ballot in every one of the fifty states."[36]

Just as Malcolm X's position on violence was grossly misinterpreted, so was his principle, "any means necessary." For Malcolm X, this principle recognizes a plurality of moral and political strategies, e.g., non-violence and counterviolence, in contrast to King's exclusive advocacy of the former.

> We're at a time in history now where we want freedom, and only two things bring you freedom—the ballot or the bullet . . . If you and I don't use the ballot and get it, we're going to be forced to use the bullet. And if you don't want to use the ballot, I know you don't want to use the bullet. So let us try the ballot. And if the ballot doesn't work, we'll try something else. But let us try the ballot.[37]

"Any means necessary," in Malcolm's view, is also a call for a contextual analysis of means-ends questions. But in deliberating means and ends, the right and necessity of self-defense must be safeguarded.

> Since self-preservation is the first law of nature, we assert the Afro-American's right to self-defense. . . . The history of unpunished violence against our people clearly indicates that we must be prepared to defend ourselves or we will continue to be a defenseless people at the mercy of a ruthless and violent racist mob. . . . We assert that in those areas where the government is either unable or unwilling to protect the lives and property of our people, that our people are within our rights to protect themselves by whatever means necessary.[38]

Finally, "any means necessary" also justifies counterviolence—

which, in the context of oppression, is self-defense. "You should never be non-violent unless you run into some non-violence. I am non-violent with those who are non-violent with me. . . . But don't die alone. Let your dying be reciprocal. This is what is meant by equality. What's good for the goose is good for the gander."[39]

It is important to identify the context in which counterviolence is legitimated. Malcolm argues from a context where there is "a history of unpunished violence" against blacks and a demonstrated failure of the government to protect the lives and property of blacks. Moreover, the society is grounded in an immoral system such as racism. "Tactics based solely on morality can only succeed when you are dealing with people who are moral or a system that is moral. A man or system that oppresses a man because of his color is not moral."[40] Further, we have a society that responds only to force or power. "The only real power that is respected in this society is political power and economic power. Nothing else. There's no such thing as a moral force that this society recognizes."[41] Finally, we have a society where violence is inconsistently sanctioned. Non-violence is not advanced as a matter of principle, as Gandhi and King did, but approved when it is advantageous to the oppressor and disapproved when it is not.

Implications for the Coming Debate

From the vantage point of its critics, liberation theology's advocacy of counterviolence is most threatening to geopolitical stability, especially where American interests are involved. For this reason, I would suggest that too much of the response of public policy makers to liberation theology reflects cold war rhetoric and logic. Approaching liberation theology as an ally of Communism is to misread the intent of liberation theology and more important, to spin out national policy that the future will show to be inept and ineffective. A more accurate reading of liberation theology's lineage and its future would tie it to the spirit and strategy of the American Revolution, the celebrated last great hope for humankind. In all of this, we must not forget that counterviolence was the foundation for the American Revolution. In the words of the *Declaration of Independence,* "Whenever any form of government becomes destructive of these ends, it is the right of the people to alter or to abolish it, and to institute new government. . . . When a long train of abuses and usurpations, pursuing invariably the same object, evinces a design to reduce them under absolute despotism, it is their right, it is their duty, to throw off such government. . . ."

One final observation is in order that should be a central focus of future examinations of liberation theology. When one inspects liberation theology's rationale for counterviolence, as well as its understanding of oppression, there will be little doubt that its theology of violence is not the most threatening feature to the status quo. Rather, its principle of authority—the affirmation of the individual as a co-equal center of freedom authority and value—is most unsettling.

I make this point for several reasons. To reach the point where the faithful give a moral rationale for counterviolence means first that their consciousness has been illuminated to see the ideological manipulations to which they have been subjected, in fundamental part through the exercise of religion. In addition, this means that they have already deabsolutized and desacralized the religious tradition and authority, making the latter the product of human power and authority which other humans can reform or eradicate. Looking at the same point from another perspective, the very fact of the existence of liberation theology, as well as its self-designation as Christian and biblical, automatically destabilizes the monopolistic authority of any Christian tradition that supports the status quo. This sets up a situation where rival interpretations of the faith not only vie with each other but force a decision as to which is authentic. This choice has already undermined the maintenance structures of oppression, even prior to developing a rationale for counterviolence. The very fact of a rival rationale, irrespective of its validity, means that the previous norms that informed America's geopolitical policies are already hopelessly outdated.

In a similar way, the oppressed's position at the bottom of the social heap is no longer connected with their salvation, but is seen as an obstacle to their highest good. At this point, the mechanism of quietism that oppression requires to maintain itself has been short-circuited beyond salvage.

In addition the analysis of violence in terms of the power to define shows us that all that the oppressed need to establish the legitimacy of counterviolence is co-equal economic, social and political power and authority, a status that they are daily assigning to themselves. All of this is the result of a new consciousness of their status as co-equal to those at the top of the social ladder.

Daily events in Latin American, South Africa, the Philippines and Afghanistan tell us that there appears no way to return them to an earlier stage of hierarchical servitude.

NOTES

1. Richard C. Brown, "Liberation Theology in Latin America: Its Challenge to the United States," *Conflict,* vol. 4, no. 1, 21, 50 (adapted). Hereafter cited as LTLA.
2. Liberation theology and Latin American liberation theology will be used interchangeably. LALT is the short hand for the latter.
3. Brown, LTLA, 21.
4. *Mission Trends No. 3,* ed. Gerald H. Anderson and Thomas Stransky (New York: Paulist Press, 1976), 1.
5. Brown, LTLA, 32.
6. Alfred Hennelly, *Theologies in Conflict: The Challenge of Juan Luis Segundo* (Maryknoll: New York: Orbis Books, 1979), 123.
7. Ibid.
8. Paul VI, Homily of the Mass on Development Day, Bogota, August 23, 1968.
9. Latin American Bishops' Third General Conference Statement, Puebla, 1979.
10. Brown, LTLA, 23–25.
11. Robert McAfee Brown, *Makers of Contemporary Theology: Gustavo Gutierrez* (Atlanta: John Knox Press, 1980), 9.
12. Brown, LTLA, 25.
13. " 'When I use a word, it means just what I choose it to mean, neither more nor less.' 'But the question,' Alice asked, 'is whether you can make words mean so many different things.' 'No,' said Humpty Dumpty, 'the question is: Who is to be the master.' " Lewis Carroll, *Through the Looking Glass,* in *The Complete Works of Lewis Carroll,* (New York: Random House, 1949), 214.
14. Gustavo Gutierrez, *A Theology of Liberation* (Maryknoll, New York: Orbis Books, 1973), ix.
15. The following are among the increasing number of exegetical studies that provide a biblical ground for liberation theology's analysis of oppression. Telsa Tamez, *The Bible of the Oppressed* (Maryknoll, New York: Orbis Books, 1982); Julio de Santa Ana, *Good News to the Poor: The Challenge of the Poor in the History of the Church* (Maryknoll, New York: 1979); Thomas D. Hanks, *God So Loved the Third World,* (Maryknoll: New York: 1984).
16. Benjamin Mays, *The Negro's God,* (New York: Antheneum, 1969), 155.

17. James Cone, *A Black Theology of Liberation,* (New York: Lippincott, 1970, 133–34.
18. Denis Collins, *Paulo Freire: His Life, Words and Thought* (New York: Paulist Press, 1977), 41.
19. Gunnar Myrdal, *Beyond the Welfare State* (New Haven, Conn.: Yale University Press, 1960), 227.
20. Jacob Burkhardt, *Force and Freedom,* (Boston: Beacon Press, 1943), p. 184.
21. Paul Tillich, *Love, Power and Justice,* (New York: Oxford University Press, 1960), 87.
22. Helder Camara, *Spiral of Violence* (Denville, N.J.: Dimension Books, 1971).
23. Robert McAfee Brown, *Religion and Violence* (Philadelphia: Westminister Press, 1973, 35. "Violence can have structural forms built into the apparently peaceful operations of society as well as overt physical expressions." SODEPAX, *Peace: The Desperate Imperative* (Geneva: Committee on Society, Development and Peace, 1969), 13.
24. George Edwards, *Jesus and the Politics of Violence* (New York: Harper and Row, 1972), 2.
25. Peruvian Bishops' Commission for Social Action, *Between Honesty and Hope* (Maryknoll: New York, 1970), 81.
26. Alfredo Fierro, *The Militant Gospel,* (Maryknoll, New York: Orbis Books, 1977), 202.
27. Ibid., 202–03. LALT could also profitably utilize the following principle to establish its claim of self-defense. No practical distinction can be made between the right of governments to use force to maintain order and the right of armed revolution to overthrow those governments when the order they maintain is anti-human." J. Andrew Kirk, *Liberation Theology: An Evangelical View from the Third World* (Atlanta: John Knox Press, 1979), 31.
28. Penny Lernoux, *Cry of the People* (Garden City, N.Y.: Doubleday & Co., 1982), 432.
29. Aquinas, *Summa Theologica,* Ia, IIae, q 96.4.
30. What Richard Brown incorrectly identifies as "pragmatism" and "Marxist Leninist dogma" is, in fact, the principle of the just war theory that asserts that the undertaking must have a reasonable chance of success.
31. Brown, LTLA, 28.
32. Jean Genet, *Ramparts,* June. 1970, 31.
33. Cited in Jacques Ellul, *Violence* (New York: Seabury Press, 1969), 33.
34. Jalles Costa, *IDOC International* (North American Edition, May, 1969), 64.
35. "It is only by the power of the gun that the working class . . . can defeat the armed bourgeoise and landlords; in this sense we must say that only with guns can the whole world be transformed." Mao Tse-tung, *quotations from Chairman Mao Tsetung* (Peking: Foreign Languages Press, 1972), 61–2.
36. *Malcolm X Speaks: Selected Speeches and Statements,* ed. George Brietman (New York: Grove Press, 1966), p. 57.

37. *Malcolm X, By Any Means Necessary: Speeches, Interviews and a Letter* by Malcolm X, ed. George Brietman (New York: Pathfinders Press, Inc., 1970), 89.
38. *Interviews,* 41.
39. *Speaks,* 34.
40. *Interviews,* 23.
41. *Interviews,* 88.

8

Religion and the Problem of Power: South Africa[1]

AUSTIN M. AHANOTU

I: Introduction

What, it may be asked, is the relevance of religion to the fight for national liberation in South Africa? The answer is simple and obvious. But like all "obvious" things it needs to be stated: Calvinism may have played a progressive role as an ideological weapon in earlier times in Europe. It was a theory developed and propagated to justify the materialist interests of the rising *bourgeoisie*. In South Africa, Calvinism, as practised by the Afrikaners, became an ideological weapon to achieve their political and social objectives.

The Afrikaner establishment had been lulled into regarding apartheid as scripturally sanctioned, thanks to the exegetical work of Professor E.P. Groenewald and the publications of Professor G. Gronjé. Both Professors argued that the scriptures taught the division of the Church of Christ on the grounds of race and color. Not that the Afrikaners were unusual in this regard. Writing about the structural social obligations of 18th century England, E.R. Norman maintains:

> The Social attitudes of the Church have derived from the surrounding intellectual and political culture, and not, as Christians themselves always seem to assume, from theological learning. The theologians have always managed to reinterpret their source in ways which have somehow made their version of Christianity correspond almost exactly to the values of their class and generation. . . .[2]

This judgment is apt in explaining the present predicament of the Church in South Africa. Between 1829 and 1881 the Dutch Reformed Church debated the issue of race relations in the Church. In 1881 the final solution to the problem was officially to create a racially separate religious establishment for members of the Reformed Church. White racial privileges in part have been moulded by the South African Dutch Reformed Church which claimed and propagated the political mythology of a "chosen people." The religious meaning of apartheid—the separation of the races—merged with the political meaning to form the basis of South African life since 1948. Excellent scholarship has shown how the Dutch Reformed Church in South Africa was vigorous in its use of Biblical assumptions in expounding the issues of race relations and politics. Afrikaner historiography traces the evolution of their "White Christian Civilization" in South Africa. This historiography owed its heritage to a vogue Calvinism—an arrogant religious conviction that God has given them the control over Africans. The National Party which came to power in 1948 utilized this vogue Calvinism to shape the political discourse in South Africa.[3]

But since the early 1950s we have been observing what might well be the cutting edge of a theological paradigm shift. The publication of *Colour: Unsolved Problem of the West* by Professor Ben Marais, though patronizing and even reactionary, challenged the Christians to seriously re-examine the issues of racism and the Churches. There were a series of theological renewals in the Christian communities of South Africa—the Reformed Ecumenical Synod at Potchefstroom in 1958, the Cottesloe Consultation of the South African member churches of the World Council of Churches (WCC) which met in 1960, Beyers Naudé who founded the Christian Institute, Black Consciousness Movement and Black Theology which had an impact on the Churches, and eventually the South African Christian Council leadership which passed from the hands of a liberal white Methodist layman John Rees to a black Anglican bishop, Desmond Tutu—in which Christians in South Africa found themselves at a juncture of events that center precisely in the question of whether it is legitimate to think theologically about the liberation of black people in South Africa. Although this is not a new question for modern Christian thought, in South Africa the introduction of such a question has brought the problem of liberation within the context of a Western prophetic tradition that has identified and criticized structures of domination in the social-political and economic order.

The revolutionary dynamics of Christian opposition to slavery, the feminist's position against the defenders of patriarchy and now the passionate opposition to the structures of domination in South Africa appeal to key theological and religious concepts in their critique of oppression. The theology of liberation has become popular in South Africa. A lot of this theology echoes the theology of liberation in the United States (James Cone), in Latin America (Sergio Torres and Gustavo Gutiérrez), in Taiwan (C.S. Song), in West Africa (Burgess Carr and Koffi Appiah-Kubi), in the Philippines (Eulalio P. Baltalzar), and in the Caribbean (Idris Hamid and Joyce Bailey). Its chief spokesmen in South Africa are Allan Boesak, Dr. Manas Buthelezi, Mokgethi Motlhabi, Sabelo Ntwasa and Desmond Tutu.

The historical development of the use of the Bible to sanction the idea of national liberation could be traced to Latin America and North America. With a combination of "Christian Sociology" and "Christian Theology", liberation theologians insist that God sides with the oppressed in their struggle for liberation. The most eminent exponents of this theology come from the Third World where extreme poverty, lack of education and oppressive structures exist in massive proportion. Their concerns focus on how to make the church more relevant to the needs of the people. On the Catholic side in Latin America, Gustav Gutierrez of Peru, though advocating radical social change, stresses love instead of class hatred.[4] Ruben Alves, the Brazilian Protestant Theologian argues that politics must become part of the new gospel of liberation, that churchmen must summon the people of the Third World to rise out of their passivity and become subjects of a new history, the builders of a new future.[5] But in building this new future, Miguez Bonino, a Methodist of Argentina warns Christians not to equate God's revelation with the history of revolution. God should not be identified with revolutionary history.[6] In North America, the God of the Exodus and Jesus the liberator are the central points of departure for theological discussion. Afro-American theologians such as James Cone and Albert Cleage would like to see more attention placed on the "underdogs" in the ghettos. They contend that the enslavement or poverty of one being is the enslavement or poverty of all. Their's is an effort to formulate a theological confrontation with "white" theology.[7]

In reaction to the policy of apartheid, white Christian liberals in South Africa have for several years fought hard to dismantle the system. They have produced historical documents and established various institutions challenging the racial and Biblical assumptions under which apartheid had thrived.[8] These documents and institutions have produced fundamental and total condemnation of the very basis of apartheid, namely that it is impossible to reconcile various racial groups within one political system. White liberal Christians reaffirmed that Christians should express their values in a social and political context in order to expose the immense suffering of the Africans, the callousness of the government and the indifference of the majority of their fellow White Christians. But the effectiveness of the message of the white liberal Christians was minimal because the liberal clergymen "almost universally tend to be more liberal than the congregation who pay the pastor's salaries."[9] The racism of the white working class which was the seed-bed of apartheid, and the failure of the Methodists, Roman Catholics, Presbyterians and Anglicans to act together especially in opposition to the 1953 Bantu Education Act are all indications of the problems confronting the white liberal Christian message of racial harmony.[10] Yet after the tragedy of the Sharpville massacre (March 21, 1960) had silenced the Black Community, it was the white liberal Christian clerics who continued to speak in the interests of the Black people since most Black South Africans felt there was not much point in talking to whites any more. The deepest significance of white Christian liberals was that they created the environment in which the church could become a major element of resistance to the policies of the state. Professor Leonard Thompson of Yale is correct when he reminded the Rockefeller Foundation's Study Commission on U.S. Policy Toward South Africa in 1982 that "the churches are a major element of resistance to the state."[11] This view is held by the majority of the African clergy. To them, "their churches have become more and more a vehicle for expression of political aspirations of black people in South Africa."[12]

There is a rise in a new self-confidence among black dissidents within South Africa. One of the functions of religion and ideology is to create a certain element of confidence in the minds of true believers. In South Africa, African Christian leadership has taken the offensive in the creation of an ideological confidence which could force socio-economic and subsequently political concessions out of the white minority government. It is this self-assured confidence that has created a revolutionary climate in South Africa.

It is the thesis of this paper that one of the most significant factors in the creation of this revolutionary climate is the confidence engendered by the whole process of de-ideologizing apartheid. Two sets of principles have clearly come on collision course. On the one hand marched the ideology of what Afrikaner Christians have called apartheid. Emerging on the other hand is black Christian leadership which is now appealing to the "revolutionary politics" of liberation theology as a way to measure the relevance of the church in South Africa.

To those who attribute great historical transformations to developments in the realm of thought, the insistence on the primacy of ideas in the transformation of South African society becomes interesting. In the tradition of Hegel and Nietzsche this viewpoint is exhilarating in its boldness of analysis. This paper examines the historical evolution and significance of the counter-ideology which has attempted to de-ideologize apartheid. The actors in this struggle to de-ideologize apartheid have been numerous but in this paper we shall focus on the Black Christian leadership in South Africa. The manner in which they perceive their role as liberators and their appeal to certain assumptions to resolve the critical problem of bondage shall be described. But more important, I hope to contribute to scholarship in the recent history of the Church in South Africa especially with regards to the role of religion as liberator.

II: National Liberation and Black Liberation Theology

The Africans have been seeking (since the first seizure of Khoi Khoi grazing lands by the agents of the Dutch East India Company in the 17th century) ways and means of resolving the crisis of bondage. There have been several phases of this struggle: the struggle between the Khoisan people and the Dutch settlers for land, water and pasturage on the Northwestern Cape (17th and 18th centuries); the conflict between the so-called "Bantu" and the Dutch and English colonialists on the Eastern frontier (18th and 19th centuries); the African Nationalist phase which subsequently led to the formation of the African National Congress (ANC) in 1913, which came to an end in 1960 when the white minority government outlawed it. More recently came the 1960s with the emergence of Black Consciousness movement which stressed the cultural and ideological independence of Africans in the formulation of their own destiny and by the 1970s Black liberation theology, as a religious manifestation of the struggle, sought to transform the political, social and economic life of the Africans. The three last phases—the nationalist, Black consciousness and Black theology—have produced fundamental ideological blueprints for dismantling apartheid.

From the beginning, religion and the art of government have

been inexorably intertwined. Religion had offered inspirational and manipulative possibilities for those who possess power and those over whom they exercise that power. Religion in this sense is used as a political mythology to legitimize power or is used as a liberating force for the oppressed. George Barany in his article "On Truth in Myths" argues that popular historical myths may draw on identical sources yet perform different functions depending on the historical and social context in which they are used.[13] Christian theology is a reality for both Afrikaner ideologues and the South African Black Christian leadership and its importance for both groups as a political tool is immense.

The Rise of Black Theology

Black theology in South Africa developed in response to challenges from the larger society. A new generation of African students have come to expect the Black Clergy to take a more radical stance in opposing the South African regime. African theological students have been trained outside the Bantu Education system and many have had quite a radical reputation which led the South African government to wage a campaign against the Federal Theological seminary at Alice. The students began to ask for a more socially, politically and economically relevant church. In spite of the passage of the Bantu Education Act which was aimed at "deconscientizing" the African student, several factors affected these African students. The increased industrialization, and its concomitant urbanization, had produced a greater number of Blacks who are secular minded in the resolution of their problems. The Civil Rights Movement and Black Power protests in the United States during the sixties and the successful liquidation of Portuguese Colonialism in Mozambique and Angola greatly influenced black attitudes and confidence in their aspirations for political and economic participation in South African life.[14] Oswald Mtshali's "Detribalised" pictures the emergence of a type of African youth who is:

> . . . clever
> not a moegie
> he never says baas
> to no bloody white man
> . . . He knows
> he must carry a pass.
> He don't care for politics
> He don't go to church

He knows Mandela
They're in Robben Island
"So what? That's not my business!"[15]

The young black people had to be mobilized, they had to be re-indoctrinated, they had to be "conscientized." In a position paper the Black students remarked:

- That African religion in its essence was not radically different from Christianity. It was the missionaries who confused the people with their new religion. By some strange and twisted logic they argued that theirs was a scientific religion and ours a superstition.
- That there is a strong case for a re-examination of Christianity to adapt it to our particular situation. Here then we have the case for Black Theology:
  1. It seeks to relate God and Christ once more to the black man and his daily problems.
  2. It wants to describe Christ as a fighting God, not a passive God.
  3. It is an important aspect of Black Consciousness Movement.

The position paper ended by advising the Black Clergy that "it is the duty of all black priests and ministers of religion to save Christianity by adopting the approach of Black Theology."[16] The challenge was thus initiated for the Black Clergy to re-examine its role in South Africa. To reenforce this challenge, white liberal Christians such as Basil Moore demanded, ". . . Where are the black churchmen who are gaining the skills to serve the people in their waterless starvation on South Africa's rural wastes to enable them to feed themselves and their children? Which black churchmen are to be found at Bantu Commissioner's offices with a real knowledge of the host of influx control laws, helping their people to find a home and hold their families together?"[17]

Although Black Theology in South Africa was born under the auspices of the University Christian Movement, it was the black clergy who defined and elaborated the claims of Black Theology.[18] Among the prominent Black Clergy who have advanced the claims of Black Theology in South Africa are Desmond Tutu, Allan Boesak, Simon Maimela, Manas Buthelezi and Bonganjals Gabo. These black clergymen are part of a vast theological current emanating from the Americas in the form of Liberation Theology. Liberation theologians contend that they are trying to prevent the churches in the Americas and Africa from choking on their own orthodoxy and folly. Black theology like its parent, Liberation Theology, is theology from the underside. Its claims include:

- That the Gospel of Jesus Christ does not only promise and bring spiritual gifts but makes a real tangible difference to the material conditions of human life.
- That Christians should be encouraged to commit themselves to political action that would lead to the transformation of the structures that have dehumanized the Africans.[19]

As time passed, the Black Consciousness Movement merged into the discussion of Black Theology. Indeed, young black clergymen gradually came to accept the objectives of the Black Consciousness Movement. Unlike their elders, these young black clergymen were "not prisoners of the Gospel."[20] Steve Biko, however, in 1970 had castigated those black ministers he had known for accepting white interpretation of the reason for black suffering in South Africa.[21] It should be noted that advocates of Black Theology have held three important seminars between 1972 and 1983 on the evolution of Black Theology within the historical context of the black struggle. In 1973 Father Sabelo Ntwasa wrote his incisive tirade on "The training of Black Ministers Today." In this article, Ntwasa deplored the unpreparedness of the black ordinands in the seminaries to confront the realities of life in South Africa. He noted:

> "At present the church has enough Uncle Toms amongst its clergy: We should work to decrease rather than increase their number. If the church is to become the church with a prophetic voice it needs prophets. These cannot be mass produced but you can at least try to ensure that those being trained are not there because they see the ministry as the gateway to a middle class life. Our life as ministers of Christ ought to be one of identification with the wretched of the earth."[22]

The Uncle Tomism and materialism of the black clergy have always been of great concern to the Association of Black Ministers. A number of the Black Clergymen had accepted positions in the civil service of the so called "Homeland" governments. The Association of Black Ministers had registered its disapproval of such activities and had indicated its intention to appeal to the Bishops to refuse to give such clergymen licenses to practice their profession.[23]

The Black Clergy was also subjected to criticism with regards to the content of their theological education. The theological schools that train Black Clergy, it was observed, had over-emphasized historical criticism rather than contextual African realities. This criticism of the content of the training of the Black Clergy is very significant especially since Western scholars themselves have even questioned the usefulness of historical criticism in modern theology. "Historical criticism of the Bible," wrote Charles Davis, "while it may still have a glorious future as a branch of history, would seem to be near the end of its career in theology."[24] The Black Peoples Congress (BPC) and the Black Clergy had an open ideological split in 1974. The Black Clergy had called for the Black Renaissance Convention that year. At this convention the BPC accused the Black Clergy of being influenced by "white money" and of performing the clandestine operation of the Central Intelligence Agency. The students of the BPC then concluded that the Black Clergy was incapable of being the custodian of the Black Consciousness Movement.[25]

The black students and the BPC were in particular addressing their criticism of the Black Clergy within the context of what church historians call "ecclesiastical colonialism." In South Africa, the political, economic and social policies of the state were also reflected in the structure of church government. European forms of church government dominated. The whites dominated and manipulated the forms of church government in order to retain power in the decision-making bodies. "Ecclesiastical colonialism" implied that black ministers were paid lower stipends than their white colleagues; that black ministers had a higher ratio of ministers to lay people; that black church buildings were less ambitious and less luxurious than those of white congregations; that black students were exposed to European teachings of Christianity without an African dimension to those teachings; and that the Black Clergy were reduced to a dependent and inferior position in church hierarchy.[26]

It is true that many of the Black Clergy depend on the financial contributions of the white churches. Indeed, the Black Clergy expects the white churches to contribute more to their projects because the white congregations are beneficiaries of the economic system of the racist regime. But as to the accusation that the Black Clergy has been influenced by "white money," there is little indication to prove that he who pays the piper dictates the tune. It has recently been confirmed that white financial contributions to black churches have dwindled as the Black Clergy aggressively pursue their projects to dismantle the apartheid system.[27] It was this fear of losing financial support from the Dutch Reformed Church (DRC) that the Black Clergy of the DRC in Africa, after declaring its opposition to the policy of apartheid, cautiously emphasized: "We do not believe that the statement of 10 Oct. 1973 . . . can disturb the relationship between the DRC in Africa and the DRC as far as mutual relations and financial help are concerned . . ."[28] By 1982 the viewpoint of the Black Dutch Reformed Churches became more radical. This viewpoint has been articulated by the Reverend Shun Govender, the Secretary of the Broederkring—the national body of the dissident reformed Black Churches in South Africa. He was one of the Black Clergymen who successfully pushed for the expulsion of the white NGK church from the World Alliance of Reformed Churches in 1982.

As to the accusation of being C.I.A. operatives, it is very noteworthy that the Black Clergy has found itself in the middle. The radical black nationalists look upon the clergy as C.I.A. operatives, and "even some black priests are now finding themselves considered by the youth as part of the enemy."[29] The Afrikaner nationalists see them as agents of the Communists.[30] It is a fact that the Black Clergy has received assistance from outside South Africa. This assistance from abroad has not been substantial; rather it is seen as a psychological boost to the clergy and their congregation. It was Hannah Arendt who observed that for an obedient Nazi who gassed millions of innocent people, his behavior stemmed partly from the fact that "there were no voices from the outside to arouse his conscience."[31] The point underscores the central purpose of the assistance given by the All African Council for Churches since 1974 and that given by the World Council of Churches since 1968 of which the special fund payments to the ANC has been highly controversial.[32] Although the Black Clergy went along in the condemnation of the activities of the WCC with regards to the special fund assistance to the ANC, they did so with the full knowledge that any signs of support for the WCC meant treason within the South African legal system.

Outside support, however significant it might be, could not transform South Africa without the African clergy taking leadership roles in the churches of South Africa. The issue of black leadership roles in the churches prompted Tutu to observe:

At this stage the leadership of the struggle must be firmly in black hands, they must determine what will be the priorities and the strategy of the struggle . . . the point is that however much they want to identify with blacks it is an existential fact . . . that they have not really been victims of this baneful oppression and exploitation. It is a divide that can't be crossed and that must give blacks a primacy in determining the course and goal of the struggle. Whites must be willing to follow.[33]

This was not racism, it was simple recognition of a brutal reality since whites generally possessed vested interests in South Africa's exploitative caste system. It was also a simple recognition that genuine leadership is a moral process in which leaders engage followers on the basis of shared values and experiences of living in the house of bondage. Tutu's observation is indicative of the fact that regardless of how sympathetic whites may be to the aspirations of the black community, only black leaders are likely to have a consistent regard for black concerns, particularly in South Africa where the whites are effectively cut off from the daily experiences and therefore concerns, of the black community. Indeed, the Azanian Peoples Organization formed in 1979 to promulgate the militant aspects of Black consciousness movement would agree with Tutu's assertion that the black people themselves in South Africa have to be in the position of leadership in the struggle and that whites in South Africa and abroad have to play only a supporting role.

The Role of the Black Clergy

We are now in a position to critically assess what the Black Clergy, once left alone in leadership role, regard as important and relevant to the Africans. In their leadership role, the Black Clergy found itself at the very center stage of the politics of liberation. The educational system has always been a powerful channel to propagate the "truths" of government, religious groups and intellectuals. In South Africa the passage of the Bantu Education Act of 1953 deprived the Black Clergy of an access to the mission schools. Having demoralized the black educators, the South African government predictably proceeded to make its own "truth" the correct view in the schools.[34] The Black Clergy in turn has turned to other channels to propagate its own "truth."

The Black Clergy reacted in different ways in resolving the question of "hypocrisy and double standards" of White Christians in South Africa. Between 1890 and 1910 there were two distinct reactions. One reaction was to remain optimistic of an eventual change of heart on the part of the racist electorate. But a growing number of the Black Clergy came to reject the teachings and beliefs of the White Christians. African nationalism in South Africa was thus expressed first through religion. In 1892 the Black Clergyman Mangena Mokone founded the Ethiopian Church with the attempt to spread the message of Psalms 68 verse 31: "Ethiopia shall soon stretch out her hands unto God," hence the name of the church. Writing in 1948 and again in 1961, Bengt Sundkler, the doyen of the African Independent Churches observed that these churches and their clergy did not assert their civil and political rights.[35] The assertion of George Shepperson in 1953 still remains correct: "Although the native church movement, on strictly Ethiopian and on 'Zionist' levels, was to grow, much of its political fervor was spent. More and more it seemed to turn itself into a safety valve."[36]

The withdrawal from the white churches, and their proclivity to retire to purely African associations were negative reactions to the continued racist policies of the South African government. The Ethiopian movement reacted with dignified protest, while the Zionists built a world apart—an emotional Utopia and were ultimately degraded to the status of a "safety valve." Martin West writing in 1975 about *Bishops and Prophets* in Soweto confirmed the continued existence of political docility in the activities of the Black Clergy of the Independent Churches.[37] And Sundkler writing in 1976 observed that Zionists set up "a hot-line to heaven."[38] It was a "Heavenly Telephone" not directed to Pretoria.

The first attempt by the Black Christian leadership to influence the course of Black Liberation came in 1913 when the African National Congress was formed.[39] The African nationalists turned to Rev. John Dube, an American trained clergy of the Congregational Church and founder of the Natal Ohlange Institute—a counterpart of Booker T. Washington's Tuskegee. In his letter accepting the presidency, Dube emphasized prudence and dutiful respect for the rulers God had placed over them. Dube's lamentation was typical of his time: "How can a government policy proclaiming itself Christian perpetrate such cruelties on the inarticulate poor? How can a professedly Christian people permit such persecution in their midst and look on unmoved . . . why must we alone of all the peoples of the earth, condemn ourselves to serfdom in order to be permitted to live in our mother country?"[40] This spirit of disillusionment characterized the period and to this generation of the Black Clergy, "ambiguity was the essence of survival" and like their counterparts in the United States, "they seem to have learnt early the constraints of dependency."[41]

Yet it was in 1946 that the Inter-Denominational African Ministers Association of South Africa was formed to achieve a more effective propagation of the Gospel and to create a forum through which African and "Colored" clergymen could speak to topical ecclesiastical and *political* issues with a united voice. Through its annual meetings they denounced the policy of racial segregation and categorically stated that the policy constituted a threat to race relations in South Africa. In 1950 there were intense pressures from an element in the Black Churches to form an African National Church and once and for all have a final split with the white churches and their society. The Inter-Denominational African Ministers Association rejected the idea.[42] It appears that those Black Clergy who advocated the formation of an African National Church were also in support of Pan-African Congress radicalism.[43]

If the policies of segregation between 1910 and 1948 disappointed the Black Clergy, the policies after 1948 killed all hopes that whites meant to do justice. Chief Albert Luthuli, teacher, lecturer, leader in the Christian Councils and Nobel laureate, President of ANC (1952–1967), like his predecessor Rev. Dube, lamented the fate of his people in the hands of White Christians. "White paternalist Christianity . . . enstranges my people from Christ. Hypocrisy, double standards and the identification of white skins with Christianity, do the same. For myself, for very many of us, nothing short of apostacy would budge us. We know Christianity for what it is, we know it is not a white preserve, we know that many whites—and Africans for that matter—are inferior exponents of what they profess. The faith of Christ persists in spite of them. But how many weak and experimental black Christians are made to stumble by the white example? How vulnerable we Christians are! . . . The churches above all were to have brought us not apartheid but fellowship one with another . . . have not many of the churches simply submitted to a secular state . . . It is not too late for White Christians to look at the Gospels and redefine their allegiance . . ."[44]

Luthuli came from the Christian liberal tradition. His plea for White Christian re-examination of the Gospel and redefinition of their allegiance was given expression by the vigorous white liberal clergy who formulated the theological constructs that affected the black nationalists and clergy alike. The period of this activity was 1948 to 1970. The non-violent means of protest was met by violence and political repression. The structural violence of apartheid intensified—population removals, migrant labor, pass laws, detention without trial, torture and deaths in detention. A society was finally created where a racist regime, supported by the DRC, inflicted intolerable pain on black people ranging from enforced poverty to unjust laws.[45] It was becoming increasingly difficult for the black community to mobilize itself because all channels of doing so were closed to them.

On the other hand, driven by the fierce edges of the perilous times, driven by common sense, the main line English speaking Christian churches accelerated the rate at which the Black clergy entered positions of authority. More black Christians were appointed in positions of authority between 1960 and 1982 than ever before in the history of the South African churches. Among these Black Christian leadership included: Bishop Alphaeus Zulu who in 1966 became the first black Bishop in charge of a Diocese (Zululand and Swaziland); the Rev. Benjamin Ngidi who in 1969 became the Chairman-elect of the Congregational Church in South Africa; Bishop Desmond Tutu who in 1978 became the first black African head of the South African Council of Churches; Sonangalisco Mkhatshwa who in 1981 became the first black Secretary General of the South African Catholic Bishop's Conference. In the Catholic Church, ten black Bishops were ordained between 1972 and 1982. The Black Bishops now constitute a third of the Bishops Conference. Similar leadership changes occurred in the Methodist Church. This shift in leadership has affected the way the churches now address the political and social and economic plight of the oppressed in South Africa. They have once again brought into focus the centrality of the black preacher in the struggle for liberation. They have joined the tradition of those Black preachers who once proclaimed "go down tell the pharaohs let my people go".

The Strategies of Black Protest

Historically, Black people under oppression have come to interpret Christianity in the light of their future emancipation. In providing their own sources for theologizing, Black Christian leadership have made Black Theology a weapon of theory and are at present attempting to make it also the property of the struggling masses. In 1969 for example, black Lutheran Bishop Manas Buthelezi and Allan Boesak called for a massive civil disobedience campaign.[46] Without debating the merits and demerits of massive civil disobedience, it is clear that when in 1977 a group of Black clergy carried out the call for civil disobedience in Johannesburg, the march was summarily smashed by the authorities.[47] One has to go back to the 1950s to explain the complete failure of Luthuli's civil disobedience. The authorities in Pretoria have established a system which does not accommodate civil disobedience. This system lacked Christian liberation and democratic scruples that must characterize an environment under which civil disobedience could flourish and succeed. Massive civil disobedience as a redemptive doctrine became an illusion in South Africa.

The ANC following the dictum that the masses must resist and fight in a thousand ways, not only with arms, has called for black South Africans to make themselves ungovernable and thereby make the institutions of apartheid unworkable.[48] In a symbolic feeling of unity in the struggle, the funerals of the victims of the recent protests have provided common grounds for Black religious leaders and the ANC. The funerals have become forums for political statements—with the ANC flag draped over the row of coffins in praise of ANC leaders, Nelson Mandela and Oliver Tambo and the underground guerilla wing of the ANC, "Unkhonto we Sizwe" (Spear of the Nation). The cortege has been led by religious leaders who eulogize the victims with impassioned appeal to Africans to avoid retaliatory violence.

Black Church leaders have been advocates of liberal options of non-violence. But the ANC has called for an intensification of attacks on strategic military and economic installations. In May 1983 the ANC attacked the South African Airforce headquarters in Pretoria. Again in keeping with their clerical duty, the Black religious leaders through Bishop Tutu declared that "The South African Council of Churches expresses its horror and condemns this act of naked terrorism."[49] After the South African government raid on supposedly ANC hide-aways in Mozambique where innocent civilians were killed, Tutu responded by deploring the SAAF strike into Maputo "as I condemned the bomb outrage in Pretoria last Friday, I do so relating to retaliatory strike into Mozambique."[50] Again, like their predecessors of the 19th and early

20th centuries the Black religious leaders find themselves in ambiguities. Bishop Tutu, for example, has recognized apartheid as a declaration of war on black people. Using historical illustrations Tutu observed:

> The Voortrekkers protested, then disengaged, then fought. Blacks have protested, have disengaged and some of them are now fighting . . . If the government continues with its policy when there will be a peaceful solution, for they are declaring war on us . . . What are Blacks then expected to do in such a situation? Fold their hands?[51]

This is a reminder that apartheid is a war machine—a war machine which need not be fuelled by foreign investments. As a war machine, the violence of apartheid is a serious reality to Africans and the Black religious leadership has to confront the issue of dismantling it through violence.

In a B.B.C.[52] interview Tutu was reminded that the liberation fighters of South Africa were "men of violence"; he replied that they are engaged in armed struggle—a different dimension of the struggle to achieve equality in South Africa. If Tutu's assertion that "apartheid is as evil, as immoral, as un-christian, in my view as Nazism," is true, the notion of the violence option in the dismantling of apartheid should be seriously discussed. Apartheid as "state violence" on the Africans introduces the notion of a "just war" on the system. In this situation revolutionaries are often involved in legitimate self-defense. Tutu, it appears is prepared to distinguish between different kinds of violence. State violence in South Africa according to the Black religious leaders made it imperative for the ANC for example, to resort to self-defense. In this sense the ANC is perfectly justified. Thus a distinction has to be made between predatory violence and the violence of resistance.

Allan Boesak had concurred with Tutu that "A situation may arise where retaliatory violence is forced upon the oppressor,"[53] although he thinks that this drastic step has to be examined in the light of the Scriptures. In an interview with *Africa Report,* Boesak attempts to clarify his viewpoint on violence: "I do not think that theology can ever justify any kind of violence . . . although there is the understanding of the Church as to why people out of their helplessness and powerlessness are driven to a situation in which they become so desperate that the taking up of the gun is the only answer. In that respect, the Church has a clear pastoral responsibility to those people."[54] While not giving a *carte blanche* to armed revolution, the Black Christian leaders have laid the blame for violence at the door of the government. The concept of "defensive violence" had led Michael Ramsay, former Archbishop of Canterbury to comment: "How can we applaud Europeans who resisted the tyranny of a Hitler and then be shocked when Africans want to resist a tyrannical regime today . . . we too easily form a habit of exculpating the violence in our own sphere of history and censuring the violence of other races."[55] The ANC has accepted violence as a redemptive instrument for bringing into being a fuller human life in South Africa. Yet the Black religious leadership has continued to insist on "persuasive pressure"—a campaign of political, diplomatic and economic pressure against the government as the last chance to avert a bloodbath. Tutu had lamented:

> Our people are rapidly despairing of a peaceful revolution in South Africa. Those of us who still speak 'peace and reconciliation' belong to a rapidly diminishing minority. And if they decide to fight, they know they can't go to the west for support. So we are paradoxically being driven into the arms of the Soviets to get our arms, by the very country [U.S.] that is concerned about Soviet expansionism.[56]

The political vocabulary of the Black religious leaders so far has been filled with mediation and reconciliation. Boesak favored reconciliation "by any means necessary" while Tutu in 1980 went further by his historic meeting with Prime Minister Botha.[57] Radical Blacks were dismayed and disappointed and in defense of his actions Tutu explained:

> Please remember the paradigms we've got to follow are biblical paradigms. Moses went to see Pharaoh not once but several times. Who are we to prejudge the grace of God? It's very difficult for me as a church leader to say 'Go to hell,' to say God's grace cannot operate on P.W. Botha.[58]

Collectively, the Black religious leaders have shied away from direct support of the revolutionary armed struggle. They even have denied any connections with the banned African National Congress. This has been a far cry from their late colleague in the now liberated Zimbabwe. Canaan Banana had put himself on line with his support of the guerilla freedom fighters in the then Rhodesia. His celebrated, emphatic irreversible shift is remarkable. His selective use of the Bible to describe the support given to African liberation fighters is worthy of being quoted in full:

Since I have been personally involved in the struggle for liberation many passages from the Bible have assumed new and compelling meanings . . . 'Greater love has no man than this, that a man lay down his life for his friends' (John 15:13) What can be more Christian than sacrificing one's life for one's fellow persons? So there is therefore a real sense in which Christian young people who offer their lives to fight for their country are bearing their crosses. They are motivated by love of what is dear to them, they sacrifice their precious lives in order to eliminate the forces of evil, becoming martyrs of freedom and saints of our time.[59]

The Black religious leadership in South Africa has not put itself in line with the aforementioned position. Yet as each year passes by they have become more and more skeptical of a peaceful transformation. Explaining this skepticism Tutu stated: "I fear more and more that change, real change in South Africa to a just, democratic non-racial society will only come violently and with bloodshed.[60]

We see Calvinist Boesak and Anglican Tutu attempting to reconcile their Christian faith to the socio-political realities of South Africa. They have become the bridge between liberalism and radicalism in the black discourse of liberation. Yet to most observers their "political stances have nearly always been a traditional liberal one, emphasizing the importance of symbolic inter-racial 'bridge building' and the avoidance of hostility toward whites."[61] To most African religious leaders the church's task is to call all men and women to conversion and reconciliation without opposing groups, without being against anyone. On the issue of armed revolution the Black religious leaders would leave Africans to make their own decision according to their own consciences and circumstances. Tutu in this regard has come to call himself a peace lover but not a pacifist.[62] Gail Gerhart has written optimistically: "As a group and individually African ministers have the potential to influence relatively large numbers of ordinary people in a population having a larger percentage of church goers."[63]

Collectively, the Black religious leaders have been consistent in their appeal to the authorities to improve the material condition of the Africans. The Inter-Denominational African Ministers Association of South Africa (IDAMASA) carried the 'Church' to the people in the field of experimental farming. They have attempted to reform the school syllabuses and mediate inter-tribal infightings.[64] Their parishoners who work in the cities have been confronting the apartheid system and the Church leaders have recognized the urgency of the problem. They have discovered that:

> When people are contracted into industrial areas, they lose contact with their churches at home, and ministers in the city usually fail to reach out to them. So our task is to conduct seminars on labor relations with clergy who minister mainly to Blacks. When these clergymen are aware of what is expected of them, what they must know, what delays equality at the industrial level they begin to relate to their parishioners in a new way.[65]

For the Black clergy to relate to their parishioners in a new way, they have to be re-oriented in their clerical training. Such re-orientation would include the material support to the poor: provisions of funds to support strikers belonging to Black Trade Unions, assistance to the families of banned persons, legal aid to those affected during the Soweto uprisings in 1976 and the rehabilitation of freed political prisoners.[66]

Ideologically this orientation of the clergy would put certain demands on the oppressed and the oppressor. If this is the case, then we need to look optimistically at the infusion of Black Consciousness ideology into the theological re-orientation of the clergy. If this movement "is a movement by which God, through Steve (Biko), sought to awaken in the Black person a sense of his (of her) intrinsic value and worth as a child of God . . . ,"[67] then Tutu will argue that the teaching of it should be included in the seminaries that train African clergy.

The writings of Richard Sincere, Jr., *The Politics of Sentiment: Churches and Foreign Investment in South Africa* and Thomas Oden, *Conscience and Dividends: Churches and the Multinationals* brilliantly examine the arguments of the pros and cons of external investment in South Africa (Sincere, Jr.) and the Third World (Oden). The debate, however, should rather focus on the limit of the commitment of these companies to oppressive governments. For example, in South Africa one might ask the question: to what extent are these foreign companies committed to finance, train and provide assistance to the regime as provided in the National Key Points Act, the National Supplies Procurement Act and the Internal Security Act of 1982? If these companies are indeed obligated to the government especially in providing the services for the Defense Ministry which in turn uses those services to suppress African resistance, a critical evaluation is needed to assess whether such companies retard or advance constructive change.

Furthermore, the Sullivan Principle which was aimed at encouraging American Companies to comply with such things as equal pay and desegregation of the work place has outlived its relevance as a policy equation. It has been replaced by the so called "Tutu Conditions." For Tutu and his supporters the Sullivan Principle would make apartheid more comfortable but would not dismantle it.

The "Tutu Conditions" gave notice that if the regime does not abolish the apartheid system within a maximum of two years he would effectively advocate disinvestment even though such an advocacy is classified as a treasonable offense in South Africa. The "Tutu Conditions" also set forth some highly desirable objectives: provision of decent housing for black workers and their families in places near their work sites; greatly increased investments in black education and training; full recognition not only of union rights but of individual workers' rights to seek jobs of their own choosing rather than being forced to accept those assigned by a government labor agency. These then are the Bishop's interim objectives. Divestment is an important weapon in the arsenal against apartheid; the Black Clergy in South Africa have understood the implications of divestment. Yet it is their recognition of the ideological potency of the struggle that the black church leaders are attempting to perfect.

The Black religious leadership has not only recognized apartheid as a war machine but they have also recognized it as a thinking machine—a theoretical affirmation of Afrikaner Dutch Reformed theology of group survival at the expense of Black people in South Africa. Through their writings, speeches and sermons, Black Christian leadership have utilized Biblical teachings as a weapon of theory to present alternatives to White Afrikaner theology which they have depicted "as the beast in Revelation 13:1." Apartheid supporters are accused of supporting a "blasphemous power." The argument to replace this "blasphemous power" has taken an ideological direction.[68]

Perhaps, the most dramatic and significant event of 1977 was the publication of Allan Boesak's *Farewell to Innocence*. This *magnus opus* of Black Theology in South Africa was addressed to both Whites and Blacks. Whites and Blacks, Boesak argues, have certain responsibilities to correct the situation in South Africa. Whites have to be willing to identify with what the oppressed are doing to serve their liberation; the oppressed on the other hand has a responsibility, for the greatest ally of the oppressor is the mind of the oppressed. As for White Afrikaner Nationalists, Boesak illustrated the hollowness of their claims that they are guided by Christian principles, and that when their claims are tested against the gospel of Jesus Christ they are wanting and can only be regarded as pseudo-religious national ideology.

Several articles and books on Black Theology in South Africa have been published since 1977. They have influenced the Black religious leaders in the following plans of pastoral action: entering into the poverty and struggle of the poor, (Bishop Tutu, for example, chose to live in Soweto rather than live in the official residence of the Bishop[69]) conscienticization as liberation education, and prophetic denunciation of the oppression and injustice of the apartheid. Black theological writings have given the Black people in South Africa an alternative political vision that is perhaps utopian. They argue that what is required is an explanation of the doctrine of equality which would bring the reality of social life into congruence with moral imperative.

The publication of Boesak's *Black and Reformed* in 1984 highlighted the personal crisis in being a Black person and a member of the Reformed Church in South Africa. This book, which is a series of speeches and sermons and letters written with one exception between 1979 and 1983, summarizes Boesak's views on violence, justice, God's action in history and the biblical stories that proclaim the good news to the poor. Reading this book, one is reminded of the sections in *Farewell to Innocence* where Boesak stressed the universality of the "Word of God":

> In its focus on the poor and the oppressed the theology of liberation is not a new theology; it is simply the proclamation of the age-old gospel, but now liberated from the deadly hold of the mighty and the powerful and made relevant to the situation of the oppressed and the poor.[70]

Boesak and the Black religious leaders have to conclude that salvation is not a separate "religious" other-worldly activity. They argue that "saving souls" is important but this cannot be achieved without dismantling the oppressive structures of society. For them Jesus opposed the exploitation of the weak by the powerful; Jesus spoke of a liberating God. For them the struggle against apartheid is not merely a struggle against an evil ideology. It is also a struggle for the integrity of the Gospel of Jesus Christ. It is in this sense that we can then start understanding the World Council of Churches and its Program to Combat Racism, and the Cottesloe Consultation with its effort to grapple seriously with the Church's responsibility after the massacre at Sharpville; then finally the declaration of apartheid as heresy in Canada in 1983 and the impassioned pleas of love and concern of people like Bishop Tutu.

The Prospects of Black Revolution

The church that the Black clerics lead is not a single, cohesive ideological content wide movement, but a congeries of groups and initiatives. The black groups at odds reflect a historical division in black South African politics. The ANC was infected with the problems of tribal differences, animosities and class differences, while its guerilla wing (Umkh) has been advocating an armed offensive since 1960. The Azania Peoples Organization has rejected white involvement in their activities; the UDF (United Democratic Front) support a multi-racial opposition to apartheid; the Inkatha movement of Chief Gatsha Buthelezi, leader of the Zulus, is accused of working within the apartheid system. Black clerics in South Africa are increasingly being pressured to take sides. But so far they have been calling for Black political unity.

Yet their modest appeals have come under severe criticism. To the revolutionaries non-violence and "persuasive pressure" have become allies of the oppressor. In their place, revolutionaries have advocated making South Africa ungovernable. A certain segment of Black religious leaders have come to question the validity of basing Black liberation on Biblical teaching. Critics[71] maintain that the Bible is a product and a record of class struggle. They now argue that the Bible is a ruling class document and represents the ideological and political interests of the ruling class; that the Bible is more inclined toward social stability than toward social transformation and liberation. To this group of Black Christians the fundamental question is not the Black versus White struggle—a racial analysis of the struggle. The struggle should be seen within the context of the oppressive and exploitative capitalist world. To them racism does not exist as a social or natural construct; racism is socially acquired—apartheid is an economic system with a racist "explanation," apartheid exists because of economic greed, cultural chauvinism and political oppression and not because of the gospel. To be fair to the ideas of Allan Boesak and Desmond Tutu, both of them see apartheid as a product of deformed capitalism. For Boesak "beyond the question of race lies the economic question. This is one of the things I have learned from our brothers and sisters from Latin America . . ."[72] For Tutu apartheid does not want to share the wealth of the nation equitably, and he "longs for a society which is not so grasping, not ruled by the laws of the rat race, but one in which there is more sharing."[73]

The United Democratic Front (UDF), a coalition of 600 groups organized to fight the new constitution, began to speak not only against white racial economic and political oppression but also spoke out against all those Blacks who collaborate with the white oppressors. For them, apartheid no longer has only a white face. One of the greatest challenges of the Black church leaders is how to respond to this new interpretation of the struggle within the context of class not race.[74] The Gospel teaching of Jesus, not Marxist theory, provides the central theme of salvation for both Tutu and Boesak and for the majority of the Black Church men. To them liberation theology is not a kind of a baptism of Marx.

In November 1979 the President of the African Provincial Synod critically assailed Black Theology: It "may be called a theology of liberation but it is not a Gospel of liberation. The Gospel is for all men good news. The theology of apartheid and liberation are essentially two sides of the same coin. That they grew out of fear of oppression in the future on one hand and the experience of oppression in the present on the other. Therefore what is "Gospel" to one is doom to another in human terms. Both came out of a struggle for political power. There is salvation in neither. . . ."[75] Critics assert that the theme of salvation lacks profound and lucid reflections in both the theology of apartheid and liberation. Yet a Christian's political commitment or lack of it derives ultimately from his understanding of salvation. To Botha and his cohorts the state is threatened by violent forces under communist leadership and an onslaught against South Africa is a total onslaught against the Kingdom of God. To Tutu and like minded Black Church men they are going to win the battle to dismantle apartheid because God is on their side. The big divide is the claim by both sides that God is on their side and that they have the absolute "Truth."

In 1980 Chester Crocker, the Undersecretary of State for Africa, commented that in political terms South Africa is not embraceable and suggested reformist solutions to apartheid. Whether the recent Botha 'reforms' are one consequence of this policy or not, the present apartheid government has recognized the potential force of the ideological and religious challenge to apartheid. The government has decided to drag its Afrikaner followers faster down the road to change (or should we say moderate the harshness of apartheid) than any Nationalist leadership has done since the party came to power in 1948.

Although the apartheid regime has recognized the need to reform, the recent reforms are introduced to make the system survive without being dismantled. The government has been making concessions since 1978 but they are small, slow and even illusory.[76] The view of Bishop Desmond Tutu on this matter is indicative of the general opinion of the Black Christian leadership. Tutu reflecting on the so called reforms observed:

> The government is attempting to give the appearance of reform. They have introduced some multiracial sport, so called international hotels and restaurants to serve all races, removed some discriminatory signs, etc. and whites are going into ecstasies about all this evidence of change. Let us dismiss it! All is merely cosmetic-superficial. They are crumbs of concession which have fallen from the master's table. We don't want these crumbs. We want to be there deciding the menu together. We don't want apartheid to be made more comfortable as would be the effect . . . As Sally Mottana, a vice-president of the SA Council of Churches put it, "We don't want our chains made comfortable, we want them removed."[77]

Boesak strongly agrees with Tutu. To him, "Apartheid can never be modified. A system as thoroughly evil as apartheid cannot be streamlined, cannot be reformed. It can only be totally and irrevocably eradicated and that's what we have to work for."[78]

III: Conclusion

The South African government has concluded that the Black Clergy has to be closely watched. The events that led to the closure in 1975 of the Federal Theological Seminary formerly in Alice and now in Pietermaritzburg—one of the most intense centers of black consciousness thinking and Black Theology—illustrate the concern of the government with the activities and ideas of the Black Clergy.[79] The government appointed two commissions of inquiry. The Steyn Commission (appointed to investigate the press and the news media) was highly critical of Black Theology, and the Eloff Commission of Inquiry (appointed to investigate the South African Council of Churches and recommend whether the church Council would be declared an "affected organization" because of its involvement in political and ecumenical issues) still has to come out with its own findings. The government has continued to harrass the Black Clergy and has tried to discredit them. The leadership of Bishop Tutu in particular came under attack. The security police—"Boss"—believes that SACC is doing the work of the banned African National Congress. A cabinet minister went further in accusing SACC of being "an agent of the underground."[80] The theological views of the Black Clergy have also come under strict scrutiny; for example, the government gave support to the Christian League of South Africa—the ultra right wing counterforce to the rising tide of Black Theology. It is believed that the Information Department of the government provided funds to the League until the end of 1979 when the Information Department itself was discredited.[81] More significant is the fact that the South African Security Police "is probably the only secret police in the world to have created a branch specializing in theological matters."[82] Vehement rejection of new paradigms by the defenders of the old is to be expected as Thomas Kuhn and others have taught us to anticipate.

But the truth is a devastating weapon. Today, the whites in South Africa have conceded that the Verwoerdian dream of complete separation of the races will never be realized. The Christian conscience of the Afrikaner is troubled but not yet enough to abandon political power over the blacks of South Africa. It is in this context that the Black clerics are advocating economic and diplomatic pressures on the government.

The contention that "if the present deadly sparring between white and black nationalists in South Africa develops into a full scale civil war, it will have to be a Christian Civil War,"[83] should be taken seriously. This viewpoint does not in any way minimize the racial and class analysis of South African history within the context of a future debacle. The political implications of the Christian message especially with regards to equality is still as subversive as ever, if taken seriously. The unfolding tragedy obliges all

Christians of the world to prepare for a possible showdown in South Africa.

The Afrikaners and the Black Clergy appeal to Christianity but, at the same time, they give entirely different and incompatible interpretations of the fundamental principles of Christianity. This is no longer a mere religious dispute. It has tremendous political impact. For black Christians, the most frightening reality in South Africa is the totality of control apartheid seeks to exercise over their lives. The Black Christian leadership could play a decisive role as the Afrikaner clerics did in the early history of their presence in South Africa. The Afrikaner resorted to arms in 1881 and 1899 against the British with the blessings of the clerical leadership of the Dutch Reform Church. Because of the dialectic ideals of African and Afrikaner nationalisms and the racial reinforcement of class distinctions between Black and White, white power, according to advocates of an armed struggle, will not abandon its privileges without a violent challenge.

If the present policy of the ANC succeeds in creating a serious cadre of armed resistance we might end up with one of the worst racial conflagrations. An all-out armed conflict would pit the Afrikaner who is bent on the survival of the Volk—his government equipped with every conceivable form of anti-personnel weaponry, including access to tactical nuclear weapons, or capability of producing such weapons—against a black population that is growing impatient and desperate to remove the chains of bondage. The fundamental role of the Black religious leaders have been to stave off the disaster by asking the United States to forego its present policy of "Constructive engagement," to forego its "neutrality" and to support the claims of the oppressed. Yet we should realistically place the Black religious leaders into an appropriate context. All peoples—especially all beseiged peoples—need "high priests" (clergymen, theologians, scholars and intellectuals) to justify, rationalize and explain their national aspirations and behavior. The Dutch in South Africa had produced their "high priests" who rationalized the way of life which became known as apartheid. The Black religious leaders have gradually become the "high priests" of African liberation. According to them the "Native Question" has become the answer. Black liberation theology was forged in the context of black disenfranchisement and seeks divine sanction for black freedom and majority rule.

There are two options open to the South Africans: peaceful

transition through reconciliation and negotiations rather than the "lousy crumbs" that have fallen from the master's table or cataclysmic collapse in which the soil of South Africa is soaked with rivers of blood to fertilize the seed of liberation. But whether freedom comes through peaceful means or through armed struggle, the liberation of the Blacks is as much a vital prerequisite to the liberation of the oppressors as the liberation of the oppressed. This fact has led Tutu to declare: "we are committed to Black liberation because thereby we are committed to white liberation. You [the whites] will never be free until we blacks are free. So join the liberation struggle."[84] His is not only an appeal to White South Africans but also an appeal to all men of good will, especially those who avow the liberal Christian message: "There is neither Jew nor Greek, there is neither bond nor free, there is neither male nor female: for ye are all one in Christ." Although the phrase "Ye are all one in Christ" has been variously interpreted, the concensus of many Christians now is that apartheid is an evil. But apartheid is more than a moral struggle. It is a legal struggle. The emancipation of black people in South Africa would come about when there is a change in their legal status. The insistence of the Afrikaner that his government is an outpost of Christianity and western democracy in Africa has been found wanting. The violence that is required to maintain apartheid negates the values of Christianity, democracy and civilization. It is against this background that any policy on South Africa should be based.

NOTES

1. The study upon which this article was originally based, was made possible by a fellowship from the National Endowment for the Humanities, Washington D.C., which allowed me to participate in the Summer Seminar at Yale, 1982. I want to express my gratitude to Professor Leonard Thompson of Yale who encouraged and assisted me in the original research.

2. E.R. Norman, *Church and Society in England 1770–1970* (Oxford 1976), 10–11.

3. For the historiography see S. R. Rither, "The Dutch Reformed Church and Apartheid," *Journal of Contemporary History,* 2, no. 4, Oct. 1967, 17–37. J. A. Templin, "God and Covenant in the South African Wilderness," *Church History,* 37, no. 2, 1968, 281–297. J. Meintjes, *The Voortrekkers: The Story of the Great Trek and the Making of South Africa* (London 1973); Marianne

Cornevin, *Apartheid: Power and Historical Falsification* (Paris UNESCO 1980). Andre DuToit, "No Chosen People: The Myth of the Calvinist Origins of Afrikaner Nationalism and Racial Ideology," *American Historical Review,* 88, No. 4, Oct. 1983, 920–952.

4. Gustavo Gutierrez, *A Theology of Liberation* (Orbis N.Y. 1973).
5. R. Alves, *A Theology of Human Hope,* (Corpus Books Washington 1969).
6. Jose Miguez Bonini, *Doing Theology in a Revolutionary Situation* (Philadelphia Fortress 1975).
7. James Cone, *Black Theology and Black Power* (New York: The Seabury Press 1969); Albert Cleage, *The Black Messiah* (N.Y. Cheed and War 1968) and *Black Christian Nationalism* (New York 1972).
8. Since the publication of *The Churches Judgement on Apartheid* (Cape Town: The Civil Rights League 1948), several books and articles have been published on the liberal wing of the Christian Church in South Africa. For a summary of the subject see John W. deGruchy, *The Church Struggle in South Africa* (Michigan 1979) and Hope and Young, *The South African Churches in a Revolutionary Situation* (N.Y. 1981). See also Trevor Huddleston, *Naught for Your Comfort* (London 1956) and Peter Randall, ed. *Not Without Honour: Tribute to Beyers Naudé* (Rowan Press 1982). Charles Villa-Vicencio and de Gruchy, *Apartheid is a Heresy* (Cape Town 1983). *The Cotteslow Consultation,* Report of the Consultation among South African member churches of the World Council of Churches 7–14 Dec. 1960; the 'Koinonia' Declaration 1977 see G. Carter, *Which Way is South Africa Going,* (Indiana 1980) 104–108. Afrikaner dissidents led by Professor B. B. Keet of the Theological Seminary of Stellenbosch published in 1956 *Whither South Africa* and in 1960 eleven Afrikaner churchmen published *Delayed Action;* the historic letter of 123 ministers and theologians of the white DRC in June 1982: "An Open Letter to the NGK" (Mss Yale Divinity Library) and comments on *The Rand Daily Mail* June 9, 1982 and *The Citizen* June 10, 1982.
9. L. Gann and P. Duignam, *Why South Africa Will Survive: An Historical Analysis* (London 1981) p. 133.
10. For a recent scholarship on South African white liberals see Paul Rich, *White Power and the Liberal Conscience: Racial Segregation and South African Liberation 1920–1960* (Manchester 1984).
11. James Young, "South African Churches: Agents of Change," *Christian Century* Nov. 24, 1982, pp. 1199.
12. *Africa Report* July-August 1983, p. 9.
13. George Barany, "On Truth in Myths," *Eastern European Quarterly,* xv, no. 3 Sept. 1981, 347–355.
14. Gail M. Gerhart, *Black Power in South Africa: the Evolution of an Ideology* (California and London 1978) especially chapter 8.
15. Oswald Mbuyiseni Mtshali, "The Detribalised" in Robert Royston, ed. *To Whom It May Concern* (Johannesburg 1973).
16. The Quest for a True Humanity, (Black Peoples Congress, Programme as adopted 13th–16th Dec. 1975 at BPC Conference, King Williamstown, East-

ern Cape Prince) Mss. Yale African Collection—pp. 20–21. Also appearing in Mothlabi, ed., *Essays in Black Theology* (Johannesburg: Project of the UCM 1972) pp. 22–27, as Steve Biko, "Black Conscienseness and the Quest for True Humanity."

17. Basil Moore, ed., *The Challenge of Black Theology in South Africa* (London C. Hurst and Co. 1973) p. 4.

18. For a bibliography of Black Theology in South Africa see *South African Outlook* Sept. 1980 and Dec. 1981.

19. C.F. Torres Sergio and Fabella, Virginia eds. *The Emergent Gospel, Theology From the Underside of History* papers from the Ecumenical Dialogue of Third World Theologians Dar-es-Soloman Aug. 5–12 1976 (Orbis 1978).

20. Joseph Lelyveld, "South Africa's Bishop Tutu," *The New York Times* Magazine March 14, 1982 pp. 44, 72.

21. Steve Biko, excerpts from his testimony in the South African Students' Organization BPC Trial, May 1976 in *Biko* p. 106.

22. Basil Moore ed., *The Challenge of Black Theology* p. 145. The problem was a Third World problem for "Blacks, Hispanics, Native Americans and Women who are hard pressed to find courses to match their sensitivities" see J. Deotis Roberts, "Liberating Theological Education: Can Our Seminaries be Served?" *The Christian Century* 100, no. 4, Feb. 2–9, 1983, p. 98.

23. Interview with Rev. Norman Montjane at Yale. 1982.

24. Charles Davis, "The Theological Career of Historical Criticism of the Bible," *Cross Currents,* XXXII, no. 3, Fall, 1982, p. 267. Dr. Basil Moore of the University Christian Movement confirms the view that the Black Clergy were unprepared for their task in the black communities. "Even black ministers," he observed, "trained in white-staffed seminaries failed largely to relate the Gospel to the situation of the black people in the pews." *A Survey of Race Relations in South Africa,* 1971, (SAIRR, Johannesburg, 1972), p. 43. His observation appeared in full in *The Black Sash,* June, 1971.

25. Report on "The Renasissance Convention held at Hammanskraal 13–16th Dec., 1974," (Mss Yale African Collections).

26. For a detailed description of ecclesiastical colonialism see Spro-cas, (acronym for the Study Project on Christianity in Apartheid Society), report *Apartheid and the Church,* (Johannesburg, 1972).

27. Leyveld, "South Africa's Bishop Tutu," p. 42.

28. "Black Ministers of the DRC: Statement on Apartheid," in H. W. Vaner Merwe et al., *African Perspectives on South Africa,* (California, Cape Town and London, 1976), pp. 318–319. However, in 1983 a Black DRC in the Cape Province decided to reject financial assistance from the white NGK church because they refused to condemn apartheid as a sin. "South Africa Church rejects White Links" *African Christian* vol. 3, no. 30, August 1, 1983, p. 4.

29. Cosmas Desmond, *Christians or Capitalists? Christianity and Politics in South Africa,* (Bowerdean, 1978).

30. *Ecunews,* June 4, 1975.
31. Hannah Arendt, *Eichman in Jerusalem,* (New York, 1964), p. 126.
32. Elizabeth Alder, *A Small Beginning: An Assessment of the First Five Years of the Program to Combat Racism,* (Geneva, 1974), WCC Central Committee Minutes of the 31st Meeting, Kingston, Jamaica 1–11 Jan., 1979, pp. 54–60, PCR, "An Ecumenical Program to Combat Racism" Ecumenical Review, 21, no. 4, (Oct. 1969), p. 348 ff; vol. 23, no. 2 (April, 1971), p. 173 ff; vol. 25, no. 4 (Oct., 1973), p. 513 ff. For a critical but highly biased analysis of the WCC see Edward Norman, *Christianity and World Order,* (Oxford and New York: Oxford University Press, 1979); and Bernard Smith, *The Fraudulent Gospel: Politics and the World Council of Churches,* (Richmond, Surrey, U.K.: Foreign Affairs Publishing Co., 1977), Ernest Lefever, defender of South African government policies, whom President Reagan had nominated in 1981 to coordinate human rights in the State Department, *Amsterdam to Nairobi: The World Council of Churches* and *The Third World,* (Washington, D.C., 1979). The claim, for example, of Lefever that the condition of the Third World cannot be changed but must be faced and endured is frivolous. *Sixty Minutes* of CBS had a segment on the WCC which was a diatribe on the Council. For a very sympathetic rebuttal, see Robert McAfee Brown, "The Gospel According to Morley Shafer," *Christian Century,* March 2, 1983, pp. 183–186. For the response of the South African public and officials see *Rand Daily,* 7 Oct. 1970; *Star,* 23 Sept., 6 and 27 Oct., 1970. For the National Party's reaction see *Hansard,* 9 Cols. 4204–5 and 11 Cols. 5474–5. It is significant to note that the cultural treaty between South Africa and Holland has been frozen since 1960. See G. J. Schutte, "The Dutch and the Afrikaner," *Times Literary Supplement,* August 7, 1981, p. 915. "The Churches in Holland deny the name of Christian to their white co-religionists in South Africa. Are not the town councillors who named a town square after Steve Biko kindred spirits of their predecessors who once baptized the square after Pretorius, the hero of Blood River?"

    A survey of the activities of the WCC and the All African Council of Churches appeared in *A Survey of Race Relations in South Africa,* 1974 (South African Institute of Race Relations, Johannesburg, 1975), pp. 43–45. Mention should be made of Canon John Collins (1905–1982) canon residentiary of St. Paul's Cathedral in London, who was the founder, president, and guiding force of the International Defense and Aid Fund for South Africa—*i.d.a.f. News Notes,* Dec., 1982, p. 1.
33. Bishop Desmond Tutu in *Frontline,* no. 5, vol. 12, (April, 1982). Driven by the fierce edges of these perilous times, driven by historical change and by common sense, the main line English speaking Christian churches have accelerated the rate at which the Black Clergy enter positions of authority.
34. If Africans were to be given totally subsidiary roles within "white" South Africa, they had to be educated to assume that position. For an excellent appraisal of what has happened to African education since 1954 see Dennis Herbstein, *White Man, We Want To Talk To You* especially the chapter on "Education for Slavery," pp. 83–109. Herbstein concludes that "the real education of South Africa's black school children only starts when they have seen through the system, when they learn how to reject it, while using it for their own purpose," p. 109.

35. Sundkler, *Bantu Prophets in South Africa,* London, 1948 and second edition London OUP, 1961).
36. Shepperson, "Ethiopianism and African Nationalism," *Phylon,* 14, no. 1, 1953, p. 16.
37. West, *Bishops and Prophets in a Black City: African Independent Churches in Soweto,* (Johannesburg, Cape Town and London, 1975).
38. Sundkler, *Zulu Zion and Some Swazi Zionists,* (Oxford Univ., Press, 1976).
39. Mary Benson, *The African Patriots* (London, 1963) and *The Struggle for a Birthright,* (Penguin, 1966) are narratives of the history of Black Nationalism in South Africa as led primarily by the ANC. For an update on Black Nationalism see Gail M. Gerhart, *Black Power in South Africa: The Evolution of an Ideology,* (California and London, 1978) and Tom Lodge, *Black Politics in South Africa Since 1945* (Longman, London and New York 1983). Foremost in the long list of African Christian leaders of the ANC were Albert Luthuli; Anton Lembede, founder of the Youth League and a devout Roman Catholic; Dr. Walter Rubusana, one of the founders of ANC and first African to be elected to Cape Provincial Council as moderator of the Congregational Union of South Africa; Dr. John Dube, American trained was a Congregational minister and founder of Ohlange Institute as the Natal counterpart of Booker T. Washington's Tuskegee; Zacheus Mahabane, a Methodist minister, who was twice president of the ANC.
40. Shula Marks, "The Ambiguities of Dependence, John L. Dube of Natal," *Journal of South African Studies,* I, no. 2, April, 1975, p. 176.
41. Ibid., p. 180.
42. Interview with Norman Montjane, a South African black clergyman at Yale, June 30, 1983. See also Edward W. Grant, *South Africa: What of the Church?* (London: Edinburgh House, 1952).
43. See P. Rodda, "The Africanists Cut Loose," *Africa South,* July-September, 1959, 23, and M. Nkoana, "On Counter-Revolution," *The New Africa,* no. 51 1968, p. 31.
44. Albert Luthuli, *Let My People Go,* (New York, 1962), pp. 45–46.
45. See Albie Sachs, *Justice in South Africa,* (London: Heineman Sussex U. Press, 1973). Sach describes how the courts have been used over the centuries to regulate and make effective race domination in Southern Africa. See also Martin Legassick, "Legislation, ideology and economy in post 1948 South Africa," *Journal of South African Studies I,* 1., Oct., 1974, pp. 5–35, and *Laws Affecting Race Relations in South Africa 1948–1976,* compiled by Muriel Horrell, (Johannesburg, 1978), Father Cosmas Desmond, *The Discarded People,* (Penguin, 1971).
46. *ECUNEWS,* 24/79, (Aug. 3, 1979) pp. 19–28 Hope and Young, *The South African Churches,* p. 93.
47. *CHURCHSOC* (The Church and Society Report of the United Congregational Church of Southern Africa) no. 18, April, 1978.
48. William Sales, "Making South Africa Ungovernable: ANC Strategy for the '80s" *The Black Scholar* Nov./Dec. 1984, pp. 2–14.

49. *ECUNEWS* vol. 5, June 1983, p. 3.
50. Ibid., vol. 6, p. 4.
51. Tutu, *Crying in the Wilderness* (London 1982) p. 42. For a recent exposition of his ideas see Tutu, *Hope and Suffering: Sermons and Speeches* (Michigan 1984).
52. B.B.C. Interview, Bishop Tutu Jan. 30, 1984.
53. Allan Boesak, *Farewell to Innocence: A Social-Ethical Study of Black Theology and Black Power* (Johannesburg: Rowen Press 1977) p. 122.
54. Interview by Margaret A. Novicki of the Rev. Allan Boesak, *Africa Report,* July-Aug., 1983, pp. 7–22.
55. Judith Vidal-Hall, "Crisis of Conscience," *South: The Third World Magazine,* May 1983, p. 12.
56. Bishop Desmond Tutu taped message to the Trans Africa Forum in the U.S. Feb. 1982.
57. Boesak on reconciliation see *Farewell to Innocence* p. 106. On Tutu's meeting with Botha see Lelyveld, "South Africa's Bishop Tutu" p. 103. Black radicals suspected that he "might be tempted to play a role in South Africa analogous to that played by Bishop Abel T. Muzorewa, the (Rhodesian) Zimbabwean-Methodist who sank his own political fortunes to be lured into an alliance with Ian Smith."
58. Ibid., p. 25.
59. Banana, *The Gospel According to the Ghetto* (Zimbabwe Mamba Press 1980) pp. 46–47.
60. *ECUNEWS* vol. 6, July 1983.
61. Gerhart, p. 295. See also David Thomas, *Councils in the Ecumenical Movement: South Africa 1904–1975* (Johannesburg SACC 1979) p. 68 where Black religious leaders offered themselves "to the white men as bridge builders into the future."
62. Bishop Tutu Interview on "Voices of Africa" Feb. 5, 1984 Voice of America Program.
63. Gerhart, p. 294.
64. Dennis Herbstein, *White Man We Want To Talk To You,* p. 70.
65. Hope and Young, *The South African Churches in Revolutionary Situation,* p. 96. See also p. 166–168.
66. Tutu, *Crying in the Wilderness,* for other current concerns see Tutu, *Hope and Suffering.*
67. Tutu, *Crying in the Wilderness,* p. 63.
68. See Z. Kameeta "The Liberated Church and True Freedom" *Church and Nationalism in South Africa* ed., Theo Sundermeier (Johannesburg: Raven Press 1975), Tutu, "The Blasphemy that is Apartheid," *Africa Report* July-Aug., 1983, pp. 4–6 and Villa-Vicencio and deGruchy, *Apartheid is Heresy.*
69. Lelyveld, "South Africa's Bishop Tutu," p. 44. See also Hope and Young, Bishop Tutu's Tripple Jeopardy," *Christian Century,* Nov. 28, 1979, pp. 1188–

9 and Creighton Lacy, " 'Love So Surprising,' South Africa's Bishop Tutu" *Christian Century* April 13, 1983 pp. 338–341.

70. Boesak, *Farewell,* p. 10.

71. For an elaboration of the position of the critics see *The Bible and Liberation* (Orbis N.Y. 1983) and E. K. Mosothoane, "The Use of Scriptures in Black Theology" in *Scripture and the Use of Scripture* (Unisa Pretoria 1979).

72. Allan Boesak, "Liberation Theology in South Africa" in *African Theology En Route* ed. by Kofi Appiah Kubi and Sergio Torres, p. 175.

73. Tutu, *Crying in the Wilderness,* p. 112.

74. See Masala and Tlhage (eds.), *The Unquestionable Right to Be Free* (Johannesburg, 1986) and *Challenge to the Church, A Theological Comment on the Political Crisis in South Africa: the Kairos Document,* October 1985.

75. Quoted in Siggibo Dwane, "Christology and liberation," *Journal of Theology for Southern Africa,* June 1981, no. 35, p. 29. For the point of view of the white DRC on Black Theology see Edmund Hill, "The Impenitent Ostrich," *South African Outlook* March 1974 and *ECUNEWS* 4 June 1975 which summarizes the report of the Commission of Inquiry into The Christian Institute. Black Theology is referred to as an "American Social Gospel" and Marxist inspired and consequently a subversive political ideology.

76. See Elizabeth Schmidt, "South Africa: Illusions of Progress or How to Integrate the Toilets While Showing up Apartheid" *Otherside* no. 110, Nov., 1980, pp. 12–16. For brilliant essays on the "New dispensation" see Allan Paton, "The Afrikaners' New Crisis of Conscience," *Newsday,* Sunday, July 10, 1983, pp. 1, 11 and Thambo Mbeki, "Reforming Apartheid Doesn't End Slavery," *The New York Times,* Monday, July 18, 1983, p. A5. For an engaging discussion of the recent abrogation of the Mixed Marriages law see N. K. Bentsi-Enchill "Apartheid Sex Change Shock: *West Africa* 22 April 1985, p. 772.

77. Baldwin Sjollema, *Isolating Apartheid Western Collaboration with South Africa* (Geneva 1982) p. 6.

78. *Africa Report* July-Aug. 1983, p. 12.

79. Gerhart p. 294. For a summary of the controversy leading to the closure and move of the seminary see *A Survey of Race Relations in South Africa* 1975, pp. 31–32.

80. Lelyveld, "South Africa's Bishop Tutu" p. 44.

81. Tutu, *Crying in the Wilderness,* p. 49.

82. Lelyveld, p. 42.

83. Ibid., p. 23.

84. *Crying in the Wilderness,* p. 28. For an examination of the moral consequences of the failure of white South Africans to give conceptual and emotional as well as legal and political recognition to South Africa's majority population see Vincent Crapanzano, *Waiting: the Whites of South Africa* (Random House 1985).

The collusion of white perception within the National Party of the Black majority is an indication of a chasm within the Volk. The National Party of Botha which is moving on with 'reforms' for limited change has been under severe challenge from the Conservative Party of Dr. Andries Treunicht which promotes itself as the keeper of the apartheid flame. Yet the general feeling is that of a character in *Waiting* who stated:

> "I don't like to think about it. Everything could have been all right. Things should have been done earlier. When I think about the future, I get scared. We are all acting out of fear, and so we are not doing the right thing. We didn't pay enough attention to the past and now no one knows what to do."

The tragic failure of "not knowing" what to do might lead to a South African apocalypse—an apocalypse the anti-apartheid movement both secular and clerical would like to avert.

NOTES ON CONTRIBUTORS

Austin M. Ahanotu is Professor of History at California State College, Stanlaus, with special responsibilities for the field of African Studies. His research and teaching are focused on the historical interactions of religion, politics and economics in the developing nations of Africa.

Harvey P. Alper is Associate Professor of Religious Studies at Southern Methodist University. He is an Historian of Religion who specializes in classical Hindu thought and the fate of traditional religions in the modern age. He is the Series Editor for the *Kashmir Saivism Series* for the State University Press of New York and has published in the areas of Saivite studies and Indian language.

Stanley Johannesen is Associate Professor of History at the University of Waterloo in Ontario, Canada. He is an American Historian who has published in the areas of the American Revolution and millennialist movements in America. He is the editor of *Historical Reflections/Reflexions Historiques* and the Director of Historical Reflections Press (University of Waterloo).

William R. Jones is Professor of Religion and Director of Black Studies at the Florida State University, having formerly served as Associate Professor and Coordinator of Black Studies at Yale Divinity School. He is a theologian with numerous publications in the areas of Black Theology and Religious Ethics including *Is God a White Racist?*

Lonnie D. Kliever is Professor of Religious Studies at Southern Methodist University, previously holding appointments in Philosophy at the University of Texas of El Paso and in Religion at Trinity University and University of Windsor. He is a philosopher of religion and culture with special interest in secularization, modernization and religion. His publications include *Radical Christianity, H. Richard Niebuhr,* and *The Shattered Spectrum.*

Bruce B. Lawrence is Professor of Religion at Duke University in the field of History of Religions with specialized competence in the religions of Islam and Hinduism in their historic and cultural settings. He serves as a consulting editor for many journals and series. His many publications include *Shahrastani on the Indian Religions* and *Notes from a Distant Flute*. He is completing an important comparative study entitled, *Fundamentalism: Christian, Jewish, Islamic*.

Richard L. Rubenstein is the Robert O. Lawton Distinguished Professor of Religion at the Florida State University. A sensitive interpreter of the human and religious prospect in the modern world, his publications span the fields of Religious Studies and Social Sciences in nearly two hundred articles and a dozen books. His best known works include *After Auschwitz, The Religious Imagination, The Cunning of History,* and *The Age of Triage*. He also currently serves as President of The Washington Institute for Values in Public Policy of Washington, D. C.

Martin Rumscheidt is Professor of Historical Theology and Church History at the Atlantic School of Theology in Halifax, Canada, having previously held a teaching position in Religious Studies at the University of Windsor. He has served on the governing boards of many professional associations and scholarly publishers. A specialist in modern European theology, his publications include *Revelation and Theology* and *The Way of Theology for Karl Barth*.

William W. Stein is Professor of Anthropology at State University of New York at Buffalo, following earlier faculty appointments at University of Miami, University of Alberta and University of Kansas. He continues to conduct primary research among highland Peruvian Indians. The published results of his field work appear in leading anthropological journals and a number of collected works which he has edited. He is currently completing two books on the Andean Campesinos.

Index

Note: Notes are indicated by (*n.*) following page number.

Index

Index

Index